OECD Studies on Water

Water Charges in Brazil

THE WAYS FORWARD

OECD
BETTER POLICIES FOR BETTER LIVES

Please cite this publication as:
OECD (2017), *Water Charges in Brazil: The Ways Forward*, OECD Studies on Water, OECD Publishing, Paris.
http://dx.doi.org/10.1787/9789264285712-en

ISBN 978-92-64-28570-5 (print)
ISBN 978-92-64-28571-2 (PDF)

Series: OECD Studies on Water
ISSN 2224-5073 (print)
ISSN 2224-5081 (online)

Photo credits: Cover © Lucas Anacleto

Corrigenda to OECD publications may be found on line at: *www.oecd.org/about/publishing/corrigenda.htm*.

Foreword

As a longstanding advocate of the Polluter-Pays and User-Pays principles, the OECD argues that economic instruments can play an important role for effective and efficient water resources management when designed and governed adequately, and when combined with other policy instruments. In particular, setting and governing abstraction and pollution charges that can deliver expected policy objectives is not an easy task and remains a necessity in several countries. A number of governments around the globe have been experiencing severe reform challenges as well as fierce resistance from users when putting in place water charges for the first time and/or raising their levels.

In the case of Brazil, the economic crisis and its social and competitiveness consequences have hampered the readiness to charge and the willingness to pay in a country that holds 12% of the world's freshwater resources and has long been perceived as "water-rich". Another reason for resistance is that many water users do not see the direct benefit from water charges and consider them an additional "tax" rather than a collective effort to improve the conditions of the river basins.

The 2014 water scarcity crisis in Brazil provided a unique momentum for change. Fierce competition across users opened up a window of opportunity to consider the use of water charges as a resource management tool to transition from water crisis management to water risk management. A dedicated policy dialogue was initiated to take stock of the state of play and to learn from international best practices.

Over the last two years, and building on the recommendations from the previous OECD report *Water Resources Governance in Brazil* (2015), the OECD and the Brazilian National Water Agency (ANA) carried out a policy dialogue with over 150 stakeholders. The aim was to discuss how water charges could contribute to sustainable and inclusive growth in Brazil, and to identify which framework conditions would be needed to effectively operationalise them.

Water charges do not operate in a vacuum and are a means to an end. They can help to promote more efficient water use and prevent and control pollution, while raising revenues to cover the costs of resource management, thus saving scarce public funds. However, water charges cannot solve the magnitude of the challenge on their own, and should be combined with regulatory, planning, monitoring and enforcement instruments and thus provide continuing incentives for users to control water availability, quality and demand.

As part of OECD's ongoing effort to support demand-driven water reform agendas, the report *Water Charges in Brazil: The Ways Forward* assesses the current state of play in Brazil and suggests policy recommendations. It also provides concrete steps to implement more effective existing water charges and to support states and basins willing to introduce water charges within their water management systems.

We look forward to forthcoming initiatives across all levels of government to foster implementation in the short, medium and long term to achieve better policies for better lives in Brazil.

Angel Gurría
OECD Secretary-General

Acknowledgements

This report is the outcome of a two-year policy dialogue between the OECD, the National Water Agency of Brazil (ANA) and more than 150 stakeholders, carried out as a follow-up to the OECD (2015) report on Water Resources Governance in Brazil. Within the OECD, this project was undertaken by the Centre for Entrepreneurship, SMEs, Local Development and Tourism (CFE) led by Lamia Kamal-Chaoui, Director, and as part of the programme of work of the Regional Development Policy Committee (RDPC).

The OECD Secretariat is grateful to ANA officials for the excellent co-operation throughout the dialogue as well as for their availability and strong commitment to engage stakeholders in the underlying consultation process. In particular, the Secretariat is grateful to Vicente Andreu, João Gilberto Lotufo Conejo, Paulo Varella, Ney Maranhão, Gisela Forattini, Ricardo Andrade, Flavia Gomes de Barros, Humberto Cardoso Gonçalves, Sérgio Rodrigues Ayrimoraes Soares, Carlos Motta Nunes, Aline Machado da Matta, Giordano Bruno Bomtempo de Carvalho, Carlos Alberto Perdigão Pessoa, Elisa Monteiro Malafaia, Marco Antonio Mota Amorim, José Luiz Gomes Zoby, Mariana Rodrigues Lirio, and Cristiano Cária Pereira. Special thanks are also conveyed to the Chancellor of the Ministry of Foreign Affairs, Mr Aloysio Nunes Ferreira, and his staff.

The policy dialogue was managed by Aziza Akhmouch, Acting Head of the Division on Cities, Urban Policies and Sustainable Development together with Oriana Romano, Policy Analyst, OECD Water Governance Programme within CFE. The policy dialogue was carried out in partnership with the OECD Environment Directorate, co-ordinated by Xavier Leflaive, leader of the Water Team. The report was drafted by Oriana Romano, Xavier Leflaive and Aziza Akhmouch, OECD Secretariat, with written contributions from Professors Arnaud Reynaud and Stefan Ambec, INRA (French Institute for Research in Agriculture) and the Toulouse School of Economics (France).

The report greatly benefitted from contributions by the following peer reviewers who have shared their country experience and expertise with Brazilian stakeholders throughout the process: Ian Barker, Founder and Managing Director of Water Policy International Ltd, formerly responsible for water management and regulation across England and Wales at the Environment Agency; Francisco Nunes Correia, former Minister of Environment, Spatial Planning and Regional Development of Portugal (2005 09) and President of the Department of Civil Engineering, Architecture and Geo resources at the Instituto Superior Técnico, Lisbon; Gonzalo Delacámara, Senior Research Fellow and Co-ordinator of the Department of Economic Analysis of Water at IMDEA Foundation and Policy Advisor for several international organisations; and Peter Gammeltoft, former Head of Unit for Water at European Commission – Directorate General for the Environment and currently President of the International Commission for the Protection of the Danube River (ICPDR). Special thanks are further conveyed to Alain Bernard, Head of Integrated Water Resources Management at the International

Office for Water (OIEAU), for his participation during the fact-finding missions and peer reviews.

The OECD Secretariat is also grateful to the 150+ stakeholders (see list in Annex F) engaged in the process across ministries, public agencies and levels of government, as well as from river basin committees and the private sector. The interviews carried out during the fact-finding (25-30 September 2016) and case study missions (6-15 February 2017) were instrumental to collecting facts and data, but also to understanding multilevel dynamics of setting and designing water charges in Brazil. Preliminary results were discussed with members of the National Council for Water Resources (CNRH) and representatives from the Ministry of Planning, Development and Management; Ministry of National Integration; Ministry of Cities; Ministry of Industry, Trade and Services; Ministry of Finance; Ministry of Environment; Ministry of Social and Agrarian Development and Ministry of Mining and Energy as well as the *Casa Civil* in the President's Office. The participation of stakeholders in the final policy seminar (19-21 June 2017, Brasilia) was also key to the discussion on interim findings, building consensus on the ways forward and co-designing an Action Plan. The OECD is also grateful to the Ministry of Industry, Foreign Trade and Services, the Piracicaba, Capivari and Jundiaí (PCJ) Consortium and the Minas Gerais Institute for Water Management (IGAM) for their written comments. Special thanks are also conveyed to the stakeholders of the three case studies that are featured in the report, namely the State of Rio de Janeiro as well as the Paraiba do Sul and the Piancó-Piranhas-Açu River Basins.

An advanced version of the report was discussed at the 9th Meeting of the OECD Water Governance Initiative (3-4 July 2017, Paris). The OECD is grateful to Bernard Barraqué (CNRS), François Brikke (GWP), Michael Eichholz (Federal Institute for Geosciences and Natural Resources, Germany), Rui Godinho (APDA), Susana Neto (University of Lisbon), Pierre Ténière-Buchot (pS-Eau), and Rob Uijterlinde (Dutch Water Authorities), who provided comments on that occasion and to Daniel Valensuela (OIEAU) for his feedback on the draft report. The report was submitted for approval through written procedure to the OECD Regional Development Policy Committee. The report was edited by Caitlin Connelly and formatted by Cécile Cordoliani. Joanne Dundon and Pilar Philip prepared the manuscript for publication. Nuno Barreiras (Instituto Superior Técnico, Lisbon) performed the translation of the report into Portuguese.

Table of contents

Acronyms and abbreviations 11

Executive summary 17

Assessment and recommendations 19

Chapter 1. Why water charges matter in Brazil 27

Rationale for water pricing 28
Practical definitions and scope 28
The use of economic instruments for water management 29
Principles for economic instruments contributing to sustainable water management 32
Note 35
References 36

Chapter 2. Water charges in Brazil — The state of play 37

The legal and institutional framework 38
Calculating water charges 41
Who does what in setting, collecting and operationalising water charges in Brazil 43
Water charges in practice: The state of play under federal and state domains 48
A tentative typology of water charges at federal and state level 52
Notes 70
References 72

Chapter 3. Practical issues for setting and managing water charges in Brazil 75

A review of international experience on abstraction and pollution charges 76
Keep it simple 91
Combining water charges with other policy instruments 93
Raising and spending revenues from water charges 97
Integrating behavioural dimensions into water charge design 100
Addressing affordability and equity issues for households 101
Addressing competiveness issues 102
Notes 105
References 106

Chapter 4. Sector–specific issues for setting and managing water charges 109

Hydropower and multipurpose dams 110
Water supply and sanitation 114
Industry 119
Agriculture 122
Notes 128
References 129

Chapter 5. Governing water charges design and implementation 133
Key principles 134
International experiences 137
Key issues in governing water charges in Brazil 145
Planning and spending issues 155
Notes 159
References 160
Annex A. The Paraíba do Sul River basin 163
Annex B. The State of Rio de Janeiro 173
Annex C. The Piancó-Piranhas Açu River basin 183
Annex D. Action Plan 191
Annex E. Charging for water abstraction and discharges – A checklist 195
Annex F. List of stakeholders consulted during the policy dialogue 199

Tables

1.1. The Polluter-Pays principle for diffuse water pollution 33
2.1. Differences between water charges and other instruments in Brazil 38
2.2. Status of implementation of water charges in interstate and state basins 51
2.3. Clusters of interstate and state river basin vis-à-vis their experiences with water charges 53
2.4. Clustering of states: Institutional framework and water charges 53
2.5. Basin committees and agencies in the State of São Paulo 62
2.6. River basins, delegated water agencies implementing water charges in Minas Gerais 63
3.1. Differentiation of water abstraction charges in France 76
3.2. Water abstraction charges in selected OECD countries 84
3.3. Pollution charges in selected countries 88
3.4. Examples of water policy instruments to address selected water-related risks 94
4.1. Empirical evidence on household water price elasticities in Europe 114
4.2. Empirical evidence on industrial water price elasticities 119
4.3. Empirical evidence on agricultural water price elasticities 123
5.1. OECD Principles on Water Governance applied to water charges in Brazil 136
5.2. Governing water charges in England & Wales and France 141
5.3. The use of resources from water charges in four interstate river basins (Year 2016) 156
B.1. Water charges in the State of Rio de Janeiro 177

Figures

2.1. The water charge implementation cycle 44
2.2. Water charges at federal and state level 49
2.3. Timeline of water charges implementation 50
2.4. Total amount charged and collected in interstate river basins and states 52
2.5. Water charges in the Paraíba do Sul River basin 55
2.6. Water charges in the PCJ river basin 57
2.7. Timeline of the institutional framework for water charges in the PCJ River basin 58
2.8. Water charges in the State of Rio de Janeiro 59

2.9. Water charges in the State of São Paulo 61
2.10. Water charges in the State of Minas Gerais 63
2.11. Water charges in the São Francisco River basin 64
2.12. Water charges in the State of Ceará 65
2.13. Water charges in the State of Parana 66
2.14. Water charges in the Doce River basin 67
4.1. Total amount collected from hydroelectric power plans subject to water use charges 112
4.2. Water abstracted and consumed by sector in Brazil 127
A.1. The Paraíba do Sul River basin 164
A.2. Water charges by type of use in the Paraíba do Sul basin 165
A.3. Proportion of water use charge by sector in the Paraíba do Sul basin 165
A.4. The water use charge cycle in the Paraíba do Sul River basin at federal level 167
A.5. Timeline of the water charges implementation in the Paraíba do Sul River basin 168
B.1. Hydrographic regions and river basin committees in the State of Rio de Janeiro 174
B.2. Water charges in the State of Rio de Janeiro (by type of users) 2016 175
C.1. The Piancó-Piranhas Açu River basin 184

Acronyms and abbreviations

ABHA	Multisectoral Association of Users of Water Resources in River Basins, *Associação Multisetorial de Usuários de Recursos Hídricos da Bacia Hidrográficas*
AESA	Executive Agency for Water Management of the State of Paraíba, *Agência Executiva de Gestão das Águas do Estado da Paraíba*
AGB Peixe Vivo	Executive Association for the Support of Water Management in Peixe Vivo River Basin, *Associação Executiva de Apoio à Gestão de Bacia Hidrográfica Peixe Vivo*
Agência PCJ	Agency of Piracicaba, Capivari and Jundiaí River Basins, *Agência das Bacias dos Rios Piracicaba, Capivari e Jundiaí*
AGEVAP	Association for Water Management in Paraíba do Sul River Basin, *Associação Pró-Gestão das Águas da Bacia Hidrográfica do Rio Paraíba do Sul*
ÁguasParaná	Water Institute of the State of Paraná, *Instituto das Águas do Paraná*
ANA	National Water Agency, *Agência Nacional de Águas*
ANEEL	National Agency for Electric Energy, *Agência Nacional de Energia Elétrica*
BAT	Best Available Technologies
BOD	Biochemical Oxygen Demand
CAERN	State Sanitation Company in Rio Grande do Norte, *Companhia de Águas e Esgotos do Rio Grande do Norte*
CBH	River Basin Committee, *Comitê de Bacia Hidrográfica*
CBHSF	São Francisco River Basin Committee, *Comitê da Bacia Hidrográfica do Rio São Francisco*
CCME	Canadian Council for Ministers of the Environment
CEDAE	State Water and Sewerage Company of Rio de Janeiro, *Companhia Estadual de Águas e Esgotos do Rio de Janeiro*
CEIVAP	Interstate River Basin Committee Paraíba do Sul River, *Comitê de Integração da Bacia Hidrográfica do Rio Paraíba do Sul*
CERB	Water Resources and Environmental Engineering Company, *Companhia de Engenharia Ambiental e Recursos Hídricos da Bahia*

CERH	State Water Resources Council, *Conselho Estadual de Recursos Hídricos*
CERHI	State Council for Water Resources of the State of Rio De Janeiro, *Conselho Estadual de Recursos Hídricos do Estado do Rio de Janeiro*
CFURH	Financial Compensation for the Use of Water Resources, *Compensação Financeira pela Utilização dos Recursos Hídricos*
CILSJ	Intermunicipal Consortium for Environmental Management of the Basins of Região dos Lagos, São João River and Costal area, *Consórcio Intermunicipal para Gestão Ambiental das Bacias da Região dos Lagos, do Rio São João e Zona Costeira*
CNARH	National Register of Users of Water Resources, *Cadastro Nacional de Usuarios de Recursos Hidricos*
CNRH	National Water Resources Council, *Conselho Nacional de Recursos Hídricos*
COALIAR	Basin Committees of Alto Iguaçu and Tributaries of Alto Ribeira, *Comitê das Bacias do Alto Iguaçu e Afluentes do Alto Ribeira*
COGERH	Company for Water Resources Management of the State of Ceará, *Companhia de Gestão de Recursos Hídricos do Estado do Ceará*
CONERH	State Council for Water Resources, *Conselho Estadual de Recursos Hídricos*
CORHI	Coordinating Committee of the State Water Resources Plan, *Comitê Coordenador do Plano Estadual de Recursos Hídricos*
CTCOB	Technical Chamber for the Water Use Charge, *Câmara Técnica de Cobrança pelo Uso de Recursos Hídricos*
CTIL	Technical, Institutional and Legal Chamber, *Câmara Tecnica de Assuntos Legais e Institucionais*
CUTE	Single Treasury Account, *Conta Única do Tesouro Estadual*
DAEE	Department of Water and Electricity of the State of São Paulo, *Departamento de Águas e Energia Elétrica do Estado de São Paulo*
DAURH	Annual Statement of Water Resources Use, *Declaração Anual de Uso de Recursos Hídricos*
DBT	Decreasing block tariff
DEFRA	Department for Environment, Food and Rural Affairs (United Kingdom)
DNOCS	National Department of Constructions Against Drought, *Departamento Nacional de Obras Contra as Secas*

DWI	Drinking Water Inspectorate (United Kingdom)
EA	Environment Agency (United Kingdom)
EU	European Union
FABHAT	Foundation Agency of the Alto Tietê River Basin, *Fundação Agência da Bacia Hidrográfica do Alto Tietê*
FABH-SMT	Foundation Agency of the Rio Sorocaba e Meio Tietê River Basin, *Fundação Agência da Bacia Hidrográfica do Rio Sorocaba e Meio Tietê*
FEHIDRO	State Water Resources Fund, *Fundo Estadual de Recursos Hidricos*
FNDCT	National Fund for Scientific and Technological Development, *Fundo Nacional de Desenvolvimento Cientifico e Tecnologico*
FRHI	Water Resources State Fund, *Fundo Estadual de Recursos Hídricos*
FUNASA	National Health Foundation, *Fundação Nacional de Saúde*
FUNDRHI	State Water Resources Fund, *Fundo Estadual de Recursos Hídricos*
GESTIN	Integrated Management System of the Paraíba do Sul River Basin, *Sistema de Gestão Integrada da Bacia do Rio Paraíba do Sul*
GIS	Geographic information system
GW	Groundwater
HR	Hydrographic Region
IBAMA	Brazilian Institute of Environment and Renewable Resources, *Instituto Brasileiro do Meio Ambiente e dos Recursos Naturais Renováveis*
IBio	BioAtlântica Institute, *Instituto BioAtlântica*
IBT	Increasing Block Tariff
ICPDR	International Commission for the Protection of the Danube River
IGAM	Institute for Water Management of the State of Minas Gerais, *Instituto Mineiro de Gestão das Águas*
IGARN	Institute of Water Management of the State of Rio Grande do Norte, *Instituto de Gestão das Águas do Estado do Rio Grande Do Norte*
ILI	Infrastructure Leakage Index
INAG	National Institute for Water (Portugal), *Instituto da Água*
INEA	State Institute of Environmental of Rio de Janeiro, *Instituto Estadual do Ambiente do Rio de Janeiro*

INEMA	Institute of Environment and Water Resources of the State of Bahia, *Instituto do Meio Ambiente e Recursos Hidricos da Bahia*
IPEA	Institute for Applied Economic Research, *Instituto de Pesquisa Econômica Aplicada*
LEMA	Law on Water and Aquatic Environments (France), *Loi sur l'Eau et les Milieux Aquatiques*
NAO	National Audit Office (United Kingdom)
NOx	Nitrogen Oxides
NRW	Natural Resources Wales (United Kingdom)
OECD	Organisation for Economic Co-operation and Development
OFWAT	Office of Water Services (United Kingdom)
OIEAU	Water International Office (France), *Office International de l'eau*
OUGC	Single Collective Management Body (France), *Organismes Uniques de Gestion Collective*
PAC	Growth Acceleration Programme, *Programa de Aceleração do Crescimento*
PAC	Public Accounts Committee (United Kingdom)
PERHI	State Water Resources Plan of Rio de Janeiro, *Plano Estadual de Recursos Hídricos do Estado do Rio de Janeiro*
PES	Payments for ecosystem services
PISF	Transposition Project of the São Francisco River, *Projeto de Integração do Rio São Francisco*
PPA	Piancó-Piranhas-Açu
PPP	Public-Private Partnership
RBAs	River Basin Authorities
RBCs	River Basin Committees
SAGE	Plans for Development and Water Management (France), *Schéma d'aménagement et de gestion des eaux*
SAIH	Automatic Hydrological Information System (Spain), *Sistema Automático de Información Hidrológica*
SDAGE	Master Plans for Development and Water Management (France), *Schémas Directeurs d'Aménagement et de Gestion des Eaux*
SEA	Secretariat of State for the Environment, *Secretaria de Estado do Ambiente*
SEFAZ	State Treasury Department, *Secretaria da Fazenda*
SEGREHs	State Water Resources Management Systems, *Sistemas Estaduais de Gestão dos Recursos Hídricos*

SEMARH	State Secretariat for the Environment and Water Resources, *Secretária de Estado do Meio Ambiente e dos Recursos Hídricos*
SEPA	Scottish Environment Protection Agency (United Kingdom)
SIA	National Integrated Water Information System (Spain), *Sistema Integrado de Información del Agua*
SIAR	Agro-climatic Information System for Irrigation (Spain), *Sistema de Información Agroclimática para el Regadío*
SINGREH	National Water Resources Management System, *Sistema Nacional de Gerenciamento de Recursos Hídricos*
SINISA	National Information System on Basic Sanitation, *Sistema Nacional de Informações em Saneamento Básico*
SNIRH	National Water Resources Information System, *Sistema Nacional de Informações sobre Recursos Hídricos*
SW	Surface Water
TFU	Fiscalisation Fee for Water Resources Use, *Taxa de Fiscalização dos Usos dos recursos hídricos*
TNMN	Transnational Monitoring Network (Danube River Basin)
TRH	Water Resources Tax (Portugal), *Taxa de Recursos Hídricos*
UK	United Kingdom
VAT	Value Added Tax
WFD	Water Framework Directive
WISE	Water Information System for Europe
ZRE	Water Distribution Areas (France), *Zones de Répartition des Eaux*

Executive summary

A policy debate on water charges in Brazil is particularly timely and relevant for a number of environmental, economic and political reasons. The country is facing a range of water issues, from risks associated with too much, too little or too polluted water, to a challenging fiscal and political context. Strengthening water charges where they exist, and considering them where appropriate, could help to drive the necessary place-based actions to safeguard water quality and quantity (e.g. pollution and excessive abstraction) and to prevent water risks from becoming barriers to Brazil's sustainable growth now and in the future. This report looks at why water charges can contribute to several current and long-term policy objectives in Brazil, and how water abstraction and pollution charges can work and deliver intended results. It outlines policy recommendations and provides a detailed action plan that identifies lead institutions that can implement actions over the short, medium and long term.

Set water charges that serve dedicated policy objectives. Abstraction and pollution charges are not currently designed to drive the behaviour of most water users (e.g. hydropower generators, industries, farmers, and utilities). They also do not reflect the opportunity costs of using water in specific basins, the risk and consequences of pollution, and the dilution capacity of rivers and water bodies. Low charges do not deliver visible benefits to water users, they hinder their willingness-to-pay, and they make any further price increases challenging. However, even though is difficult for public authorities to set the abstraction or pollution charge at a rate that covers the entire environmental and opportunity costs, methodological issues for calculating charges should not postpone water charges implementation. Simple proxies can be used to set water charges and send economic signals to water users that pave the way for the use of more sophisticated methodologies and rate calculations. To maximise benefits for water management and revenue raising, and to minimise the transaction costs of setting and managing charges, water charges should target users who abstract or pollute most (although in the longer term, a fair and inclusive approach is required).

Build capacities. River basin committees and water agencies should enhance their skills in carrying out economic analysis as a basis to guide decisions for setting water charges and measuring their impact on affordability and competitiveness, which should be documented and addressed. Government agencies at federal and state levels should provide guidance on setting charges and on spending revenues from charges. Guidance may include general rules, such as lower bounds for abstraction or pollution charges, list of pollutants to be controlled and monitored (mandatory and river-specific), rules for expenditure spending and publishing of accounts. The National Water Resources Council could define clear rules to establish minimum and maximum rates for abstraction and pollution charges, which could then trickle down at state level to adapt to local circumstances.

Enhance the knowledge and information base for water charges. Without a solid knowledge and information base, any assessment of needs, efficiency and effectiveness of economic instruments will remain subjective. In Brazil, the availability of good, accessible data and information on water varies across states, which makes decision-making somewhat challenging. The process could be improved with a better understanding of who gets water, where and when, and who pays for what. Information systems across basins, local, state and federal levels should provide comprehensive, robust and up-to-date data on the state and quality of environment and water resources, including pressures on water resources.

Strengthen the institutional framework for water charges and manage water charges at the right scale. Institutional arrangements can be adjusted to make the best of existing structures and processes. The democratic process whereby charges are set within river basin committees can be thwarted by vested interests. River basin committees are becoming places of resistance, whereby the most vocal users are able to voice their opinion on water charges and preserve the *status quo*. This is why a decision-making process that helps manage trade-offs across users and neutralise *consultation capture* is much needed. River basin committees could have a stronger consultative rather than deliberative role. Governments (federal and state) should be accountable for following their recommendations on setting and implementing water charges, and they should provide explanations or justifications if otherwise. Finally, co-ordination across delegated water agencies within and across states would be needed when implementing charges at state and federal levels, given the differences in terms of governance models, regulations and enforcement rules. One solution could be to create a single water agency in interstate river basins.

Deploy water charges in combination with other policy instruments and coherently with actions foreseen in river basin plans. Charges on their own cannot solve the magnitude of water challenges in Brazil and should be designed and implemented in co-ordination with other policy instruments such as water allocation regimes and water quality standards. Water charges should be considered in the context of water resources management plans that effectively set priorities and levels of ambition, guide infrastructure development, and are accompanied by sustainable financing strategies and expenditure programmes. Finally, any reform of existing or new water charges should come with proper monitoring and regulatory capacities. Unintended consequences, such as trade-offs between different water sources, should be documented.

Consider accompanying measures when reforming or deploying water charges. The potential impacts of water charges on the affordability of water bills and on the competitiveness of industrial and agricultural users should be documented, including through robust economic and evidence-based analysis. In addition, these issues are better addressed through targeted accompanying measures – eventually financed through recycling some of the revenues generated by water charges – than through blanket exemptions or discounts.

Facilitate spending that contributes to enhanced water security and show the benefits to users. Revenues from water charges are not directly used to finance expenditure programmes that benefit water users in the basins where they are levied. Users do not perceive the benefits of paying the charge, thus undermining the legitimacy of the instrument and users' willingness to pay. This is why expenditure programmes should be commensurate with revenue raising capacities and deliver visible benefits to water users in the basin. Spending rules should be amended so that agencies can effectively spend the money collected through water charges in a reasonable timeframe.

Assessment and recommendations

Recent and ongoing droughts in Brazil create a momentum to think about different policy instruments that can contribute to water security and sustainable growth now and in the future. Water abstraction and pollution charges are among the instruments that can help the country to transition from water *crisis* management to water *risk* management, while setting incentives to use water efficiently and reducing the qualitative pressure on water resources.

This report sets out a case for change based on an assessment of the state of play of water charges in Brazil and identifies implementation challenges. It suggests ways forward to improve the current system building on international good practices. It acknowledges the efforts of the six interstate river basins and six states in Brazil where water charges have been instituted to date, as well as the challenges faced by other countries in terms of institutional capacity, hydrological complexity, and level of economic development, amongst others, which all affect the political choice of implementing water charges.

The report highlights the need for water charges to operate within an effective water regulatory regime inclusive of abstraction and discharge. It argues that without effective charges and regulation, water pollution, wastage and misallocation will hinder economic growth and improvements in social welfare. Likewise, not charging or charging insufficiently for water, can be more costly in terms of jobs, growth and impacts on individual users than having charges that "bite". Lastly, how revenues from water charges are spent is an essential part of the efficiency, effectiveness and political acceptability of any charging system. This is why the report goes beyond the consideration of the *level* and *structure* of the charges to focus on the *process* of setting up and enforcing charges, as well as on *expenditure* management.

Water charges in Brazil: The state of play

The water charge (*cobrança*) is a price for the use of a common-pool resource, set by basin committees in a participative manner involving water users, civil society, and public authorities. The main objective is to point out the economic value of water, while encouraging its rational use and preserving its quality. Those holding permits (*outorgas*) for using water for economic purposes are subject to water charges. In practice, sectors subject to water abstraction and pollution charges in Brazil are water supply and sanitation utilities, industry, hydropower and agriculture.

The process for setting and operating water charges at federal and state level is similar across the country: the river basin committees (interstate or within states) submit the charge for approval to the federal (Conselho Nacional de Recursos Hídricos, CNRH) or state (Conselhos Estaduais de Recursos Hídricos, CEHRs) water resources councils. National (Agência Nacional de Águas, ANA) or state agencies (e.g. executive bodies of State Secretariats for the Environment) are in charge of billing and collection, and delegated water agencies (in the form of private organisations, associations, foundations, consortia) manage revenues, which are spent in the basins according to the actions foreseen in the river basin plans.

River basins at federal and state levels have different experience vis-à-vis water charges in Brazil. However, some common features do exist despite different levels of maturity in institutional frameworks. Interstate river basin committees and states in which charges are implemented can be clustered into the following tentative categories: "pioneers", "followers", "inspirational", "newcomers" and "aspirants".

- The **pioneers** include the Paraíba do Sul River basin, the Piracicaba, Capivari, Jundiaí (PCJ) River basin and the State of Rio de Janeiro. The Paraíba do Sul River Basin was the first pilot for water charges in Brazil and helped to fill in some important legislative and operational gaps. In the PCJ River basin, a consortium of 40+ municipalities and major water users, applied a voluntary water charge scheme (*cobrança voluntária pelo uso da água*) as a pilot experience that paved the way for the implementation of water charges in 2006. The State of Rio de Janeiro was the first state, after the State of Ceará, to implement water charges as foreseen by the National Water Resources Management System (Sistema Nacional de Gerenciamento de Recursos Hídricos, SINGREH).
- The **followers** include the São Francisco River basin and the States of São Paulo and Minas Gerais. In these cases, debates on the implementation of water user charges started way ahead actual implementation. The double jurisdiction over state and federal rivers is particularly important for these three cases: the São Francisco is a huge basin involving the Federal Government, the Federal District and the States of Minas Gerais, Goias, Bahia, Pernambuco, Alagoas and Sergipe; the State of Minas Gerais cuts across several interstate river basins, each of them having their own delegated water agencies; the State of São Paulo, whose legal framework for water management dates back to 1991 – namely before the 1997 Federal Water Law – is part of the Paraíba do Sul river basin and the PCJ river basin.
- The **inspirational** case is the State of Ceará, characterised by a longstanding experience and sophisticated centralised institutional framework for water charges, where river basin committees have less deliberative functions than in other states. This centralised system was put in place given the need for the redistribution of financial resources among basins in the state. Water charges are used to finance both administrative costs and the operation and maintenance of the water infrastructure. It is a model for other states, although conceptually different and difficult to replicate.
- The **newcomers** include the Doce, Paranaíba and Verde Grande River basins and the States of Parana and Paraíba, which only recently started implementing water charges. Their experience is relatively limited and some bottlenecks still remain to be addressed. In Paranaiba and Verde Grande, water charges came into effect in March and April 2017.
- The **aspirants** include those states and basins where discussions for implementing water charges in the future are currently taking place (e.g. Piancó-Piranhas-Açu River basin and the State of Rio Grande do Norte).

Until 2016, about BRL 548 million were raised by charging for the use of water resources under federal domain and around BRL 1.5 billion under state domain. At federal level, these revenues are able to cover about 10-15% of the financing need to implement actions foreseen in water resources plans, such as studies, projects or construction works. As a consequence, additional financial resources are needed.

Uneven implementation of water charges in Brazil

Water abstraction and pollution charges can serve economic and financial functions amongst which incentivising behavioural changes to improve water-use efficiency and reducing pollution; socialising the benefits of using a collective resource; and catalysing funding for water management.

Where they exist, water charges in Brazil are established at levels that are too low to drive behavioural change of most users (hydropower generators, industries, farmers, and utilities) and to finance water resources management functions. Revenue that is generated is not perceived to directly benefit users or to finance expenditure programmes in the basins where the charges are levied. Moreover, as the structure and level of charges are similar across the country, they do not reflect local circumstances or changes in water availability over time. The charges also do not reflect the opportunity costs of using water in specific basins, the risk and consequences of pollution, or the dilution capacity of rivers and water bodies. Finally, objections to water charges mostly build on arguments of affordability and competitiveness. These arguments, which can be overstated and misdirected as social and economic consequences, are not assessed with appropriate granularity (large groups of users are exempted, whereas some subgroups might be able to pay).

Water charges are therefore currently a sensitive subject because of the different needs and interests across users and beneficiaries at large. Their decision-making and implementation process through the river basin committees, (national or state) water councils and (delegated) water agencies is rooted on bottom-up considerations but also has some drawbacks that hinder their effectiveness and efficiency.

- First, decisions on the level of charges are predominately political, resulting from negotiation amongst stakeholders within river basin committees. This process brings with it the risk that vested interests may prevail given that the stakeholders involved are also water users who at the end will pay the charge. While in theory, the committee is the most legitimate platform to build consensus across users, in practice it is becoming a place of resistance, trying to avoid charges.
- Second, although it is often recognised *ex post* that charges are generally able to deliver neither economic nor financial objectives, national or state councils tend to endorse automatically charges proposed by committees, with a few exceptions only. In practice, clearer criteria for the approval by (national or state) councils of the proposed water charges by the river basin committees are lacking. It follows that the discussion within the river basin committees (or other platforms) on the political objectives achievable by the charges remain vague and inconclusive.
- Finally, delegated water agencies are subject to heavy procedural rules for public expenditures, slowing down the expenditure process.

Ways forward for water charges to deliver

This report provides some policy recommendations to better set and govern water charges for sustainable growth in Brazil.

Set water charges that serve clearly stated policy objectives

A well-designed water charge drives the behaviour of water users: abstraction charges promote water use efficiency and pollution charges make pollution costly and promote clean technologies and practices. In addition, revenues from charges cover the costs of water management, including infrastructure that contribute to water quantity and quality management. Charges should be designed, and set in reference to, such policy objectives: what is the level of ambition when it comes to protecting water users from risks of scarcity, floods or pollution? These objectives should be set by water resources management plans, most appropriately at basin level.

However, setting the level of an abstraction or pollution charge such that it covers exactly the cost of the environmental and opportunity costs is an almost impossible task for public authorities. Methodological issues for calculating charges should not postpone implementation of water charges; to overcome these difficulties, proxies should be used.

Target large users and polluters first and reflect local conditions

Water charges do not need to be universal to be fair and equitable. In practice, a very large proportion of water is used by a small group of water users. Similarly, a few water users generate a large share of polluted effluents. Transaction costs to cover smaller users or polluters can be high compared to the benefits in terms of water resources management and revenues raised. Hence, to minimise transaction costs, water charges should be targeted to large users and heavy polluters, at least at an early stage.

Minimising transaction costs and targeting payers requires a reliable inventory of users and uses, as well as clear rules for exemption. This is why a staged approach to the deployment of water charges is needed in Brazil, with an initial focus on large water utilities, manufacturing units in water-intensive industries, hydropower plants and large farms growing water-intensive crops.

An efficient charging regime should also reflect the severity of consequences of water abstraction and pollution emissions, in a particular catchment or basin, taking into account competition to access the resource and the opportunity cost of using it, and the dilution capacity of the water body.

Build capacities

Technical capacities can be built in two ways. First, river basin committees and agencies should gain experience with economic analysis. This is a requisite to approximate the opportunity cost of using water, and the cost of pollution, two items which serve as a basis to set charges. Economic analysis is also required to support assessment of the impacts of water charges on the competitiveness of selected industries or farmers, or on the budget of poor households. It is also required to assess the economic benefit of improved water resources management in a particular basin or catchment. Robust economic analysis can support informed discussions in councils, beyond ideological or misconceived statements.

Second, states councils and basins committees would benefit from clear guidelines on how to set and implement economic instruments. Federal authorities (the ANA or the CNRH) could consider setting general rules, such as lower bounds for abstraction or pollution charges, list of pollutants to be controlled and monitored (mandatory and river-specific), rules for expenditure spending and publishing of accounts. The decentralised nature of the system would, however, need to be preserved, with river basin committees then deciding on the specific modalities for adapting these guidelines to their context.

Enhance the knowledge and information base for water charges

Implementing water charges requires a good understanding of how water is used and valued by competitive users. Without a solid knowledge and information base, any assessment of needs, efficiency and effectiveness of economic instruments will remain subjective. However, the availability of good, accessible data and information on water varies across Brazilian states, preventing effective decision-making in terms of who gets water, where and when, and who pays for what. It prevents a common understanding of the state of the water resources, the pressures, as well as the actions needed to protect and improve the resource.

In Brazil, at the level of the national and state councils, estimates of the impacts of water charges on the cost structure of water users are carried out based on secondary data in order to verify that the levels agreed within the river basin committees cause very low impacts. The current state of play may actually reflect the low willingness to charge rather than affordability issues. The lack of data or projections on users' ability to pay and wider needs of the basin has led to the implementation of rates that are generally similar across different basins and fail to reflect local conditions.

Information systems across basins, local, state and federal levels should provide comprehensive, robust and up-to-date data on the state and quality of environment and water resources, including pressures on water resources. Parts of the revenues from water charges could be allocated to strengthening the capacity to monitor water abstraction and pollution in Brazil. Focus could be set first on the major users and polluters.

Strengthen the institutional framework for water charges

Experience of OECD countries shows that river basin committees are best-placed to identify and try to reconcile diverging interests after thorough consultation of all those who have a stake in the outcome at a given scale. However, a realistic distinction between the role assigned to stakeholders in the "consultation" and "decision-making" process needs to be made. There is a need for an open and documented policy debate on the effectiveness of current "deliberative" bodies in water resources management (river basin committees) and their capacity to be outcome- and result-driven. Historically, this conversation has been difficult given the history of councils created throughout the country in different policy domains. A stronger consultative role of the river basin committees and greater devolution of deliberative and executive powers to water agencies would match decision-making to capacity and accountability lines, and result in less unimplemented decisions. This does not imply deflating the role of the national and state water resources councils or overlooking the role of basin committees. It would require water agencies to consult with the "advisory" councils and the committees, and give thorough explanations when they do not follow their advice, in order to guarantee transparency and accountability. Another requisite is that water agencies be totally neutral and independent from any vested interests from water users in order to have such deliberative roles.

Manage water charges at the right scale and enhance co-ordination

In Brazil, the double dominion over state and federal rivers has consequences on the implementation of water charges. Water charges in several cases are applied and governed at both state and federal levels. The issue of scale includes differences in terms of charge rates across states and federal waters, the cost of inaction and the related consequences on water quantity and quality when charges are not applied, and the lack of harmonisation for audit and accountability processes across levels of government.

Another issue concerns divergent governance models and charging systems to which delegated water agencies need to adapt, when delivering executive functions in different states. As such, it is important to facilitate co-ordination across agencies and harmonise regulatory measures and levels of enforcement. At interstate level, a single delegated agency could favour co-ordinate use of financial resources.

Develop river basin plans that drive water charge decisions

River basin plans should drive decisions on the level of abstraction and pollution charges and the use of revenues when they are earmarked for water expenditures in the basin.

River basin plans should identify the priority areas for action on water resources management on the basis of objective criteria that would take into account primarily health risks, social issues, the environment and the economy. They should quantify realistically the financial resources needed to take action, and list specific actions that can help drive behaviour change and foster water use efficiency. River basin plans could also specify which measures should be financed by the public administration and which ones would fall under the private domain. They should be accompanied by strategic financial plans, tailored to an agreed action plan and affordable timescales for implementation.

Water charges should effectively address the issues of scarcity and pollution and be co-ordinated with other policy priority. This is why river basin plans should be integrated with other plans (e.g. for agriculture development or sanitation) as they can contribute to enhance water security.

Deploy water charges in combination with other policy instruments

Water charges should be considered in combination with other policy instruments such as water allocation regimes or water quality standards. In addition, awareness raising campaigns and nudging can enhance users' willingness-to-pay for improved water management and improve the efficiency of water charges. Nudging is a way to influence water users' behaviour by providing more information about water stress and water quality.

Water charges deliver best when water use (abstraction and pollution) is monitored and regulations are enforced. There is room for improvement in Brazil. Sound inspection and control mechanisms, as well as sanctions and penalties in case of non-compliance, should be strengthened to make the entire system more robust and credible.

Consider accompanying measures, when reforming or deploying water charges

A reform of existing charges or the deployment of new ones can be costly for water users. Accompanying measures can facilitate the transition towards more efficient water uses or cleaner technologies or practices. For instance, best available technologies and best practices could be promoted. Investment in such technologies could be facilitated by financial support, eventually financed by recycling some of the revenues of water charges. Such support should be time-bound, targeted and assessed.

Facilitate spending that contributes to enhanced water security and show the benefits to users

The reason why water charges in Brazil do not bite or are considered irrelevant is because their collection lacks purpose and is viewed by users as a mere fiscal instrument. For example, sometimes revenues are allocated to investment programmes (e.g. water supply and sanitation infrastructure) that are several orders of magnitude larger. The perception by users in these cases is that their contribution has no added-value. In other cases, collected funds, when used, are scattered across minor expenses that the payers do not view as important, which also affects users' willingness to pay.

Poor performance in the allocation of revenues from water charges hinders the legitimacy of the instrument and fuels resistance to increase rates and revenues. In the Brazilian context, there is a good rationale to expedite disbursement of revenues from water charges, and to ensure they generate tangible benefits for water users in the basin. At the moment, it is difficult to justify that parts of the revenues should be saved to manage future water crises.

Revenues from water charges should be allocated to expenditures in line with the initial objectives set for charging and where they can make a difference. For instance, it is counterproductive to allocate revenues from water charges to large infrastructure projects to which their contribution is minimal: users will infer that charges are ineffective.

Chapter 1

Why water charges matter in Brazil

This chapter makes the case for a more systematic use of economic instruments as a response to water challenges in Brazil. It explains the rationale for using economic instruments for sustainable water management and sets principles for setting and governing such instruments. The remainder of the report will focus on two specific economic instruments, namely abstraction and pollution charges.

Rationale for water pricing

The OECD (2015a) argued that Brazil should continue to promote water use efficiency to alleviate pressures on all surface and groundwater resources, especially where water is scarce and competition between sectors intensifies, whilst taking into account the need for environmental flows. Economic policy instruments (e.g. water abstraction charges) have a role to play.

Similar issues relate to water quality. Urbanisation and increased demand for water reinforce the need to collect and treat effluents of wastewater. The same applies to industries and, in similar ways, to agriculture. To this end, OECD (2017) recommends that governments combine regulatory, information-based and economic instruments to provide continuing incentives for water users and polluters to reduce quantitative and qualitative pressure on water resources.

It follows that economic instruments can play a significant role in support of achieving water policy objectives in Brazil while setting incentives for different sectoral users (e.g. agriculture, energy, etc.) to use water efficiently now and in the future. OECD, 2015a showed that, where they exist, water charges are established at levels that are too low to drive behavioural change or to provide a significant source of finance for water policy. Moreover, their design (e.g. flat rates) and charge exemption for some sectors may be inappropriate in specific situations. For instance, social and economic consequences are not properly assessed, transparency in the collection and use of revenues is a challenge, and enforcement is weak in many cases.

Recent and ongoing droughts in Brazil, and heightened attention to water management in the political agenda, provide the momentum to think about the different policy instruments, including water charges, to ensure they contribute to water security and sustainable growth in Brazil. Reduced availability of long-term renewable water resources, combined with the increasing demand due to growing population, especially in urban areas, intensifies competition across sectors. Poor management of competing demands for water between sectors and weak controls on polluting discharges compound the challenge of natural scarcity. Climate change is altering hydrological conditions, increasing uncertainty and the frequency of extreme events. Left unaddressed, the impact of these challenges will restrict economic growth and social welfare improvements; therefore, a bold change is urgently needed sooner to increase resilience and to embrace a long-term view.

Practical definitions and scope

This report focuses on setting and governing abstraction and pollution charges in Brazil. It provides an overview on how they currently operate and provides suggestions on how they could be improved to support attainment of water policy objectives. The discussion extends to an analysis of how they could be combined with other policy instruments (regulation, or information-based ones) and policies (e.g. energy efficiency, food security, urban development, etc.) to achieve the best results. Tariffs for water services, in particular water supply and sanitation, are not covered by this report, except in so far as abstraction and pollution charges are likely to be reflected in water bills for final users.

The report takes into account the following:

- Water abstraction and pollution charges are a pricing instrument but should not be conflated with tariffs for water supply or sanitation services: they reflect some of the costs associated with using or polluting water. While economic theory argues that charges should reflect the value of using water, *value* and *charges* are two distinct concepts. In the same vein, *charges* are not equal to *costs*. Charges should reflect a series of costs associated with the use of freshwater resources. This reflection is partial at best and charges therefore do not equate to costs. However, charges can be used to fund the costs of managing water resources and regulating activities that impact upon water availability and quality.
- Economic instruments can play a critical role in managing water risks at least cost for the community. Water security is the management of four water-related risks, which hinder social well-being and economic growth: i) too much water, ii) too little water, iii) too polluted water, and iv) resilience of freshwater ecosystems. In addition, the lack of access to safe water and sanitation puts a high cost on social, economic and environmental development in Brazil. OECD (2013) argues that water-related risks need to be addressed in a co-ordinated way, and OECD (2015a) argues that governance responses also need to be tailored to the level of risks.
- For water charges to deliver, it is crucial to take into account the overall governance system in which they are set and implemented. To this end, OECD (2015b) Principles on Water Governance call, amongst others, for clarity and co-ordination on *who does what* in setting, implementing and regulating water charges; appropriate *scale*, policy *coherence*, adequate technical, human and financial *capacity* to collect and disburse revenues from charges; consistent *data and information* to guide, assess and improve water charges; *transparent* practices for budgeting and accounting; robust *regulatory* frameworks to ensure enforcement and compliance with water charges; *stakeholder* engagement to raise awareness on risks and secure the buy-in for charges; as well as regular *monitoring and evaluation* to assess if charges they fulfil the intended outcomes.

Policy attention is often focused on the *level* of abstraction and pollution charges. The report will argue that levels or rates are important features of water charges. However, the *structure* of the charge matters as well, as different structures (e.g. a flat rate or increasing block charges; how different pollutants in the effluent are charged) will affect the behaviour of water users differently. Two other features of a charging system deserve attention and will be addressed in the report: 1) the *process* of setting and enforcing charges; in particular, the modes of engaging with stakeholders matter; and 2) the management of *expenditure*, since how revenues from water charges are spent is an essential part of the efficiency, effectiveness and political acceptability of a charging system.

The use of economic instruments for water management

In a perfectly competitive market, the price given by the market through interaction between buyers and sellers leads to an efficient solution, and the optimal allocation of water is automatically achieved. Yet with water, and specifically due to its environmental uses and associated externalities (water as a common pool resource and a source of pollution), prices have to be established. Water charges (both abstraction and pollution charges) have to be set to correct inefficiencies resulting from individual behaviours. For instance, the market does not adequately manage common pool resources where access is open and there is no property right. These resources are subject to overuse (high rivalry in consumption) in situations of scarcity where strong common property resource institutions or resource user groups are not in place (OECD, 2015c).

From the economic theory point of view, water charges should reflect infrastructure and transaction costs, environmental costs, and opportunity costs; however, in practice they are not always fully represented. The design of the charge scheme should, to the extent possible, take into account these costs despite existing challenges to adequately reflect them.

- *Infrastructure and transaction costs* can include costs such as the cost of irrigation and storage infrastructure, wastewater treatment plants, sewerage networks, energy costs, and administrative, monitoring and data analysis costs. They depend on technological choices, infrastructure design and financing, and operation and maintenance and asset management. Revenues from water charges would not usually cover the cost of investment or operation and maintenance (this is typically the role of tariffs for water-related services). However, where an asset benefits more than one sector, such as a reservoir which is used to regulate river flows for the benefit of water supply, industry and agriculture, then it would be appropriate for abstraction charges to cover the operational and financing costs. Charges can also cover the administrative and technical costs of managing and regulating water resources for the benefit of all users.
- *Environmental costs* correspond to damage induced by water abstraction or pollution. For example, too much groundwater abstraction may cause saline intrusion in coastal aquifers, or reduce river flows. Excessive surface water abstraction may result in reduced environmental flows and ecosystem functioning, and require expensive infrastructure in some sectors to allow them to ensure secure water supplies. Note that the same level of pollution can generate different levels of externalities, depending on features of the receiving water body (e.g., dilution capacity, instream water quality levels) and potential uses downstream (recreational, drinking water, or others) (Box 1.1). Industry and public water supply can incur significant increased treatment costs to ensure that the abstracted water meets their quality standards.
- *Opportunity costs* of using water represent the foregone opportunities of alternative water uses. These costs are incurred when one water user or polluter affects the use of the resource by any third party. For example, higher water withdrawal by a city might affect the quantity of water available to downstream irrigators, thus imposing costs on these users. There are also opportunity costs associated with exclusion of other potential users in areas where water quality is unsuitable for use. Technically the opportunity cost is defined as the value of the water in its highest value alternative use. Opportunity costs are typically higher where water is scarce and competition to access is fierce. They are also higher when water is being used for low value uses, preventing access for higher value uses. If property rights are in place and tradable, the market value of water would reflect opportunity costs.

Box 1.1. Economic, social and environmental impacts of water pollution

Water pollution is costly, with many economic costs entailed, including: i) water treatment and waterborne health costs; ii) degradation of ecosystem services; iii) impacts on economic activities such as agriculture, fisheries, industrial manufacturing and tourism; iv) reduced property values; and v) opportunity costs of further development (OECD, 2017). For example, in the United States, drinking water impacts from nitrogen pollution are estimated at USD 19 billion per year (Sobota et al., 2015). In England, the total cumulative cost of water pollution (point and diffuse sources) was estimated at GBP 700 – 1300 million per year (National Audit Office, 2010). Water quality impacts to economic, social and environmental values are presented in the table below. Water users through their water bill usually pay the cost of treating water pollution to enable domestic, commercial and industrial use. The costs of cleaning up polluted water resources and restoring freshwater ecosystems are often afforded by tax payers.

Impacts of water pollution: Economic, social and environmental

Impact	Examples
Human health	Polluted water is the world's largest health risk and continues to threaten both quality of life and public health. Associated with this are health service costs, loss life expectancy, and emergency health costs associated with major pollution events.
Ecosystem health	Damage to freshwater and marine ecosystems (e.g. fish kill, invertebrates, benthic fauna, flora, habitat degradation) and loss of ecosystem services, which may require investment in additional or different grey infrastructure alternatives to replicate these services.
Social values	Prohibition from recreational use (e.g. swimming, fishing, kayaking), beach closure, impacts on aesthetics, cultural and spiritual values.
Agricultural productivity	Exclusion of contaminated water for irrigation results in increasing water scarcity. Irrigation with contaminated water causes damage to, and reduced productivity of, pasture and crops, contamination of soil, impacts to livestock health and production, and scouring of infrastructure.
Industrial productivity	Exclusion of contaminated water for industrial use results in increasing water scarcity. Scouring of infrastructure and clean-up costs from spills/accidents.
Commercial fisheries	Direct and indirect fish kill, contamination of shellfish.
Urban and domestic use	Increased water treatment and inspection costs, maintenance costs from scouring and premature ageing of infrastructure, increased wastewater treatment costs with implementation of stricter regulations. Emergency and clean-up costs from spills/accidents.
Tourism	Losses in fishing, boating, rafting and swimming activities to other tourism activities or to other ventures with superior water quality.
Property values	Waterfront property values can decline because of unsightly pollution and odour.

Source: OECD (2017), *Diffuse Pollution, Degraded Waters: Emerging Policy Solutions*, OECD Publishing, Paris, http://dx.doi.org/10.1787/9789264269064-en.

The general principle for setting water charges is to reflect the *externalities*[1] that water abstraction (or water pollution) by one user causes to third parties and the environment. From an economic point of view, the existence of externalities makes the case for the intervention of authorities that implement charges so that water users are able to internalise these environmental costs when deciding on the volume of water to be abstracted (or pollution discharged). Charging users for the environmental and scarcity costs induced by water abstraction or use is essential for achieving cost recovery. For instance, this is the rationale for Article 9 of the Water Framework Directive in Europe (European Commission EC – Water Framework Directive – 2000/60/EC). The charge should also enhance the efficiency of water allocation across users, where "efficiency is concerned with maximising the welfare that is obtained from a resource by allocating it to its most valuable economic use" (OECD, 2011).

Water charges are sources of revenue that can be used to reduce distortionary taxes (double dividend) or to finance public goods. They can be used for regulating and managing the resource. This could include operational or even capital costs, where an investment benefits multiple users (e.g. from a new reservoir to cleaning up a discharge from an abandoned mine discharge). The income could pay off a loan, or reimburse a Public Private Partnership. Water charges are not intended to cover the investment needs in the water supply and sanitation sector, which are booming due to demographic growth and the willingness to achieve universal coverage. This is an issue not only for Brazil. By 2050 in the OECD, USD 6.7 trillion will be needed for investments in water supply and sanitation (OECD, 2015b). Water charges (abstraction and pollution charges), beyond those needed to recover investment and operating costs, may serve two main purposes: i) to incentivise behavioural changes to improve water-use efficiency and reduce pollution; and ii) socialise the benefits of using a collective resource.

Water abstraction and pollution charges are best used alongside with several policy instruments. Economists usually distinguish between "command-and-control" and "market-based" regulations (Sterner and Coria, 2012). Command-and-control regulations refer to technical restrictions on economic activities that aim at reducing pollution and resource use. They include banning the most dangerous products, imposing "end-of-pipe" pollution treatments, setting a cap on wastewater discharges or pollution concentration on water streams. Public authorities "command" some restrictions on the production process, which are then "controlled" and enforced with penalties in cases of non-compliance.

In turn, market-based regulations refer to instruments that rely on market mechanisms to induce a reduction in pollution or resource extraction. It is usual to distinguish between *price* and quantity instruments. Water abstraction and pollution charges are "pricing" market-based instruments, since a price is assigned to the volume of water extracted or to wastewater discharged. Water markets or tradeable emission permits are "quantity" market-based instruments. Two situations then happen: with *pricing* mechanisms, regulators set the price and quantity adjusts accordingly; with *trading* mechanisms, regulators cap the quantity and the price adjusts through the market. A last family of instruments is based on *information* and includes environmental certification, product labelling, nudges and information conveyance.

Principles for economic instruments contributing to sustainable water management

The following set of principles for water resources management should be considered when designing abstraction and pollution charges.

The Polluter-Pays principle creates conditions to make pollution a costly activity and to either influence behaviour to reduce pollution, or generate revenues to alleviate pollution and compensate for social costs (OECD 2012a). Examples include pollution charges, taxes on inputs (such as fertilisers and pesticides) and sewer user charges. The Polluter-Pays principle should not be accompanied by conflicting subsidies, tax advantages or other measures that encourage polluters to pollute, or assist polluters in bearing the costs of pollution, thereby creating distortions in the market (OECD, 1972;

1974). While there is a case for a public subsidy to address the accumulated damage caused by historical pollution (particularly when polluters are no longer around to pay), the Polluter-Pays principle should be the first line of defence in securing water quality and incentivising behaviour change.

The Polluter-Pays principle is commonly used for the control of point source pollution (see Box 3.5 for a definition). Several challenges result in the Polluter-Pays principle not frequently being applied in the control of diffuse pollution. They include difficulties with identifying and targeting polluters, determining reliable estimates of pollution costs, poor enforcement of existing regulations, and strong political opposition. Possible ways to overcome these barriers are listed in Table 1.1.

Table 1.1. The Polluter-Pays principle for diffuse water pollution

Barriers	Solutions
Difficulties with identifying and targeting polluters	Computer modelling as a cost-effective alternative to directly observing individual diffuse pollution emissions. Taxes on inputs (e.g. fertilisers, pesticides, cleaning products) or land use (e.g. paved urban surfaces, livestock numbers, intensive land use). Collective accountability at catchment level.
Difficulties with determining reliable estimates of pollution costs	Economic modelling and scientific monitoring to inform costs and justify action (new data sources are available). Market mechanisms to reveal pollution costs and differentiated abilities to cope with them.
Poor enforcement of existing regulations	Computer modelling as a cost-effective alternative to directly observing individual diffuse pollution emissions. Taxes on inputs (e.g. fertilisers, pesticides, cleaning products) or land use (e.g. paved urban surfaces, livestock numbers, intensive land use). Collective accountability at catchment level.
Strong political opposition	Economic modelling and scientific monitoring to inform costs and justify action (new data sources are available). Stakeholder engagement. Collective accountability at catchment level. Connecting with higher-level policy priorities.

Source: OECD (2017), *Diffuse Pollution, Degraded Waters: Emerging Policy Solutions*, OECD Publishing, Paris, http://dx.doi.org/10.1787/9789264269064-en.

The Beneficiary Pays principle allows sharing of the financial burden of water management. It takes account of the high opportunity cost related to using public funds for the provision of private goods that users can afford. A requisite is that private benefits attached to water resources management are inventoried and valued, beneficiaries are identified, and mechanisms are set to harness them (OECD 2012a). For example, wastewater treatment plants help to protect water quality in rivers and lakes, and green infrastructures, such as wetlands and forested catchments, and to deliver ecosystem services such as water purification. Benefits include city residents provided with quality drinking water; reduced water treatment costs for utilities and health systems and downstream industrial and agricultural users; improved business for fisheries and tourism operators; and benefits for recreational users, waterfront property owners, the environment, and society at large. However, it can be a challenge to find mechanisms to ensure that the beneficiaries pay for the true value of their benefits.

Equity should be considered with regards to who bares the costs and benefits of policy reform fall upon and the needs of future generations. Disproportionate costs to users, whilst important, should not be overstated. Where high levels of taxes have been applied to chemical inputs to comply with the Polluter-Pays Principle, often coupled with a mix of other policy measures, they have usually led to reductions in input use without loss of farm production or income (OECD, 2012b). Due consideration of the Equity principle for water quality management financing should also be given for public subsidies (OECD, 2009). Equity and fairness in burden sharing do not preclude efficiency.

Policy coherence is required to ensure initiatives taken by different policy sectors do not have negative impacts on water availability, quality and freshwater ecosystems, or increase the cost of water management. Multiple policy sectors affect water quantity and quality, particularly the management of diffuse water pollution – for example, urban development, agriculture, climate, natural resources, forestry, energy, conservation and human health. The potential synergies and complementarities among the sectors should be used to guide formulation of effective options to maximise gain, optimise co-benefits, and avoid negative impacts. Policy coherence would entail the following actions:

- Remove subsidies that encourage land use change or intensification that can augment water-related risks.
- Look for win-win solutions such as NOx reductions to improve air and water quality and reduce greenhouse gas emissions.
- Integrate water pollution control with air pollution control, land use management, and water quantity management.

When considering new policy in other sectors that may have potential impact on water security (e.g. agriculture, urban development, energy, climate, mining, etc.) it is important to identify their impacts on water, freshwater ecosystems, the economy and social welfare, and their underlying driving factors (e.g. market, information, institutional and enforcement failures, and perverse subsidies). Strengthening valuation of water in environmental impact assessments can help identify trade-offs and co-benefits. The decision to commit to a new policy can be guided by a benefit-cost assessment framework that measures whether the potential benefits of water management, adjusted to account for risks, outweigh the potential costs. International experience and lessons learned from previous policy successes and failures should be applied.

In practice, the interactions of the above-mentioned principles can be problematic. For instance, when the equity principle is invoked to diminish the cost paid by polluters, second or third best solutions to pollution challenges that result can sometimes crowd out more effective policy options (such as the use of pollution charges). Moreover, the Beneficiary Pays principle is often conflicting with the Polluter-Pays principle: lax definitions can lead to apparent contradictions. This is the case, for instance, when poorly defined Payment for Ecosystem Services schemes result in sharing the cost of pollution. Farmers who use water wisely may be penalised vis-à-vis others if the less virtuous ones receive a larger incentive to change their behaviour (see OECD, 2012b).

Note

1. Quoting OECD (2011): "The presence of these negative externalities means that individuals do not take into account the full cost of their decisions when extracting water and only take into account the personal cost of withdrawing water, not the cost this will have on others. This creates a wedge between the marginal cost of water withdrawals faced by individuals and the marginal cost of water withdrawals faced by society, and this divergence leads to over-extraction of the resource."

References

National Audit Office (2010), "Tackling diffuse water pollution in England", report by the Comptroller and Auditor General, HC 188, Session 2010-2011, United Kingdom.

OCDE (2017), *Diffuse Pollution, Degraded Waters: Emerging Policy Solutions*, OECD Publishing, Paris, http://dx.doi.org/10.1787/9789264269064-en.

OCDE (2015a), *Water Resources Governance in Brazil*, OECD Publishing, Paris, http://dx.doi.org/10.1787/9789264238121-en.

OECD (2015b), "OECD Principles on Water Governance", www.oecd.org/cfe/regional-policy/OECD-Principles-on-Water-Governance-brochure.pdf.

OECD (2015c), *Water Resources Allocation: Sharing Risks and Opportunities*, OECD Publishing, Paris, http://dx.doi.org/10.1787/9789264229631-en.

OECD (2013), *Providing Agri-environmental Public Goods through Collective Action*, OECD Publishing, Paris, http://dx.doi.org/10.1787/9789264197213-en.

OECD (2012a), *A Framework for Financing Water Resources Management*, OECD Publishing, Paris, http://dx.doi.org/10.1787/9789264179820-en.

OECD (2012b), *Water Quality and Agriculture: Meeting the Policy Challenge*, OECD Publishing, Paris, http://dx.doi.org/10.1787/9789264168060-en.

OECD (2011), *Towards Green Growth*, OECD Publishing, Paris, http://dx.doi.org/10.1787/9789264111318-en.

OECD (2009), *Managing Water for All: An OECD Perspective on Pricing and Financing*, OECD Publishing, Paris, http://dx.doi.org/10.1787/9789264059498-en

OECD (1974), *Recommendation of the Council on the Implementation of the Polluter – Pays Principle*, 14 November, C(74)223, http://acts.oecd.org/instruments/showinstrumentview.aspx?instrumentid=11&instrumentpid=9&lang=en.

OECD (1972), *Recommendation of the Council on Guiding Principles concerning International Economic Aspects of Environmental Policies*, 26 May 1972, C(72)128, http://acts.oecd.org/instruments/showinstrumentview.aspx?instrumentid=4&instrumentpid=255&lang=en&book=false.

Sobota J.D. et al. (2015), "Cost of reactive nitrogen release from human activities to the environment in the United States", *Environmental Research Letters*, Vol. 10/2, pp. 14, http://iopscience.iop.org/article/10.1088/1748-9326/10/2/025006/pdf (accessed September 2017).

Sterner T. and J. Coria (2012), *Policy instruments for environmental and natural resource management*, RFF Press, Routledge, New York.

Chapter 2

Water charges in Brazil — The state of play

This chapter describes how water charges currently operate in Brazil. It presents the legal and institutional framework for water charges and reviews the experience of federal and state governments, grouping them in five clusters: pioneers; followers; inspirational; newcomers; and aspirants. The chapter highlights several common challenges in terms of setting clear objectives for water charges, developing plans that can drive decisions, putting in place an adequate information system and making the most of collected revenues for the benefit of water users.

The legal and institutional framework

What is a cobrança?

The water charge (*cobrança*) is a price for the use of a common-pool resource, set within the basin committees in a participative manner by water users, civil society, and public authorities (ANA, 2014). The main objective is to point out the economic value of water, while encouraging its rational use and preserving its quality. It is levied on users who abstract raw water or discharge effluents directly into water bodies. Established by the Federal Water Law 9433 of 1997 (Box 2.1), water charges are one of the water management instruments included in the National Water Management System (Sistema Nacional de Gerenciamento de Recursos Hídricos, SINGREH), together with water resources plans; water quality classification of water bodies; water permits; and water resources information system (art. 5).

The *cobrança* is neither a tax (*imposto*), a fine (*multa*), nor a tariff *(tarifa)*, such as the tariff for water supply (ANA, 2014). It can be seen as an *economic compensation for using the share of the water "commons"* (Braga et al., 2005). It does not relate to services or investments and it is subject to implementation rules for public revenues (Canali, 2010). From a perspective, two different branches of law regulate taxes (tax law) and public prices (financial law) (Pompeu, 2000) (Table 2.1).

Table 2.1. Differences between water charges and other instruments in Brazil

		Fee (*taxa*)	Tariff (*tarifa*)	Special assessments (*contribuição de melhoria*)	Public price (preço publico)
Instrument		Fiscal	For public services	Fiscal	Patrimonial
Calculation basis		Basic public service	Public service through concession or permission	Projects promoting equity gains for third parties	Use of the public good or service through authorisation
Measurement of use or service	**Yes**		X	X	X
	No	X			
State of use or service	**Effectively provided**	X	X	X	X
	Mandatory	X			
Implementation instrument		Law	Executive Decree	Law	Contract or Normative Resolution
Competent authority for collection		Public authorities	Service provider	Public authorities	Public authorities
Possibility of delegation		Only to a public body	To private providers	Only to a public body	Only to a public body
Validity		From January 1st	From the validity of the decree	From 1 January	From the validity of a contract
Practical examples		Inspection fee (taxa de fiscalização)	Water and Sewage Services	Asphalt road services	Water charges

Source: ANA (2014), "Cobrança pelo uso de recursos hídricos, Capacitação em Gestão de Recursos Hídricos", Vol. 7, Brasília.

Box 2.1. The relevant legal framework for water charges in Brazil: A synthetic overview

- **Civil Code, 1916**: Allows for a charge on the use of a public good, according to the federal, states and municipal law (art.68)
- **Water Code, 1934**: Allows for a charge on the use of water resources (art. 36). It considered water as private property when situated on private land
- **Federal Constitution, 1988**: Exclusion of water as private property and consolidation of the double dominion
- **National Environment Policy, 1981 (Act 6938/81)**: Obligation for the polluters to compensate for environmental damages and pay for the exploitation of environmental resources with economic purposes
- **Water Law No. 9 433/ 1997**: Establishment of water charges
- **Law No. 9 984/ 2000:** Creation of the National Water Agency (Agência Nacional de Águas, ANA) and definition of its roles including implementing, together with the river basin committees, the water charges for the use of water in the federal domain
- **Law No. 10881/2004**: Regulation of management contracts between ANA and delegated water agencies
- **CNRH Resolution No. 48/ 2005**: General criteria establishing mechanisms and rates of water charges
- **State legislations**: Replication of the objectives established by the Water Law No. 9 433/ 1997

Recently, the National Water Resources Council (Conselho Nacional de Recursos Hídricos, CNRH) has started discussing how to improve the Resolution No. 48/2005 establishing general criteria for water charges in Brazil. The Technical Chamber for water charges (Câmara Técnica de Cobrança pelo Uso de Recursos Hídricos, CTCOB) of the CNRH has already held seminars with stakeholders from several states, water use representatives and civil society to investigate challenges and hear proposals for improvement. Various stakeholders share the view that water charges should incorporate issues of local interest. The discussion could potentially take into account issues such as general criteria for defining clear objectives of charges at basin level; the financial sustainability of river basin committees and agencies; the updates of water charges' levels; lower bounds for rates, the automatic adjustment of water charges based on inflation and procedures for efficiently using revenues. It is expected that findings from this OECD report will contribute to future debates on the topic, building on the fruitful exchanges and dialogue with the representatives from the CNRH and the CTCOB during the seminars held by the OECD delegation and the ANA in Brazil in September 2016, February 2017 and June 2017.

Source: ANA (2016), "Background report on setting and governing economic instruments for water policy in Brazil", Brazil.

Water charges: What for?

The Federal Water Law 9433/1997 attributes a double role to *cobrança:* an *economic* one, aiming to send signals for rationalising water uses and internalising environmental costs; and a *financial* one, as revenues can be used to finance interventions foreseen by the river basin plans, such as recovery and preservation of water bodies. More specifically, art. 19 of the Water Law identifies three objectives of the *cobrança*: i) to recognise water as an economic good[1] and to give users an indication of its real value;

ii) to encourage a rational water use; iii) to raise resources to finance programmes or interventions included in the plans. Clearly, charging does not privatise the use of water that is an inalienable public domain good (Bronzatto and Amorim, 2012). The Water Law implies that water is a good belonging to the public domain and a *limited natural resource* endowed with economic value (art.1). The logics behind is that water is a scarce good (economically scarce in relative terms) by definition, reflecting both water depletion due to anthropogenic and natural causes, as well as multiple, alternative competitive uses, respectively in water scarce and water abundant contexts.

Revenues from water charges should be used in the watershed where they are generated. The 1997 Federal Water Law established that 7.5% of revenues should cover implementation and administrative costs of the National Water Resources Management System (Sistema Nacional de Gerenciamento de Recursos Hídricos, SINGREH). The remaining 92.5% should be devoted to studies, programmes and projects included in the river basin plan. According to the *Water Pays for Water* principle, inspired by the French system, water charges originally sought to create a financially autonomous water management system (ANA, 2014). Earmarked revenues represent an incentive for stakeholders, gathered in the river basin committees, to build consensus on the needs and actual use of water charges. The rationale is that water users or polluters would be more willing to pay if they could see concrete benefits in return; however, currently, one of the most important issues is that the "service" that the charge buys is not evident and benefits are not immediate.

Who pays the cobrança*?*

According to the 1997 Federal Water Law, those holding permits (*outorgas)* for using water for economic purposes are subject to water charges (art. 20). Permits are granted for: i) freshwater and groundwater withdrawal for final consumption or production processes; ii) effluent discharge into water bodies from sewage and other liquid for the purpose of dilution, transportation or final disposal; iii) hydropower generation; iv) other uses that alter water quantity or quality of water bodies. There are also exemptions, such as in the case of negligible abstraction and storage of water to meet the needs of small population groups in rural areas (art. 12). River basin committees establish the thresholds below which users are exempt from requesting the permits (and thereafter, exempt from paying the *cobrança*), which are approved by the National Water Resources Council (Conselho Nacional de Recursos Hídricos, CNRH) (Box 2.3).

In practice, sectors subject to water charges are: water supply and sanitation, manufacturing, hydropower and agriculture. The Government grants permits, according to the priorities established in the water resources plans for preserving multiple water uses (art.13), while controlling water quality and quantity (art.11). The integrated approach between permits (*outorga*) and charges (*cobrança*) formalises the link between command and control and economic instruments (ANA, 2014).

Box 2.2. Water abstraction charges for small users: International examples

In **France**, below established water volume thresholds, water users are exempt from paying abstraction charges. These thresholds vary according to the water agency, the type of resource (groundwater/ surface water) and the scarcity of water. For example, in the Rhône-Méditerranée-Corse River basin, water users abstracting less than 10 000 m3 per year are exempted from paying abstraction charges. The threshold is reduced to 7 000 m3 in areas facing water scarcity problems.

Box 2.2. Water abstraction charges for small users: International examples (*cont.*)

In **England** and **Wales**, some classes of small user have been exempted from charging (and in some cases, regulation) entirely, e.g. a borehole for household use only. For small volume users the charge below a de minimis exclusion would in any case be too small to be seen as any sort of incentive, and is only viewed as a mere bureaucratic exercise. A charge should also reflect a service, and most small users will get little or no service other than knowing that their abstraction has been registered. They will not be inspected (or should not be — enforcement should be risk-based and small users will almost always be low risk) and so the perception of the charge is negative. The same applies for diffuse (as opposed to point-source) pollution — the high variability in time and space makes attribution of sources of pollution complex; the high transaction costs associated with dealing with a large number of heterogeneous polluters call for other sorts of incentives or regulation, such as nutrient trading, or payment for ecosystem services for reducing pesticide use.

In **Portugal**, the abstraction charge for surface and groundwater water is applied regardless of the purpose of the water use and public or private nature of users. However, there is a threshold related to the means of extraction. If the abstraction is done by a pumping system with a power of less than 5 HP, no payment is required, unless otherwise established in the river basin plan and justified by the special sensitivity of the affected area. This exemption essentially contemplates small farmers.

In **Spain**, at the central level, the competent authority (Ministry of Agriculture, Fisheries and the Environment, Central Government of Spain) may include some exemptions. River basin authorities shall issue within three months, in a mandatory way, and prior to the resolution to be adopted, a motivated report to provide the rationale for whatever exemption.

In **Latin American countries**, very often, several water users are exempted from paying abstraction charges. However, when calculating what actually has to be paid, that exemption should be effective at taxable event level, not at base level. This distinction is relevant: as per the former, anyone withdrawing or polluting water should be subject to the levy; as per the latter, this does not imply everyone has to pay, but it will depend on other decisions (allowances, etc.). As per the new groundwater management, Peru is currently discussing a service tariff (not a use tariff) that levies those water users with a well of their own and excludes agricultural groundwater users.

Source: Ian Barker, Peer-Reviewer, Water Policy International Ltd (England and Wales); Gonzalo Delacámara, Peer-Reviewer, IMDEA Water Institute (Spain and Latin America); Francisco Nunes Correia, Peer-Reviewer, Technical University of Lisbon (Portugal); Arnaud Reynaud, Expert, Toulouse School of Economics (France).

Calculating water charges

The calculation of water charges in Brazil is basically similar across river basins where charges are applied. In a simplified formula, three variables are multiplied (ANA, 2016):

- The basis of calculation includes each type of use: abstraction, consumption and discharge. The annual volume of water *abstracted* is quantified by the licensed annual volume or through a weighed sum of the licensed annual volume and the metered annual volume; the water *consumed* is calculated as the difference between the volume abstracted and discharged; the *discharge* takes into account the pollutant load in the discharged wastewater effluent;
- The unit price, which is generally based on investment programmes contained in the river basin plans and operational costs of water agencies;

- The coefficients take into account specific goals and adjustments to the formula. They include, for instance: water quality classification of water bodies, according to their main category of water uses; volume of water actually used in relation to the permitted volume; water loss ratio in the sanitation sector; and payment capacity of the agricultural sector.

In interstate river basins, water abstraction charges' calculation is based on the volumes specified both through the permits and the volumes measured by the users themselves. The latter are declared to the ANA by means of the Annual Declaration of Water Resources Use (Declaração Anual de Uso de Recursos Hídricos, DAURH), available online. Users are subject to inspections by the ANA, done it usually through water samplings in the most critical basins. The calculation of the annual charges from water volumes reflecting the permits is conceived as a means to potentially encourage users to request lower volumes of entitlements, which could reduce the pressure on water resources in the medium and long term. Leakage rates are also self-reported by users. The ANA has the prerogative of checking and disregarding the data.

This system suffers from some limitations: First, water charges set on self-reported water abstraction can be considered as a viable option only if inspections and audits of reported water abstraction are conducted and if fines and penalties are in place and enforced. Second, the calculation of annual charges based on permits may create some perverse effects. Since users know they will be charged based on their permits and not on their actual water use, they may have no incentive to reduce water abstraction below permitted values. Although in the medium or long term, there may be a beneficial effect if the user requests decrease in their permitted values, depending on the level of charges.

Choosing the volume of water abstracted as the basis for charging is a usual approach. However, abstractions should be measured against a standard that gives confidence that the measurements can be used as a basis for charging. Therefore, a meter or other measurement device is required to measure the volume of water that is abstracted: meters should be calibrated and sites routinely monitored for compliance. The accuracy of the volumetric information should be submitted as the basis for billing.[2] This is not the case in Brazil. Meters are not always installed, especially in the agricultural sector. Instead, a strategic use of metering (e.g. for large users, in case of water scarcity) can help monitor water abstraction. If abstracted water cannot be metered, then authorities must rely on other mechanisms to approximate water use. Examples include charging irrigated surfaces on a per hectare basis or hydroelectricity production on a per megawatt-hour basis. Another issue is when part of the water abstracted is returned to the environment. If the water that is returned is of the same quality, and if it is returned close to where it was abstracted, then the charge should reflect return flows and be based on the volume of water used (and not returned to the environment in the catchment). This, however, may be difficult to quantify since it could require a meter to measure water abstraction and a meter to measure water that is returned to the environment. In some cases, such as industrial uses, it may be possible to reach agreement about the proportion of water incorporated in the product, or lost through evaporation.

Pollution charges are generally based on the volume of discharged water. This volume is rarely monitored, except for industries and hydropower generation. For households, it is often approximated by the volume of water used. The pollution load is often estimated on the basis of the control of a limited set of pollutants. Even though water charges are based on polluter-pay principles, in practice, there are can be difficulties in implementing these principles (see Chapter 3). Currently, in Brazil, the only charged pollutant load is the organic load related to the Biochemical Oxygen Demand ($BOD_{5,20}$). However, it is a poor proxy for pollution load for many discharges since other pollutants in effluent streams increasingly cause damages to the environment and human health, whilst increasing the cost of water treatment. Therefore, monitoring BOD should gradually be supplemented by monitoring a range of other substances to be included in the terms of discharge permits and within the basis for charging. Incorporating new parameters would require an adequate monitoring system, reliable knowledge and registration of sources of pollution, all of which are linked to information systems.

Further attention should be devoted to the capacity of different users to pay (poor households, farmers, selected industries) and to the economic, social and environmental consequences of high or low water charges, which are rather poorly documented. These factors make a difference in some instances, e.g. when cheap water diverts a valuable resource from valuable uses, or leads to costly supply augmentation measures; or when poorly designed pollution charges fail to minimise pollution and lead to higher treatment costs for users downstream. Additional considerations apply to how abstraction and pollution charges are used for specific uses — hydropower, water supply and sanitation, industry, and agriculture —, which are discussed in Chapter 4.

Who does what in setting, collecting and operationalising water charges in Brazil

The water charge implementation cycle represented in Figure 2.1 shows key steps and responsible authorities at federal and state level. The process for setting and operating water charges at federal and state level is similar. In most cases, the river basin committees (interstate or within states) submit water charge values for approval to the Federal (CNRH) or State (CEHRs) Water Resources Councils. National (ANA) or state agencies (e.g. executive bodies of State Secretariats for water resources and the Environment) are in charge of billing and collection. The funds raised are then managed by delegated water agencies (in the form of private organisations, associations, foundations, consortia) that in principle allocate spending in the basin according to the actions foreseen in the river basin plans.

Setting a water charge is the outcome of both a *political* and *technical* process within the river basin Committees (ANA, 2014). It is a political decision to start implementing water charges in the river basin, but the level of charges should be backed up by technical analyses. The Federal Water Law foresees that the delegated water agencies would propose the values of charges to the river basin Committee; however, in practice, a technical group within the river basin committee carries out this function. The proposal is then discussed with the stakeholders within the river basin committee and finally submitted to the national or state water councils. This system has the advantage of the bottom-up, consensus-based and participatory drive for what remains a very sensitive area in water management. But it also has some drawbacks that hinder its effectiveness and efficiency: even though charges are proposed *in primis* through technical analyses, eventually the decision on the level of charges is predominately political, as it is the result of a negotiation (*pacto*-agreement) amongst stakeholders. Given that the stakeholders involved are also water users who at the end will pay the charge there is a risk that vested interests may prevail. Another issue concerns the robustness of technical analyses: in some situations, economic assessment is at best based on a calculation, *ceteris paribus*, of the impact of the charge on water users' costs, while no assessment of the wider impacts on competitiveness is carried out, nor on the savings for the users that this is likely to stimulate.

Figure 2.1. The water charge implementation cycle

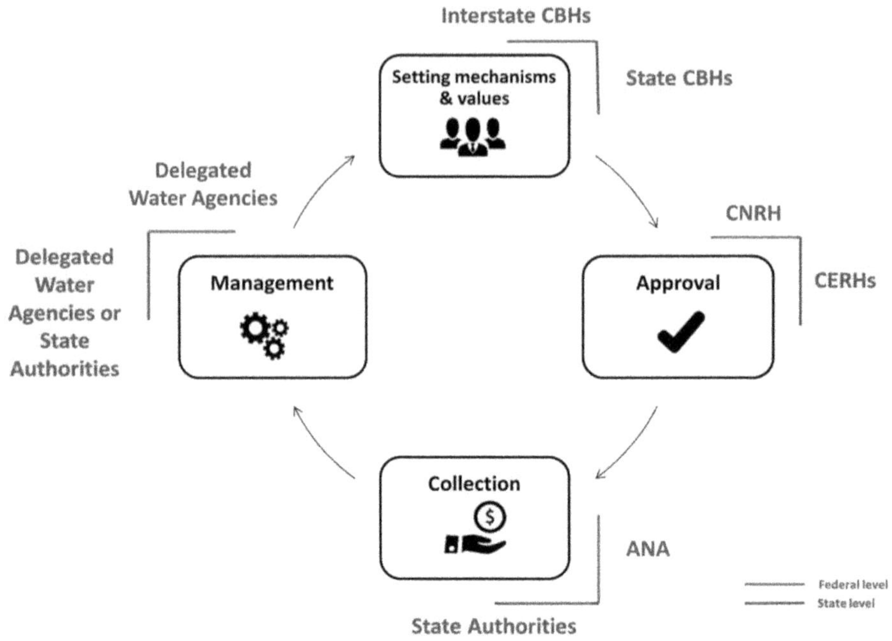

Notes: State Water Resources Council, Conselho Estadual de Recursos Hídricos – CERHs; National Water Resources Council, Conselho Nacional de Recursos Hídricos – CNRH; National Water Agency, Agência Nacional de Águas - ANA; River Basin Committees, Comitê de Bacia Hidrográfica - CBHs.

Source: Authors' elaboration.

Resolution CNRH No. 48/2005 establishes general rules for mechanisms and prices that should apply at federal or state levels alike. However, each river basin committee is allowed to propose alternative mechanisms to better reflect local circumstances. Mechanisms and prices for water charges proposed by the (interstate or state) Basin Committees are then submitted for approval to the (national or state) water councils.

The (national or state) water council is in charge of reviewing proposals on water charges. In practice, the approval process of water charges is seldom challenged and councils endorse the proposals they receive, whether at federal or state levels. At the federal level, the ANA evaluates proposals submitted by the interstate river basin committees, providing a technical analysis of the proposal, which is subsequently submitted to the Technical Board of Water charges (Câmara Técnica de Cobrança pelo Uso de Recursos Hídricos, CTCOB) within the CNRH. Legal aspects are then analysed by the Board of Legal Affairs (Câmara Tecnica de Assuntos Legais e Institucionais, CTIL). Approval is given following a plenary discussion in the CNRH. Historically, most proposals made by the interstate river basin Committees have been backed up by the technical notes provided by ANA. At state level charges are proposed by state river basin committees and approved by state water resources councils. Executive water and environmental agencies at state level can support the decision by the Council with technical analyses (ANA, 2016). Box 2.3 illustrates the experience of National Water Councils in France and in Spain.

Box 2.3. The role of National Water Councils in France and Spain

In **France**, the National Water Committee was created in 1964 as a consultative body of the Ministry of Environment by the first Law on water (Law No. 1245/ 1964). Recent Laws in 2006 and 2007 have amended its compositions. It is composed by 156 members, including representatives of various levels of government (central, regional, local), presidents of river basin committees, water user members and experts. The National Water Committee provides its view on water policies, laws and regulations, as well as on water infrastructure projects at national level of major regional infrastructure projects. It is also consulted on the price of water charged to users and the quality of public water and sanitation services. The National Water Committee has played an important role in proposing and in setting national guidelines to river basin committees on who has to be charged and on the maximum threshold to be applied.

In **Spain** the National Water Council was established in 1985 by the Regulation of the Public Administration of Water and Hydrological Planning (amended by the Royal Decrees 117/1992 and 1383/2009). It is mainly a consultative body composed by the Ministry of Agriculture, Food and Environment, as well as by regional, basin and local authorities. Water users and professional associations are also represented. The 1992 Decree suggested the inclusion of professional organisations representing the agricultural sector. The role of the Council is to produce mandatory reports on national and basin water resources plans; on issues concerning water uses by interstate basins; plans and projects of common interest on agrarian, urban, industrial and energy management or land use planning, before the approval of the Government and also to make proposals to various levels of government relatively to innovation technology in water conservation, treatment and recovery. Some inconsistencies were flagged in the approval of the national water plan after the approval of plans at basin levels. In fact the role of the national plan is to provide internal consistency to all the river basin management plans. The National Water Council does not provide guidance to river basin committees.

Source: Arnaud Reynaud, Expert, Toulouse School of Economics (France); Gonzalo Delacámara, Peer-Reviewer, IMDEA Water Institute (Spain); Hispagua Sistema Español de Información sobre el Agua (n.d.), Consejo Nacional del Agua, http://hispagua.cedex.es/instituciones/consejo_nacional_agua (accessed August 2017); Comité national de l'eau (n.d.), Le rôle du Comité national de l'eau, www.comitenationaldeleau.fr/role (accessed August 2017).

The ANA and state authorities are in charge of collecting revenues from water charges, respectively at federal and state levels. At state level, water charges are collected by the Company for Water Resources Management of the State of Ceará (Companhia de Gestão de Recursos Hídricos, COGERH), the State Institute of Environmental of Rio de Janeiro (Instituto Estadual do Ambiente do Rio de Janeiro, INEA), the Institute for Water Management of the State of Minas Gerais (Instituto Mineiro de Gestão das Águas, IGAM), the Paraná Water Institute (ÁguasParaná-Instituto das Águas do Paraná, Paraná), the Executive Agency for Water Management of the State of Paraíba (Agência Executiva de Gestão das Águas do Estado da Paraíba, AESA) or by the Department of Sanitation and Water Resources of the State of São Paulo (Departamento de Águas e Energia Elétrica, DAEE of the Secretaria de Saneamento e Recursos Hídricos do Estado de São Paulo-SSRH). Since charges are linked to the permit system, a comprehensive and up-to-date users' registry is key to accurately billing states according to their water use. This data must be properly synchronised with the National Registry for Water Resources (Cadastro Nacional de Usuarios de Recursos Hidricos, CNARH) to cross-check the relevant information for interstate basins. The charge is calculated and billed after obtaining data from users and receiving final approval of the mechanisms and values.

Delegated water agencies are designated by river basin committees to manage revenues. Revenues from water charges are considered as public resources and subject to the same controls as for managing public assets and funds. Non-refundable financing is the only model adopted by the delegated water agencies to disburse the funds. Even if the Federal Water Law does not exclude it explicitly, delegated water agencies cannot grant funds to private entities even if when their projects match activities foreseen by the river basin plans.

At federal level, such agencies are non-profit institutions charged by the CNRH to provisionally act as competent water agencies (Box 2.4). The ANA charges, collects and transfers the full amount to such agencies via a management contract signed with the delegated water agencies (contracted parties) and the river basin committees (consenting parties). The delegated water agency is then expected to disburse the resources as foreseen by the interstate river basin committee. Management contracts are also signed at state level between state institutions collecting revenues and delegated water agencies in charge of disbursing them according to river basin plans.

Regulation of delegated water agencies differs across states (Box 2.4), e.g. they are foreseen by the legislation in the States of Rio de Janeiro, Minas Gerais and Bahia, but not by the States of Ceará, Paraná and Paraíba. In the latter cases, the same functions are carried out by state authorities responsible for water management (see below further description of each state). In the State of São Paulo, water agencies were created in the form of foundations or where water agencies do not exist, the functions are carried out by the state authority responsible for water management, which is the DAEE. Until 2011, delegated water agencies disbursed revenues directly to municipalities; however, perceived lack of capacity on the part of the part of the municipalities triggered the delegated water agencies to spend funds directly.

Box 2.4. The delegated water agencies

According to the art. 44 of the 1997 Federal Water Law, water agencies are in charge of:

- implementing water charges through delegation;
- analysing and issuing opinions on the projects and works to be financed with resources generated by the collection of water charges and sending them to the financial institution responsible for the administration of these resources;
- monitoring the financial administration of the resources collected with the collection for the use of water charges;
- proposing to the respective river basin committees the plan for applying the resources collected.

Art. 43 establishes that the creation of a water agency is subordinated, among others, to the financial viability guaranteed by the collection of water charges. Even though art. 53 established that the Federal Government would, within one hundred and twenty days from the publication of the Law, submit to Congress a bill regarding the institution of water agencies, in practice they have never been created. However, the 1997 Federal Water Law foresaw for the National Water Council the possibility of temporarily delegating to no-profit organisations the functions of water agencies. These organisations could take the form of: consortia and river basin associations of municipalities; regional, local or sectorial associations of water users; technical, educational and research organisations interested in the field of water resources; NGOs whose objectives are the defence of diffuse and collective interests; other organisations recognised by the National Water Council or by the State Water Resources Councils (art. 47).[1] Consequently the Law 10 881/2004 regulated the management contracts between ANA and the delegated water agencies, through which ANA was able to fully transfer to them the revenues collected from water charges. The CNRH Resolution 48/2005 established that water charging is conditioned to the existence of a (delegated) water agency, in charge of managing the revenues collected from water charges. At state level, when delegated water agencies are not foreseen by the Law the same functions are carried out by state authorities.

Box 2.4. The delegated water agencies (*cont.*)

Delegated water agencies in interstate and state river basins

Interstate River Basin	Name of delegated water agencies[2]	Comment
Paraíba do Sul	Pro-Management Association of the Paraíba do Sul River Basin (Associação Pró-Gestão das Águas da Bacia Hidrográfica do Rio Paraíba do Sul, AGEVAP)	In this basin, waters are shared among the States of São Paulo, Minas Gerais, Rio de Janeiro and the federal government. AGEVAP acts as delegated water agency for the whole basin at federal level. At state level, the AGEVAP is a delegated water agency only for the States of Rio de Janiero and Minas Gerais, but not for São Paulo, in which the same functions are carried out by the DAEE, within the State Secretary for Sanitation and Water Resources.
Piracicaba, Capivari, Jundiaí (PCJ)	PCJ Foundation Agency (Fundação Agência PCJ das Bacias Hidrográficas dos Rios Piracicaba, Capivari e Jundiaí: Agência das Bacias PCJ)	In the basin, waters are shared among States of São Paulo, Minas Gerais and the federal government. The Agência das Bacias PCJ is the agency with foundation status to the State of São Paulo and acts as delegated water agency for the Federal Government and for the rivers basins's portions that belong to the State of São Paulo. It does not act as delegated water agency for the State of Minas Gerais, in which the same functions are carried out by the IGAM.
São Francisco	Peixe Vivo Executive Association for the Support of Water Management (Associação Executiva de Apoio à Gestão de Recursos Hídricos Peixe Vivo, Agência Peixe Vivo)	In the basin, waters shared between the federal government and the Federal District, the States of Minas Gerais, Goias, Bahia, Pernambuco, Alagoas and Sergipe. The Agência Peixe Vivo acts as delegated water agency for the Federal Government and the State of Minas Gerais (the only state in which water charges are implemented so far).
Doce	BioAtlântica Institute (Instituto BioAtlântica, IBio AGB Doce)	In this basin, waters are shared among the States of Minas Gerais and Espiritu Santo. IBio AGB Doce acts as delegated water agency for the federal government and the State of Minas Gerais.
Paranaiba	Multisectoral Association of Water Resource Users of the Araguari River Basin (Associação Multissetorial de Usuários de Recursos Hídricos da Bacia Hidrográfica do rio Araguari, ABHA)	In this basin, waters are shared among the States of Goias, Minas Gerais, Mato Grosso do Sul and the Federal District. ABHA acts as delegated water agency for the federal government and the State of Minas Gerais.
Verde Grande	Peixe Vivo Executive Association for the Support of Water Management (Associação Executiva de Apoio à Gestão de Recursos Hídricos Peixe Vivo, Agência Peixe Vivo)	In this basin, water management is shared between the Federal Government and the States of Minas Gerais and Bahia. The Peixe Vivo agency acts as a delegate water agency for the federal government. The basin committee, which in this case is a single one for both the states, has submitted the proposal for collection to the water councils of both states, but it has not been approved yet.

Box 2.4. The Delegated water agencies (*cont.*)

State	Name of Delegated Water Agencies	Comment
Rio de Janeiro	• Associação Pró-Gestão das Águas da Bacia Hidrográfica do Rio Paraíba do Sul, AGEVAP • Consórcio Intermunicipal para Gestão Ambiental das Bacias da Região dos Lagos, do Rio São João e Zona Costeira, CILSJ	Currently, there is no movement in the State of Rio de Janeiro towards the creation of water agencies.
Minas Gerais	• Associação Executiva de Apoio à Gestão de Bacias Hidrográficas Peixe Vivo, Agência Peixe Vivo • Associação Multissetorial de Usuários de Recursos Hídricos da Bacia Hidrográfica do Rio Araguari, ABHA Gestão de Águas • Instituto BioAtlântica, IBio AGB Doce • Associação Pró-Gestão das Águas da Bacia Hidrográfica do Rio Paraíba do Sul: AGEVAP	Currently, there is no movement in the State of Minas Gerais towards the creation of water agencies.
São Paulo	• Fundação Agência das Bacias Hidrográficas dos Rios Piracicaba, Capivari e Jundiaí: Agência das Bacias PCJ • Fundação Agência da Bacia Hidrográfica do Alto Tietê: FABHAT • Fundação Agência da Bacia Hidrográfica do Rio Sorocaba e Médio Tiete	The State of São Paulo created three agencies with foundation status. For the other river basins, the DAEE, within the State Secretary for Sanitation and Water Resources carries out some water agency functions.
Ceará	No delegated water agency	The COGERH is responsible of the use of revenues from water charges
Paraná	No delegated water agency	The State Law 16242/2009 does not foresee water agencies, whose functions became part of the legal competencies of the state water resources management authority, *Instituto das Águas do Paraná.*
Paraíba	No delegated water agency	The State Law does not provide for the establishment of water agencies. Functions are carried out by the State Executive Agency of Water Management, *Agência Executiva de Gestão das Águas do Estado da Paraíba* (AESA).

Notes: 1. According to ANA (2016): "This temporary delegation model has been perpetuated and the establishment of a real water agency has not materialised yet. It is possible that the main reason is the fear that the water agency will be an institution governed by public law rather than private law".

2. All the delegated agencies operating in interstate river basins have management contracts with ANA.

Source: ANA (2016), "Background report on setting and governing economic instruments for water policy in Brazil", Brazil.

Water charges in practice: The state of play under federal and state domains

Water charges may not be needed everywhere in Brazil. They require a place-based approach depending on states and basins' exposure to water-related risks. However, irrespective of risks, they represent a source of revenue to cover costs of management and monitor the effects of anthropogenic activities on water resources quality and quantity. When taking stock of the current implementation of water charges, only a limited number of jurisdictions[3] have experience in that area (Figure 2.2):

- At federal level, water charges have been instituted in the Paraíba do Sul River basin (since 2003), the most important source of water for the State of Rio de

Janeiro; the Piracicaba, Capivari and Jundiaí (PCJ) River basin (since 2006), which supplies the metropolitan region of São Paulo through the Cantareira System, as well as the municipalities of the Piracicaba river basin, located downstream of the Cantareira System itself; the São Francisco River basin (since 2010), which covers seven states with contrasted hydrological, demographic and economic features; the Doce River basin (since 2011), located in the region with the largest complex of steel production in Latin America; finally, water charges were implemented in the Paranaíba and Verde Grande River basins in 2017 (Figure 2.3 shows the timeline of water charges implementation).

- At state level, water charges are applied in six states: the State of Ceará was the first one to implement water charges in 1996 and today water charges are implemented in the all management units. Revenues have been used to recover the costs of operation, maintenance and administration of water infrastructure. Rio de Janeiro was one of the pioneering states in issuing water permits and charges. Water charges have been implemented by law since 2004 in all management units. The State of São Paulo endorsed a specific law providing for water charges. Implementation began in 2007 and now concerns 9 out of 22 management units. In the State of Minas Gerais, water charges started in 2010 and they are currently established in 12 out of 36 management units. In the State of Paraná, water charges started in 2013 in one of the 11 management units. The State of Paraíba started operating water charges in 2015 in the management units of Litoral Norte, Paraíba e Litoral Sul, not included in the Piancó Piranhas Acu River Basin, in which discussions about water charges have just started (Table 2.1).

Figure 2.2. Water charges at federal and state level

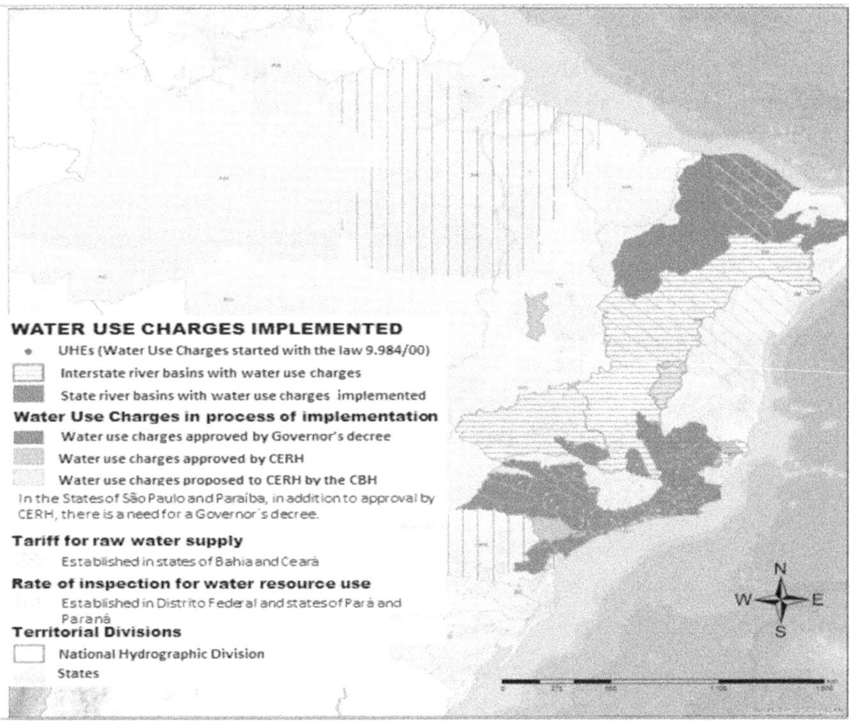

Source: ANA (2017), "Cobrança pelo Uso de Recursos Hídricos no Brasil", http://arquivos.ana.gov.br/institucional/sag/CobrancaUso/Cobranca/CobrancaPeloUsodeRecursosHidricosnoBrasil.pdf.

Figure 2.3. Timeline of water charges implementation

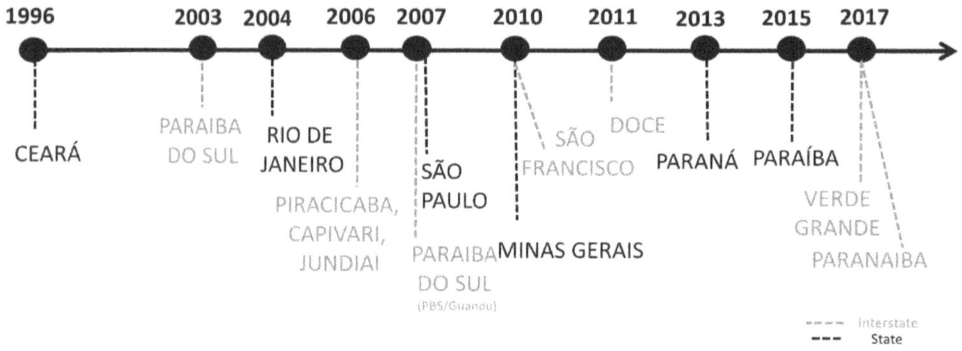

Source: Authors' elaboration.

The hydrological complexity of the area in which water charges are applied and the institutional framework is in place affect the technical and political choice of implementing them. Brazil is a diverse country in terms of institutional capacity, performance, hydrological characteristics and level of economic development, amongst others. In 2014, the ANA clustered the 27 states that adhered to the National Water Management Pact in four classes (from A to D), according to their respective degree of complexity in water management and the corresponding institutional model. For the 27 states, these clusters reflect different degrees of complexity – from low to very high – according to the scope, intensity, number and dispersion of conflicts. They also involve different degrees of institutional complexity and required management actions that range from basic to advanced. It is worth noting that the implementation of water charges was featured only in the "most advanced" class (OECD, 2015).

Geographically speaking, water charges have been implemented in the Southeast and in the Northeast of Brazil (Table 2.1). The Southeast is the richest region in the country and hosts 13% of the total available water sources and 57% of the population. It suffers from water pollution, especially in urbanised and industrialised metropolitan areas, which has increased since the drought of 2014. The Northeast is a poor region hosting 3% of total available water sources and 29% of the total population. It is characterised by a high level of water scarcity. It shows low rates of sewage collection and treatment, respectively 6.5% and 14.7% (ANA, 2015). Since 2012, the region has been facing the most severe drought ever registered.

Table 2.2. Status of implementation of water charges in interstate and state basins

Intestate River Basin	Status of water uses charges	States within the River Basin (*in bold where the charges have been applied for state waters*)	Degree of implementation of charges in the State[1]	Typology from the National Water Management Pact (Class)	Geographical area
Paraíba do Sul	Implemented	**São Paulo**	41%	D	Southeast
		Minas Gerais	33%	D	Southeast
		Rio De Janeiro	100%	D	Southeast
Piracicaba, Capivari and Jundiaí	Implemented	**São Paulo**	41%	D	Southeast
		Minas Gerais	33%	D	Southeast
Doce	Implemented	**Minas Gerais**	33%	D	Southeast
		Espirito Santo	0%	C	Southeast
Rio Grande	Not implemented	**Minas Gerais**	33%	D	Southeast
		São Paulo	41%	D	Southeast
Paranapanema	Not implemented	**São Paulo**	41%	D	Southeast
		Paraná	9%	C	South
Paranaíba	Implemented	Goiás	0%	B	Central-West
		Mato Grosso do Sul	0%	B	Central-West
		Minas Gerais	33%	D	Southeast
		Distrito Federal	0%	C	Central-West
São Francisco	Implemented	**Minas Gerais**	31%	D	Southeast
		Bahia	0%	C	Northeast
		Pernambuco	0%	C	Northeast
		Alagoas	0%	B	Northeast
		Sergipe	0%	B	Northeast
		Goiás	0%	B	Central-West
		Distrito Federal	0%	C	Central-West
Verde Grande	Implemented	**Minas Gerais**	33%	D	Southeast
		Bahia	0%	C	Northeast
Piancó-Piranhas-Açu	Not implemented	Rio Grande do Norte	0%	B	Northeast
		Paraíba	75%	C	Northeast

Notes: 1. Percentage (%) of management units where the charge is implemented on the total number of units.

The State of Ceará, where water uses charges are applied since 1996 does not belong to an interstate river basin and therefore it is not reported in this table. Classes are: Class A: Low water conflicts; basic institutional framework; Class B: Medium water conflicts-Intermediate institutional framework; Class C High water conflicts – Developed institutional framework; Class D Very high water conflicts – Advanced institutional framework.

Source: ANA (2016), "Background report on setting and governing economic instruments for water policy in Brazil", Brazil; OECD (2015), *Water Resources Governance in Brazil*, OECD Publishing, Paris, http://dx.doi.org/10.1787/9789264238121-en.

The average rates currently in use by interstate river basins[4] are BRL 0.02/m³ for water abstraction, BRL 0.02/m³ for water consumption and BRL 0.11/ kg BOD for discharge of organic loads. These rates are not automatically adjusted for inflation. After the initiation of water charges in Brazil (Paraíba do Sul River basin, 2003), unit prices have basically remained at the same levels and were adopted for the Piracicaba, Capivari, Jundiaí (PCJ) (from 2006) and for the São Francisco River basins (from 2010). In the Doce River basin (from late 2011), slightly higher prices were adopted. Due to the double dominion, there may be more than one price in place within a given basin: one for federal waters and another (if not several others) for state waters. However, in practice, although established by different committees and councils, water charges in Brazil are overall similar in terms of their values.

Until 2016, about BRL 548 million were raised by charging for the use of water resources under federal domain[5] and around BRL 1.5 billion under state domain (Figure 2.4). At federal level, these revenues are able to cover about 10-15% of the financing need to implement actions foreseen in water resources plans, such as studies, projects or construction works. As a consequence, additional financial resources are needed to fill financing gaps (ANA, 2016). It is estimated that at federal level, 5% of users charged (large users) contributed 92% of the total charged. This scenario is similar to other countries (e.g. France), where focusing on big users allows to reduce transaction costs for collection, monitoring and enforcement of small users activities. In most cases, the gap between the amount collected and charged was below 10% with the exception of the State of Paraíba where the gap was 90%.

Figure 2.4. Total amount charged and collected in interstate river basins and states

BRL million; from the first year of implementation in each basin* to 2016

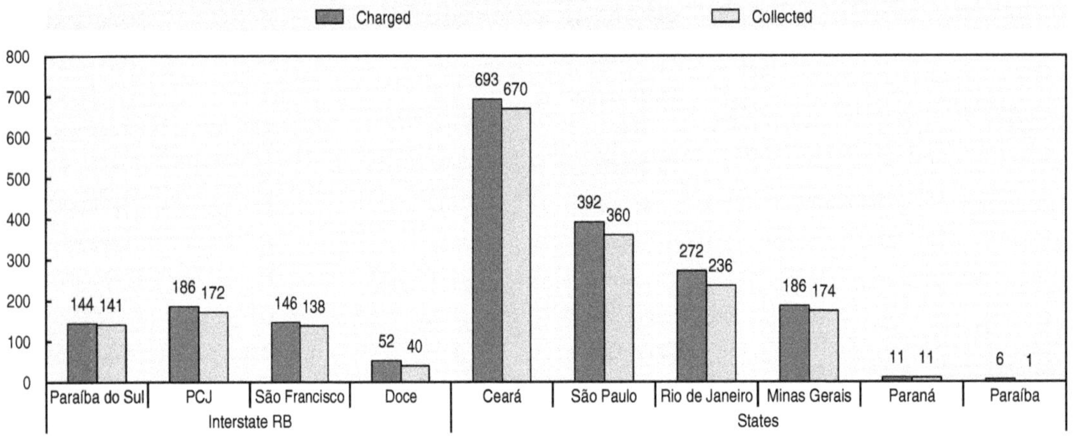

Notes: Water charges starting date: Ceará, November 1996; São Paulo, January 2007; Rio de Janeiro, January 2004; PCJ, January 2006; Minas Gerais, March 2010; Paraíba do Sul (excluding Guandu major diversion project), March 2003; São Francisco, July 2011; Doce, November 2011; Paraná, September 2013; Paraíba, January 2015.

Source: ANA (2017), "Valores Cobrados e Arrecadados", www2.ana.gov.br/Paginas/servicos/cobrancaearrecadacao/cobrancaearrecadacao.aspx (accessed August 2017).

A tentative typology of water charges at federal and state level

River basins at federal and state levels have different experience vis-à-vis water charges in Brazil. However, they share some characteristics that allow the following classification synthesised in Table 2.3. A schematic view of the typology is provided below at macro level and more developments are detailed for each cluster. This typology also reflects the level of maturity in the institutional framework, which was captured by the management map carried out by the ANA for the implementation of the National Pact for water management mentioned above. Table 2.3 matches the clustering of states done for the implementation of the National Pact for Water Management and that for water charges.

Table 2.3. Clusters of interstate and state river basin vis-à-vis their experiences with water charges

Cluster	Interstate RB Water charges applied for water under federal domain	States Water charges applied for water under state domain
Pioneers	Paraíba do Sul PCJ	Rio de Janeiro
Inspirational		Ceará
Followers	São Francisco	São Paulo Minas Gerais
Newcomers	Doce Paranaíba Verde Grande	Parana Paraíba
Aspirants	Piancó-Piranhas-Açu	Rio Grande do Norte

Source: Authors' elaboration.

Table 2.4. Clustering of states: Institutional framework and water charges

States	Typology from the National Water Management Pact (Class)	Typology according to the implementation of water charges
Rio De Janeiro	D *very high complexity, advanced institutional framework*	Pioneer
Ceará		Inspirational
São Paulo		Follower
Minas Gerais		Follower
Paraná	C *high complexity, developed institutional framework*	Newcomer
Paraíba		Newcomer
Rio Grande do Norte	B *medium complexity, intermediate institutional framework*	Aspirant

Source: Authors' elaboration based on OECD (2015), *Water Resources Governance in Brazil*, OECD Publishing, Paris, http://dx.doi.org/10.1787/9789264238121-en.

- The **pioneers** are the Paraíba do Sul River basin, the PCJ River basin and the State of Rio de Janeiro. The Paraíba do Sul River basin was the first pilot for water charges implementation in Brazil, which provided insight into how to fill important legislative and operational gaps. In the PCJ River basin, a Consortium of 40+ municipalities and major water users applied a water charge voluntary scheme (*cobrança voluntária pelo uso da água)* as a pilot experience that paved the way for the implementation of water charges in 2006. The State of Rio de Janeiro was the first state, after Ceará, to implement water charges as foreseen by the SINGREH.
- The **followers** are the São Francisco River basin and the States of São Paulo and Minas Gerais. In these cases, debates on the implementation of water user charges

started way ahead their actual implementation. The double dominion is particularly important for these three cases: São Francisco is a huge basin involving the Federal Government, the Federal District and the States of Minas Gerais, Goias, Bahia, Pernambuco, Alagoas and Sergipe; the State of Minas Gerais cuts across by several interstate river basins, each of them having their own delegated water agencies; the State of São Paulo, whose legal framework for water management dates back to 1991 – namely before the 1997 Federal Water Law – is part of the Paraíba do Sul and the PCJ River Basins.

- The **inspirational** case refers to the State of Ceará, characterised by a longstanding experience and sophisticated centralised institutional framework for water charges, where river basin committees have less deliberative functions than in other states. This centralised system was put in place given the need for the redistribution of financial resources among basins in the state. Water charges are used to finance both administrative costs and the operation and maintenance of the water infrastructure. It is a model for other states, although conceptually different and difficult to replicate.
- The **newcomers** are those that only recently started implementing water charges, namely the Doce, Paranaíba and Verde Grande River basins and the States of Parana and Paraíba. Their experience is relatively limited and some bottlenecks still have to be dealt with. In Paranaiba and Verde Grande, water charges started to be operative respectively in March and April 2017. In both cases, billing will start in 2018.[6]
- The **aspirants** are those where discussions for implementing water charges in the future are currently taking place (Piancó-Piranhas-Açu River Basin and the State of Rio Grande do Norte).

The pioneers

Paraíba do Sul River Basin

The Paraíba do Sul River basin was the first one implementing water charges under federal domain in 2003. It represented a benchmark for river basins at state and interstate level, which have followed relatively similar methodologies and rates. From 2007, the Paraíba do Sul River basin employed the methodology developed by the PCJ River basin in 2006. Since 2003 to 2016, the Paraíba do Sul River basin has collected about BRL 141 million (excluding revenues from the Guandu transfer) (Figure 2.5). However, according to the average annual revenues and the investment programmed in the river basin water resources plan to 2020 (COPETTEC, 2007), 470 years would be needed for meeting the overall investment needs (Bernardes and Broch, 2015). In 2016, abstraction and consumption (quantitative use) represented 83% of the total charged, while BOD (qualitative use) accounted for the remaining 17%. As per users, about 98% of the revenues collected come from sanitation and industry users. Other sectors, including agriculture, contribute to 2%. Over a period of ten years (since 2003), the number of payers increased from 186 to 417 (ANA, interview 2017).

Figure 2.5. Water charges in the Paraíba do Sul River basin

(BRL million, 2003-2016)

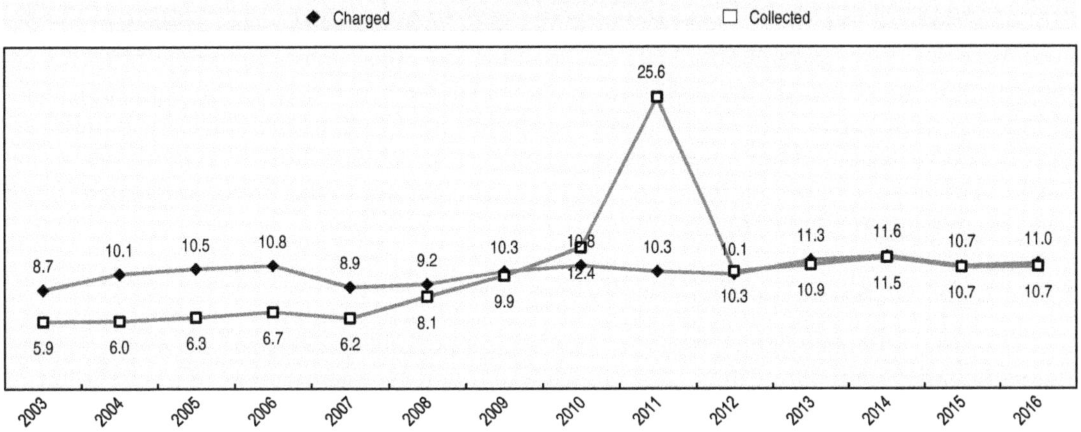

Notes: The higher volume collected in 2011 is explained by the fact that the ANA was able to transfer to the AGEVAP an additional BRL 14.5 million, due to the a judicial decision, which made the National Steel-maker Company (Companhia Siderúrgica Nacional,CSN) pay what was due from 2003 to 2009.

Source: ANA (2017), "Valores Cobrados e Arrecadados", www2.ana.gov.br/Paginas/servicos/cobrancaearrecadacao/cobrancaearrecadacao.aspx (accessed August 2017).

The Interstate River Basin Committee of the Paraíba do Sul River basin (Comitê da Bacia Hidrográfica Interestadual do Rio Paraíba do Sul, CEIVAP) was created in 1996. It has responsibilities on federal rivers across the States of Rio de Janeiro, São Paulo and Minas Gerais. Regarding the institutional organisation for water charges, roles are allocated as follows: the CEIVAP sets water charges, the ANA collects them, and the AGEVAP manages and disburses revenues according to the actions foreseen in the interstate river basin plan. The AGEVAP, the delegated water agency, was created in 2002 and is a non-profit organisation. Further information is provided in Annex A.

Beyond the CEIVAP, in the Paraíba do Sul River Basin, at state level there are other seven state committees: one in São Paulo, two in Minas Gerais and four in Rio de Janeiro. These river basin committees set the charges for water under state domains, then the Environmental State Institute (Instituto Estadual do Ambiente, INEA) in Rio de Janeiro, the Institute for Water Management (Instituto Mineiro de Gestão das Águas, IGAM) in Minas Gerais, and the Department of Water and Electricity (Departamento de Águas e Energia Elétrica, DAEE) in São Paulo collect the charges. Concerning the management of revenues at state level, the INEA and the IGAM have management contracts with the AGEVAP, as the delegated water agency. In the case of the State of São Paulo, water agency functions are carried out by the DAEE, within the State Secretary of Sanitation and Water Resources (Secretaria de Saneamento e Recursos Hídricos do Estado de São Paulo, SSRH). According to the management contract between INEA and AGEVAP, 10% of revenues from water charges collected through the implementation of water charges in the State of Rio de Janeiro are transferred to the AGEVAP, while the rest is transferred to the State Water Resources Fund (Fundo Estadual de Recursos Hídricos, FUNDRHI). In the case of the State of São Paulo, revenues are fully transferred to the State Water Resources Fund (Fundo Estaduao de Recursos Hidricos, FEHIDRO) (ANA, 2014).

The pilot experience of the Paraíba do Sul River basin provided an opportunity to solve ambiguities in the national legislation and to clarify the relationship across levels of government regarding management of revenues from water charges (Abers and Keck, 2013). Prior to the pilot, before water charges management was delegated to the AGEVAP for disbursement, the ANA had to fulfil that role, generating some concerns on the return to the basin of the revenues, once transferred to the National Treasury. This pioneering experience with water charges resulted in the identification of a number of new questions around water revenue management, for instance, how to avoid funds being used for other purposes than those related to water, specific to the basin, and stated in the river basin plan (ANA, 2016).

Piracicaba, Capivari, Jundiaí (PCJ) River Basin

The PCJ Interstate River basin is another pioneering experience in water charges implementation and interesting case for intermunicipal co-operation. The river basin includes the States of São Paulo and Minas Gerais. The PCJ Committee was inspired by the French system, in particular the experience of the Seine/Normandy Basin (Greater Paris) (see Chapter 5).

In 1989, municipalities in the Piracicaba and Capivari River basin created a consortium called Inter-municipal Consortium of the Piracicaba and Capivari Rivers basins. In 2000, it incorporated also the Jundiaí River basin, becoming the PCJ Consortium, which includes also large water users. The Consortium is a non-profit association, created to raise awareness and manage watershed protection funds to improve water quantity and quality. It is also responsible for determining river basin plans. Today, the consortium has 42 municipalities and 30 companies from the sanitation and industry sector as major water users.

In the late nineties, a discussion on water charges was initiated to rationalise the use of water and raise awareness. In 1999 the Consortium PCJ set a voluntary charging scheme, paving the way for the implementation of water charges in 2006. Although almost symbolic (BRL 0.01/m3 of abstracted water), the amount charged aimed to raise awareness over rational water use amongst members of the Consortium. This voluntary programme ended in 2005, a year before water charges were put in place.

As in the Paraíba do Sul and Doce River Basins, the implementation of water charges was gradual: water users paid 100% of the charged amount only after the third year of implementation (60% for the 1st year and 70% for the 2nd). The amount charged was BRL 0.01/m3 of abstracted water; BRL 0.02/m3 for not returned water and BRL 0.10/kg BOD. About 95% of revenues from water charges proceed from 19% of users. The major contribution (86%) came from the sanitation sector, followed by industry (14%). The first rates increase since their implementation in 2006 was eight years later in 2014. In 2007, the PCJ Committee modified mechanisms for agricultural uses, such as multiplier coefficients according to the irrigation technology adopted, as well as differentiated payment mechanisms (ANA, 2014).

Figure 2.6. Water charges in the PCJ river basin

(BRL million; 2006-16)

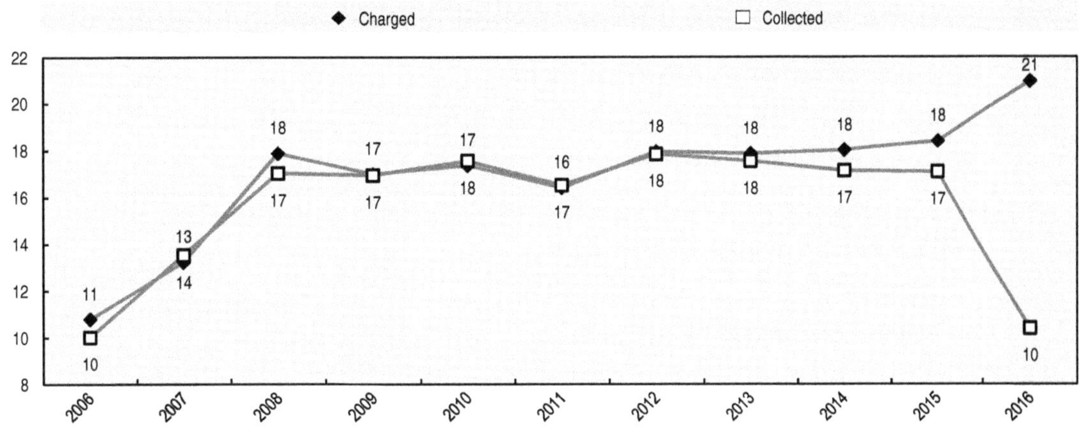

Source: ANA (2017), "Valores Cobrados e Arrecadados", www2.ana.gov.br/Paginas/servicos/cobrancaearrecadacao/cobrancaearrecadacao.aspx (accessed August 2017).

In 2005, the PCJ River basin committee nominated the PCJ Consortium to perform water agency functions for the rivers under federal domain (Figure 2.7). In five years a reduction by 40% the volumes of permitted water was achieved (PCJ Consortium, interview 2017). The PCJ basin agency foundation replaced the Consortium in 2011 as delegated water agency. The PCJ basin agency foundation is responsible for the implementation of water charges, according to programmes, projects and works foreseen in the river basin plan, approved by the PCJ Committee. The PCJ basin agency foundation[7] is the water agency for the river basin's portions of the States of São Paulo and delegated water agency for the federal government, but not for the State of Minas Gerais, in which the same functions are carried out by the IGAM. This implies that at state level, revenues collected through water charges in rivers in the State of São Paulo are transferred to FEHIDRO and administered by the PCJ Basin Agency Foundation, which receives 10% of this funding to cover its governance and operational costs. On the other hand, revenues collected through water charges in rivers under the domain of the State of Minas Gerais are fully transferred to the IGAM.

Figure 2.7. Timeline of the institutional framework for water charges in the PCJ River basin

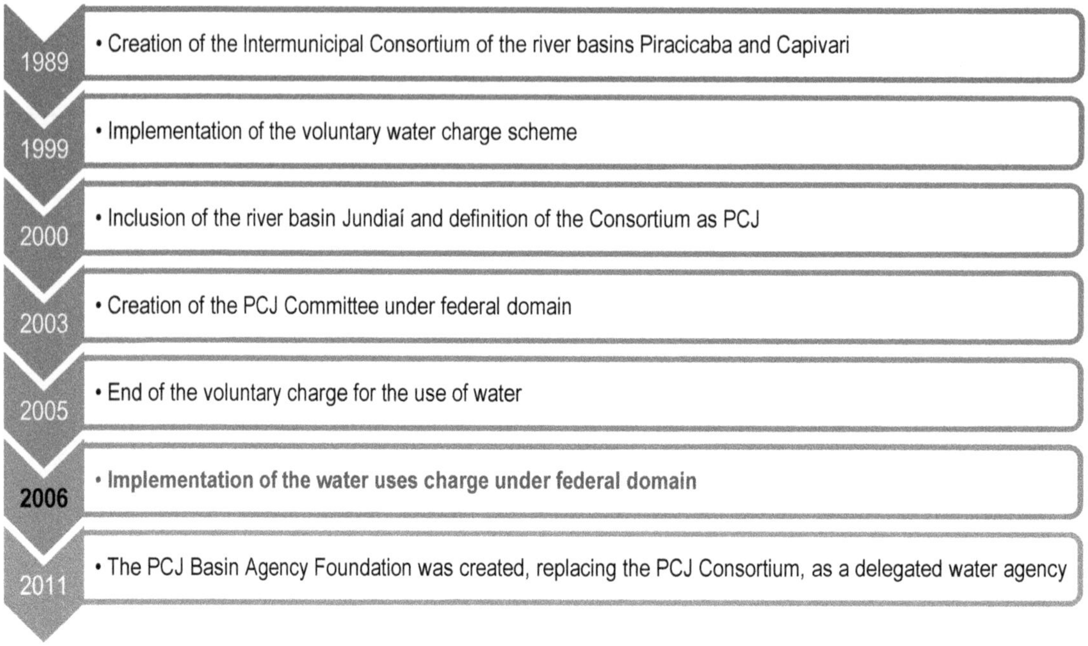

Source: Authors' elaboration, based on ANA (2014), "Cobrança pelo uso de recursos hídricos, Capacitação em Gestão de Recursos Hídricos", Vol. 7, Brasília.

As it is the case in other basins, the PCJ Committee established a methodology for prioritising the use of funds. The methodology consists of scoring projects according to criteria developed by a technical group and available online. Projects are eligible if they cover one of the eight thematic groups foreseen by the river basin plan: database, records, studies and surveys; water resources management; programme for rational use of water resources; recovery of the quality of water bodies; multiple use of water resources; conservation and protection of water bodies; prevention and protection against extreme hydrological events; and technical training, environmental education and social communication. There are 11 technical chambers in PCJ involving more than 600 people. They represent platforms for dialogue to discuss best practices and build a common vision. Revenues annually collected within the PCJ basin are returned to the basin to implement these projects, excluding the administrative costs of the agency (the latter are covered by 7.5% of revenues at federal level and 10% from the State of São Paulo). The multi-year budgeting for disbursement, a common practice in basins, in PCJ runs currently from 2017 to 2020. The PCJ agency offers technical assistance to municipalities to compile their plans and get access to funds, which is a challenge especially for small municipalities.

The amount charged is not able to cover investment needs, or to truly trigger a behavioural change. The yearly collection is about BRL 16 million against an overall project investment need of BRL 4 billion (at current levels of charging, it would take 250 years to cover investment needs). On the one hand, progress has been made in terms of completed projects and reducing the volume of permitted water by 40%; although, not necessarily linked to the implementation of water charges. Conflicts over water uses are amongst the major challenges for the basin, which has been threatened by water scarcity. The area hosts the third largest industrial park in the country, generating one of the largest

GDP; a significant irrigated area and a population of 5.5 million people. Regarding the sanitation gap, charges are not able to help reduce the investment liability for basic sanitation and they are actually not meant to do so. In fact, there is an unbalance between the (little) revenues from the water charges and the huge investment needs in the sanitation sector. In practice, revenues from water charges can be more effectively spent for other uses aiming at improving water management in the basin. The legislation itself advocates that water resources, sanitation and environment systems are interconnected; however, it is unclear how to allocate resources and responsibilities to make this happen in practice. The issue of investment backlogs can only be solved by an ambitious and sustainable national sanitation policy and sound enforcement mechanisms.

The State of Rio de Janeiro

Rio de Janeiro was one of the pioneering states in issuing water permits and charges. Water charges for state waters have been implemented by Law (No. 4 247/03) since 2004. In 2016, the annual collection was around BRL 24 million, which is below 2.5% of what it would take to meet the needs of the State Water Resources Plan (Plano Estadual de Recursos Hídricos do Estado do Rio de Janeiro, PERHI) (Acselrad et al., 2015) (Figure 2.8).The collection increased particularly after 2010 when the sanitation company (Companhia Estadual de Águas e Esgotos do Rio de Janeiro, CEDAE) started to pay for water use. The value of charges has stagnated from 2003 to 2016, when all the management units saw their charges doubled (Lagos São João being the exception). In 2016, the sanitation sector contributed to the collection of 83% of the total revenues collected, followed by industry (10%) and thermoelectric (4%), although there were relevant differences within the state (ANA Database, 2017).

Figure 2.8. Water charges in the State of Rio de Janeiro

by management unit; BRL million; 2007-2016

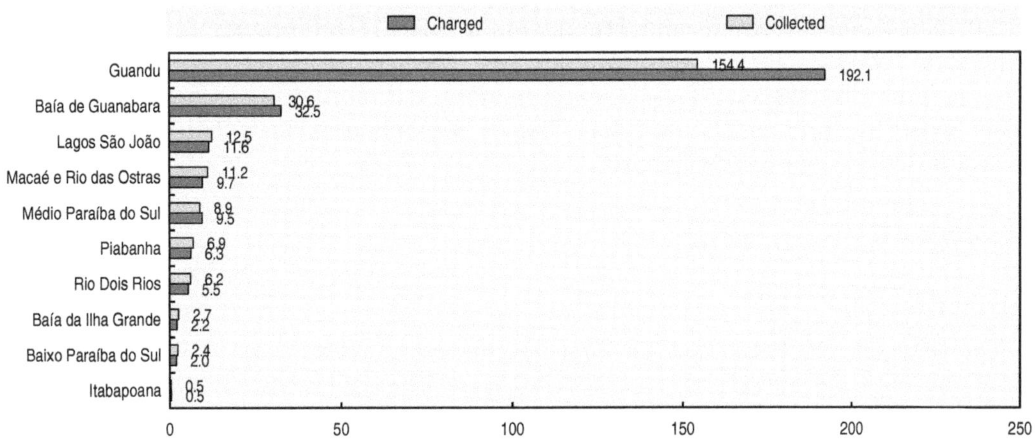

Source: ANA (2017), "Valores Cobrados e Arrecadados", www2.ana.gov.br/Paginas/servicos/cobrancaearrecadacao/cobrancaearrecadacao.aspx (accessed August 2017).

The case of Rio de Janeiro presents some distinctive features. First, water charges were established by law (No. 4247/03) across the whole state even where river basin committees were not yet established. Second, there is a significant earmarking of the funds to the sanitation sector. In fact, the law foresees that at least 70% of the amount collected on urban water and sanitation services must be invested in urban wastewater treatment systems until the achievement of a coverage of 80% in the river basin (see case study on the State of Rio de Janeiro in Annex B).

The institutional framework for water charges is defined as follows: the Secretary of State for the Environment (Secretaria de Estado do Ambiente, SEA) proposes and guides public policies related to the implementation of water charges. The INEA, the executive body of water resources is responsible for the collection; basin committees have the legal prerogative to define the methodology, criteria and rates, for a subsequent approval by the State Council for Water Resources (Conselho Estadual de Recursos Hídricos do Estado do Rio de Janeiro, CERHI). The INEA holds also monitoring and inspection powers. Revenues are managed by delegated water agencies, including the AGEVAP (ANA, 2016).

According to the 2003 Law, revenues collected from water charges for the use of water resources, recorded as FUNDRHI funds, should be implemented in the region or in the river basin where they were generated. The FUNDRHI is organised in sub-accounts, allowing the autonomous management of the financial resources by each river basin. Funds can be used in projects altering the quality, quantity or flow regime of water bodies only in the public interest and after approval by the respective river basins.

The economic crisis of the State of Rio de Janeiro has been posing serious challenges especially concerning the use of revenues for water management purposes. Even though the situation is gradually improving and the state has seen a recent doubling of the charges collected, it seems unlikely that significant additional state or federal funds for hard and soft infrastructure water-related needs will be available in the short to medium term. The state is a very urbanised and industrialised, as such presenting conflict over water uses. In the future, water charges can play a key role, as a water management instrument, to effectively achieve water security goals. Therefore, they should not systematically be geared to investments where they can realistically make no difference given the huge needs and backlogs, such as in the case of sanitation. According to the PERHI, investments need in sanitation amount at BRL 10 billion, which represents 64% of the total expenses foreseen by the Plan (e.g. the overall water management system costs, including for instance those for information and monitoring, represent 5% of the overall expenses foreseen by the Plan). Annex B explores further challenges and ways forward for the case of Rio de Janeiro.

The followers

The State of São Paulo

The State of São Paulo was the first one to pass a Water Law in 1991 (No. 7663), before the national framework was put in place. The 1991 law identified bulk water charges as instrument of state policy (art. 14). In 2005, the state endorsed a specific law (No. 12 183/ 2005) providing for water charges, with features such as general criteria and upper limits to levels of charges. Water charges were gradually implemented: in Paraíba do Sul and PCJ from 2007; in Sorocaba e Médio Tietê from 2010; in Baixada Santista from 2012; in Baixo Tietê from 2013; in Alto Tietê from 2014 and in Tietê Batalha, Tietê, Jacaré and Ribeira de Iguape, Litoral Sul from 2016. In the other ten basins water charges have been proposed, but not yet implemented (SigRH, 2017a). Therefore, water charges implementation now concerns 9 out of 22 management units. Decree No. 50667/2006 regulates water charges for urban and industrial uses.

Figure 2.9. Water charges in the State of São Paulo

by management unit; BRL million; 2007*- 2016

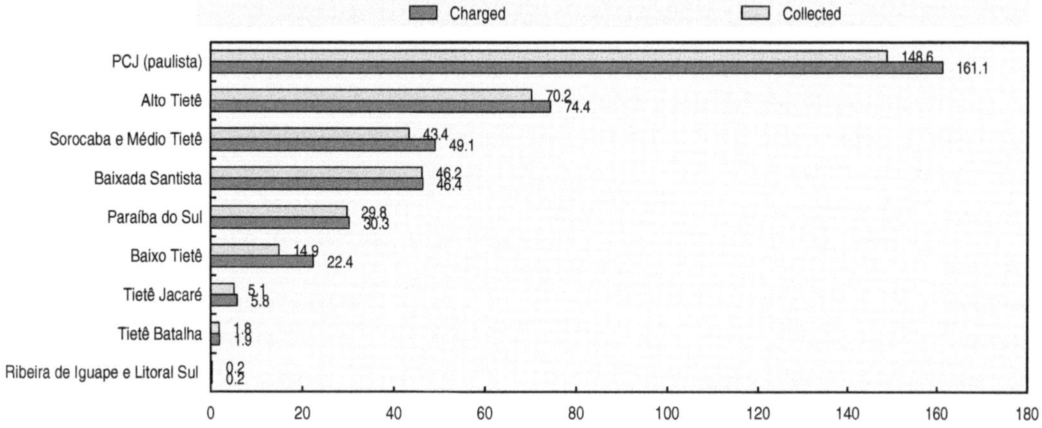

Notes: Water charges implemented in Paraíba do Sul and PCJ from 2007; in Sorocaba e Médio Tietê from 2010; in Baixada Santista from 2012; in Baixo Tietê from 2013; in Alto Tietê from 2014 and in Tietê Batalha, Tietê / Jacaré and Ribeira de Iguape / Litoral Sul from 2016.

Source: ANA (2017), "Valores Cobrados e Arrecadados", www2.ana.gov.br/Paginas/servicos/cobrancaearrecadacao/cobrancaearrecadacao.aspx (accessed August 2017).

As in other cases, revenues are too low to meet the needs of the river basins in São Paulo. A total of BRL 360 million has been collected in the state from 2007 to 2016 (Figure 2.9). Some concerns have arisen in terms of how resources are used and distributed. According to the Upper Tietê River Basin Agency Foundation (Fundação Agência da Bacia Hidrográfica do Alto Tietê, FABHAT), after two years of water charges implementation, members of the basin committee are showing concern about the issue of the allocations of revenues and adjustments might be needed in the future. Regarding the State Water Resources Plan (Plano Estadual de Recursos Hídricos, PERH), changes have been adopted as a consequence of the recent law No. 16 337/ 2016. The law clarifies competences of the State Water Resources Council, the Coordinating Committee of the State Water Resources Plan (Comitê Coordenador do Plano Estadual de Recursos Hídricos, CORHI) and the river basin committees. It calls for greater integration between the actions foreseen in PERH and in the Plurennial Plan (PPA) and includes the private sector as beneficiary of incentives for the implementation of projects in compliance with the PERH.

According to the 2005 Law, entities responsible for water charges are the granting authority DAEE or the water agencies. Revenues collected are accredited into the State Fund for Water Resources (FEHIDRO). The Law No. 10 020/ 1998 foresees the creation of water agencies in the institutional form of foundations. They should be created only in hydrographic basins when issues related to water resources justify so. Thus far, three water agencies were created (SigRH, 2017b) (Table 2.5):

- The Foundation of the Piracicaba, Capivari and Jundiaí River Basin Agency (PCJ Basin Agency) which manages FEHIDRO's financial resources in the corresponding river basin;

- The Upper Tietê River Basin Agency Foundation (FABHAT), which elaborates all the technical studies to support the river basin committee in the definition of the water charges, as foreseen by the law;
- The Sorocaba and Meio Tietê River Basin Agency Foundation (Fundação Agência da Bacia Hidrográfica dos Rios Sorocaba e Médio Tietê, FABH-SMT), which was established in 2003, and is responsible of managing water charges since September 2014. Before then, functions were carried out by the DAEE, which continues to support FABH-SMT when needed.

Table 2.5. Basin committees and agencies in the State of São Paulo

River Basin	Delegated water agencies
River Basin Alto Tietê (CBH-AT)	FABHAT
River Basin Piracicaba, Capivari e Jundiaí (PCJ)	Agência PCJ
River Basin Sorocaba e Médio Tietê (CBH-SMT)	FABH-SMT

Source: Authors' elaboration based on information accessible at: SigRH (2017a.), Agência de Bacia, http://www.sigrh.sp.gov.br/agenciadebaciaapresentação (accessed August 2017).

In absence of an official water agency, the functions are carried out by the DAEE within the State Secretariat of Sanitation and Water Resources of the State of São Paulo.

The State of Minas Gerais

In the State of Minas Gerais, water charges started in 2010 and are currently established in 12 out of the 36 management units. The state is located in seven interstate river basins, each with its own delegated water agency to manage revenues from water charges where they are applied: Paraíba do Sul, Piracicaba, Capivari and Jundiaí, Doce, Rio Grande, Paranaíba, São Francisco and Verde Grande. As it happens at Federal level and in the case of Rio de Janeiro, the Minas Gerais State Law No. 13199/1999 foresees the need of an institution to be allowed by the State Water Resource Council to temporarily act as a water agency. In this case, the State of Minas Gerais delegated the management to several entities: the Agência Peixe Vivo; the ABHA; the IBio AGB Doce; and the AGEVAP (Table 2.6).

Since 2010, more than BRL 173 million has been collected at state level (Figure 2.10). About 6% of users account for 90% of the amounts charged in the State of Minas Gerais. The implementation of water charges by the Doce River basin considered a milestone for the state water management system. Since then, charges have been applied in additional six river basin committees included in the Rio Doce Basin. Moreover, the integration of the river basin committees allowed the establishment of the IBio AGB Doce as delegated water agency. In fact, before the integration only two basin committees had the financial viability to do so. In 2014, 31% of small users were exempt from the payment. Inspections on illegal use of water led to estimate that about 40% of illegal users are small users, bringing no additional income due to the exemptions (GECOB/IGAM, 2016). In Minas Gerais, 92.5% of revenues are used for implementing the river basin plans, while 7.5% should cover the administrative and technical costs of water agencies. However, the amount generated by water charges is not sufficient for the agencies to properly execute their roles. One of the major concerns is the ability to use the collected revenues for more ambitious projects, e.g. beyond studies and planning, to improve water quality and control water quantity. In addition, the disconnect between city master plans and river basin plans (as is often the case in Brazil given the low level of engagement of municipalities in water resources management as described in OECD 2015) also hinders synergies towards greater water efficiency.

Table 2.6. River basins, delegated water agencies implementing water charges in Minas Gerais

Federal basins	State basins	Delegated water agencies or state authorities carrying out functions of water agency
Rio Doce	Piranga	IBio
	Piracicaba	
	Santo Antonio	
	Suacui	
	Caratinga	
	Manhuacu	
Paranaiba	Araguari	ABHA
Paraiba do Sul	Preto e Paraibuna	AGEVAP
	Pomba e Muriae	
Piracicaba e Jaguari	Piracicaba e Jaguari	IGAM *
Sao Francisco	Para	Agência Peixe Vivo
	Rio das Velhas	

Note: * IGAM is a State Management Authority.

Source: IGAM (n.d.), Cobrança pelo uso de Recursos Hídricos, http://www.igam.mg.gov.br/gestao-das-aguas/cobranca-pelo-uso-de-recursos-hidricos (accessed August 2017).

Figure 2.10. Water charges in the State of Minas Gerais

by management unit; BRL million; 2010-15

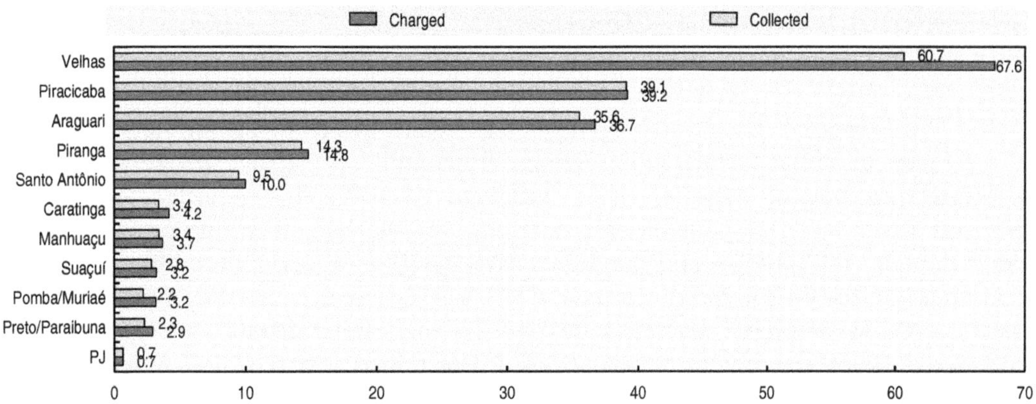

Notes: Water charges implemented: in PJ, Velhas, Araguari in 2010; in Piranga, Piracicaba, Santo Antônio, Suaçuí, Caratinga, Manhuaçu in 2012; in Preto/Paraibuna and Pomba/Muriaé in 2014.

Source: ANA (2017), "Valores Cobrados e Arrecadados", www2.ana.gov.br/Paginas/servicos/cobrancaearrecadacao/cobrancaearrecadacao.aspx (accessed August 2017).

São Francisco River Basin

Although actually applied in 2010, the São Francisco River basin committee (Comitê da Bacia Hidrográfica do Rio São Francisco, CBHSF) started considering the implementation of water charges in 2001, two years after its creation. From 2010 to 2016, the total amount collected was BRL 137 million (Figure 2.11). About 7% of the users represent approximately 95 % of the total revenue. About 66.7% of basin collection is concentrated in the transposition of the Sao Francisco River (Projeto de Integração do Rio São Francisco, PISF). Water charges rates in the São Francisco River Basin have remained the same since 2010; however, a review of rates is currently ongoing. The agricultural sector is charged 40 times less than other sectors. After seven years of implementation, there is no analysis of results of water charges implementation in this basin (ANA, 2016).

Figure 2.11. Water charges in the São Francisco River basin

BRL million; 2010-16

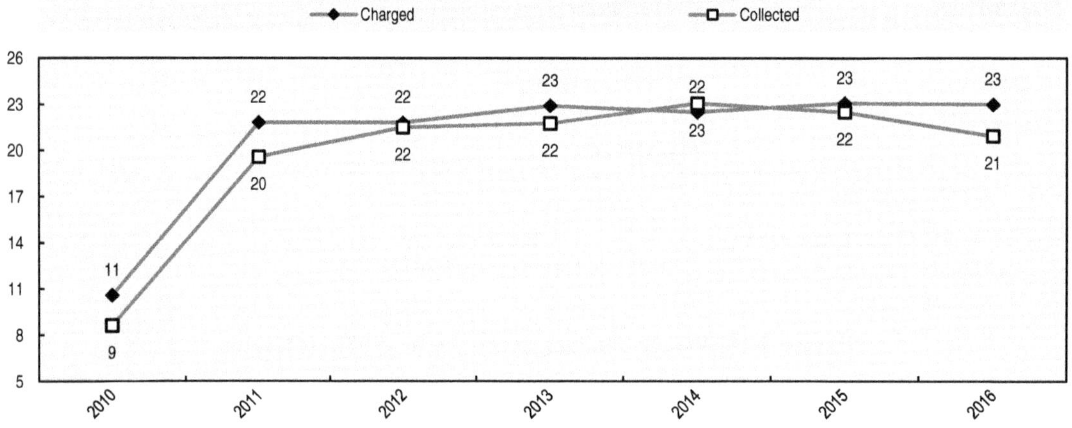

Source: ANA (2017), "Valores Cobrados e Arrecadados", www2.ana.gov.br/Paginas/servicos/cobrancaearrecadacao/cobrancaearrecadacao.aspx (accessed August 2017).

The São Francisco River basin involves the federal government, the Federal District and the States of Minas Gerais, Goias, Bahia, Pernambuco, Alagoas and Sergipe. Unlike other interstate basins, there are two interstate river basin committees in the São Francisco River basin responsible for charging for the use of water resources under federal domain: the CBHSF and the Verde Grande River Basin Committee (Comitê da Bacia Hidrográfica do Rio Verde Grande, CBH Verde Grande). The São Francisco River Basin is shared amongst several states which made the debate on water charges challenging. Given this complexity, the basin determined that it would only charge for water in federal rivers, except for the Verde Grande River. The delegated water agency in charge of managing resources from water charges is the association Agência Peixe Vivo. Mechanisms approved for charging were the same used in other basins. Unit prices were the same as those adopted in the Paraíba do Sul River basin (ANA, 2014). Besides in the federal domain, water charges exist only in the State of Minas Gerais.

The inspirational case

The State of Ceará

The State of Ceará was the first one to implement water charges in 1996. Its experience is unique, representing a model for other states, although difficult to replicate. Ceará, one of the poorest states in Brazil, adopted a centralised model for water charges management. The body responsible of water charges implementation is the Water Resources Management Company (Companhia de Gestão de Recursos Hídricos, COGERH), created in 1993. It is both a provider of raw water supply and holds water agency's functions (ANA, 2014; Formiga Johnsson and Kemper, 2005).

Water charges are used to finance both the COGERH's administrative expenses and the operation and maintenance of the water infrastructure for which it is responsible. This centralised system was put in place given the need for the redistribution of financial resources among basins in the state, which had not been easy to implement under a decentralised setting, except for the case of Fortaleza Basin. River basin committees have less deliberative functions than in other states: prices are not suggested by Committees but by the government. In fact, rates for water charges are defined through technical analysis from the COGERH and the State Council for Water Resources (Conselho Estadual de Recursos Hídricos, CONERH). The latter has seven regional offices (*gerencias interioranas*).

The objective of water charges is to recover the costs of operation, maintenance and administration of the hydraulic infrastructure. As such, they are not meant to remunerate investments. Water charges are applied for urban water, sanitation, industrial and agricultural uses. For irrigation, they are applied progressively. Charges are differentiated by type of users, considering their payment capacities, thus containing inter-sectoral and extra-sectoral subsidy mechanisms including subsidising agriculture by charges incurred to the industry. Charges are calculated on the actual volume but the amount charged varies yearly and according to the climate conditions, e.g. in period of drought, charges are greater to compensate for the increase in costs of pumping. The total collected since 1996 is BRL 670 million, most of which has been collected in the Metropolitana River basin (BRL 464 million), which is not included in Figure 2.12.

Figure 2.12. Water charges in the State of Ceará

by management unit; BRL million; from 2008 to 2016

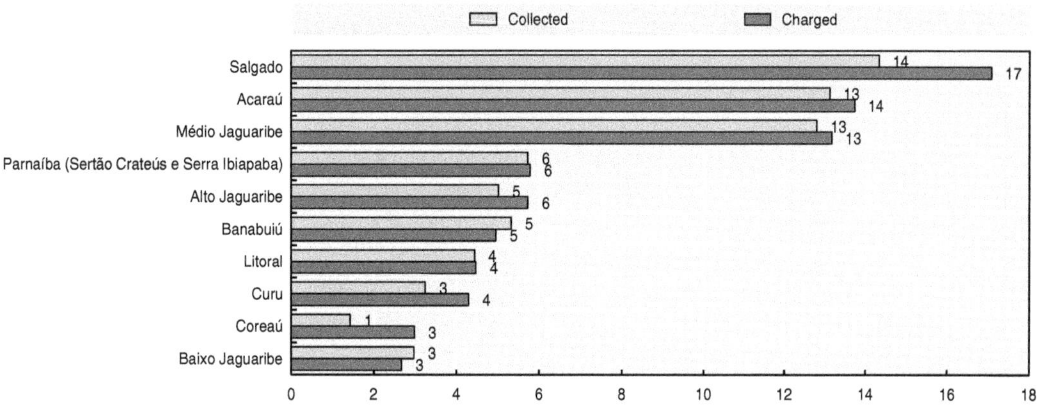

Note: From 1999 to 2007 disaggregated data by river basins are not available.

Source: ANA (2017), "Valores Cobrados e Arrecadados", www2.ana.gov.br/Paginas/servicos/cobrancaearrecadacao/cobrancaearrecadacao.aspx (accessed August 2017).

From 2012 to 2015 users billed increased by over 400%. Amongst the users, in 2016, the sanitation sector was the biggest contributor (55%) followed by industry (44%). Irrigation contributed only 1% of the total collected revenues (ANA Database, 2017). The result is that the degree of cross-subsidisation within the state for water management costs is enormous, both among user sectors (from industries to the domestic and irrigation sectors) and regionally (from the metropolitan basin to the other basins) (Formiga Johnsson and Kemper, 2005).

The state has been successful in raising revenues from water charges; however there much remains to be done for enhancing water security. The drought is raising new challenges, and opportunities such as: co-operation between the water and power sector through a contingency tariff; discussions on the update of possible water charges to enable future water reuse, on the allocation of tradable water rights and on cross-sectoral subsidy mechanisms (Interviews, Brasilia 2017). For the system to be resilient in the face of drought, water charges should be set in a way that does not overlook the achievement of "economic" objectives.

The newcomers

The State of Paraná

In the State of Paraná, water charges started in 2013 in one of the eleven management units. The Alto Iguaçu e Afluentes do Alto Ribeira basin, where charges have been applied, represents a pilot testing experience. The state counts about 4 000 users granted with permits for abstraction and discharge. When water charges are implemented in all the state units, revenues are projected to reach BRL 20 million/year. Total investments for the next 30 years would require an amount of BRL 2.92 billion, of which BRL 2.42 billion for environmental sanitation and the rest for tackling pollution of industrial origin. Most of the river basin committees have completed their plans or are near to completion.

The Water Institute of Paraná holds water agency's functions. A Water Resources State Fund (Fundo Estadual de Recursos Hídricos, FRHI/ PR) was created in 1999 and regulated through the Decree 9131 in 2010.[8] The Water Charges Technical Chamber within the river basin committee (COALIAR) created in 2007, monitors the implementation of the charges in the basins.[9]

Figure 2.13. Water charges in the State of Parana

BRL million, 2013-16

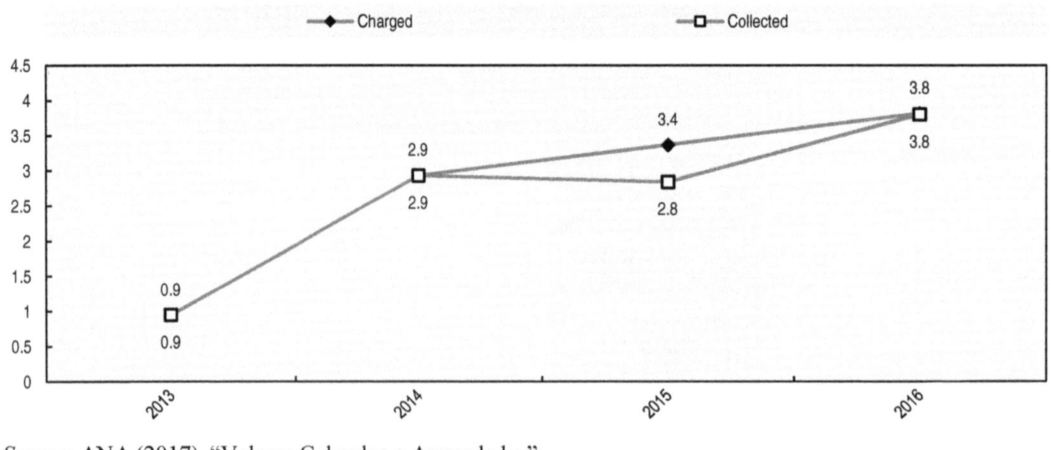

Source: ANA (2017), "Valores Cobrados e Arrecadados", www2.ana.gov.br/Paginas/servicos/cobrancaearrecadacao/cobrancaearrecadacao.aspx (accessed August 2017).

In the Alto Iguaçu e Afluentes do Alto Ribeira basin, BRL 10 million was collected between 2013 and 2016. As in other states, the rates applied were almost symbolic: BRL 0.01 cent/ m3 of water captured directly from rivers; BRL 0.02 cent/ m3 for groundwater abstraction and BRL 0.10 / kg of BOD discharged in the river. The agricultural sector is exempt from payment. Since 2013, 70+ industries and large users have been charged for water use.[10]

Doce River Basin

Under federal domain, the Doce River basin implemented water charges in 2011. Doce River basin encompasses the States of Minas Gerais and Espirito Santo. Technical analyses were carried out by the ANA to support the decision on mechanisms and prices within the committee. The study took into account different revenue scenarios in order to be able to meet the interventions needed for the water resources within the river basin plan. Nevertheless, the decision was eventually political and the unit prices were different from those proposed (ANA, 2016).

From 2012 to 2016, the total revenue was about BRL 39 million. As they stand, charges are able to cover less than 10 % of the needs. As for the São Francisco, in the Doce River basin, the volumetric charge for agricultural users is 40 times smaller than other sectors as well. The Bioatlântica Institute IBio holds delegated water agency's functions for the federal government and the State of Minas Gerais. Prioritised planning actions are foreseen in the multi-year implementation plan (2016-20). This initiative for multi-annual planning inspired by the CEIVAP, PCJ Committees and CBHSF aims to streamlining and improving the disbursement of raised funds.

Figure 2.14. Water charges in the Doce River basin

BRL million; 2012-16

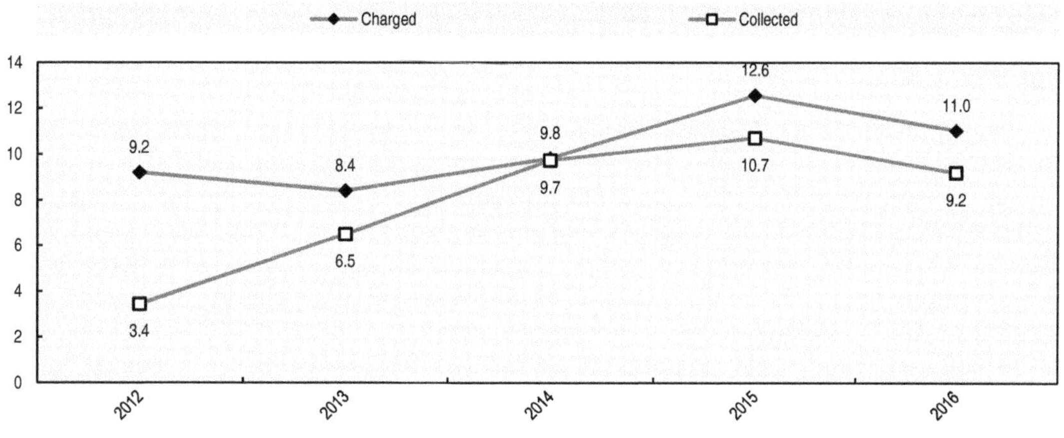

Note: Data for the years 2011 and 2012 have been merged.

Source: ANA (2017), "Valores Cobrados e Arrecadados", www2.ana.gov.br/Paginas/servicos/cobrancaearrecadacao/cobrancaearrecadacao.aspx (accessed August 2017).

One of the main challenges is due to the double dominion and overlapping jurisdictions: IBio finds challenging to manage contracts with federal and state entities, which is costly and poses difficulties in terms of human capacities (Interviews, Brasilia 2017). State and federal governments have different approaches and *modus operandi* concerning how the funds should be spent and inspections should be carried out: e.g. the

State of Minas Gerais tends to apply much stricter inspections for disbursement. The imminent renewal of the contract will be an occasion to discuss the efficiency of this model and possible ways forward. In 2016, the collapse of a dam caused the release of 40 million tonnes of sediments into the river, with financial consequences.

The State of Paraíba

The State of Paraíba implemented water charges in 2015 in all management units except those located in the Pianco Piranha Acu River basin. Water charges are regulated by the state law (No. 6.308/ 1996), but as in the States of Ceará and São Paulo, they became operational only after a government decree (No. 33613/2012). The state law does not provide for the establishment of water agencies. The Executive Agency of Water Management of the State of Paraíba (Agência Executiva de Gestão das Águas do Estado da Paraíba, AESA) is the executive agency of the Basin Committees. For water quantity, the state depends on reservoirs funded through general taxation. Irrigators are the bigger water users; however, they may have greater exemptions depending on the region of the state where they are installed. The value of 100 cubic meters varies between BRL 0.3 and BRL 1.50 according to the use.[11] Irrigators pay a fee for the use of common infrastructure,[12] excluding dams.

Revenues are not sufficient to support operational costs of the river basins plan. Up to 2016, a total of BRL 1 million was collected against the BRL 6 million originally charged. Framework conditions are in place for water charges, but the drought made it politically and socially difficult to accept and then to collect revenues. The low levels of collection would require greater inspections and enforcement. Compared to the current charge of BRL 0.01/m, it is estimated that a charge of BRL 0.46/m^3 would be needed to implement the water resources plan.[13] Possible next steps would foresee a revision of the current charge rates and the exemptions thresholds. Importantly, collection should be shielded from political interference. Exemptions should be public, based on robust analysis of affordability issues and liable of contestation (OECD, 2017, forthcoming).

Paranaíba River Basin

The Paranaiba River basin is shared amongst the States of Goias, Minas Gerais, Mato Grosso do Sul and the Federal District. Water charges were approved in 2016 by the CNRH and started in 2017. The amounts collected by the ANA will be fully transferred to the ABHA.[14] Some of the deadlocks for the implementation of the charges and items discussed within the river basin committee concerned the use of funds and where. One of the conditions for the Federal District to be in favour of water charges implementation was the possibility to have access to revenues generated. At present, 60% of the revenues to be collected from water charges are earmarked for priority actions located in the Federal District. However, this provision is to be revised in 2020. The Federal District is the largest representative in terms of population in the area, but the smallest in terms of territory of the river basin.

Verde Grande River Basin

In the Verde Grande River basin, a São Franciso river's tributary, billing will start in 2018 for waters under the federal domain. In this river basin, a single river basin committees (CBH Verde Grande) is responsible for suggesting proposals on mechanisms and values of water charges both under federal and state domains (States of Minas Gerais and Bahia). The basin committee has submitted the proposal for collection to the water councils of both states, but it has not been approved yet. Water charges are operated by the public institution responsible for water management in each State: IGAM in the State of Minas Gerais and the Institute of Environment and Water Resources of the State of Bahia, Instituto do Meio Ambiente e Recursos Hidricos da Bahia-INEMA) and by the ANA at federal level. The legal framework in States of Minas Gerais and Bahia allows the delegation of water agency's functions to a single entity, which, however, should be subject to the *modus operandi* of each of these units of the federation (ANA, 2016). The CNRH appointed the Peixe Vivo Agency, the same agency that operates for the São Francisco River basin committee, as the delegate entity of the Verde Grande River Basin.

The aspirants

Piancó-Piranhas-Açu River Basin

Water charges are not yet implemented in the Piancó-Piranhas-Açu (PPA) interstate river basin. Since 2015, water charges have been implemented only for the water uses under the domain of the State of Paraíba, although not in the Piancó-Piranhas Açu River basin area, and not yet in the State of Rio Grande do Norte, where technical and legal studies on the subject are currently under preparation. Uncertainties of water availability and intermittent rivers have been the main obstacles to the implementation of the water charges so far. However, the project of water transfer from the Sao Francisco River to the Piancó-Piranhas Açu River basin opened up the discussion about paying for water. Additional details are reported in Annex C.

The State of Rio Grande do Norte

In the State of Rio Grande do Norte, the legal and institutional framework for water charges is in place. However, they have not been applied yet. The 1996 State Law (No. 6 908, modified in 2003) includes economic instruments for water. Currently, a technical and legal chamber within the Executive Agency (Instituto de Gestão das Águas do Estado do Rio Grande Do Norte, IGARN) is working towards the future implementation of water charges.

During the last five years of drought, IGARN concluded that technical solutions were not enough to solve all the problems and that strong institutions and management instruments were needed as a response to the water crisis and for greater water security. Infrastructure construction represented a key response for mitigation, allowing people and economic activities to be supplied with water during water scarcity periods. However, issues remain especially regarding the financing of infrastructure (*who pays for what?*) and the democratic access to water (*who has the right to access the water?*). Since 2012, the IGARN has been in charge of issuing permits for water use. From 2012 until 2015, 500 permits were issued, reaching a cumulative number above 2000 in 2016. The IGARN has inspection responsibilities for the regular use of water; however enforcement is challenging. Although the number of permits has rapidly increased over the last five years, there is significant room for improvement towards a regulated use of water, in terms of greater enforcement, which is seen as an instrument for water security and not as a mere form of punishment.

Other experiences

The Federal District created an inspection fee for monitoring the use of water resources by water users (*Taxa de Fiscalização dos Usos dos recursos hídricos*, TFU). Since 2006, the State of Bahia has been charging for the supply of raw water from some reservoirs. By law, 20% of revenues go to the INEMA and 80% to the Water Resources Environmental Company (*Companhia de Engenharia Ambiental e Recursos Hídricos da Bahia,* CERB), mainly for administration, operation and maintenance of water infrastructure of these reservoirs. In the State of Pará, those using water as an input in production processes or for the purpose of exploitation or economic benefit have been paying a fee for control, monitoring and inspection of these activities since 2015. In 2016, the State of Paraná also created this fee for control, monitoring and inspection.

Notes

1. What makes water an economic good is not the fact that a charge is levied but rather both its relative scarcity (beyond physical scarcity or abundance it has alternative uses that compete) and its contribution to utility / well-being.
2. This is responsibility of the competent body in charge of granting permits.
3. At federal level, according to art. 38 of Law 9433/97 and art. 6 of CNRH Resolution 48, the water charge (*cobrança*) is applied only if river basin committees decide to do so.
4. Paraíba do Sul, Piracicaba, Capivari and Jundiaí, São Francisco and the Doce River Basins (ANA, 2016).
5. At federal level in 2016, almost 2 900 users were charged.
6. The proposal was approved even though the technical note by ANA raised concerns regarding the ability of water charge (very low) to cover the financial needs for the activities foreseen in the river basin plan.
7. Agência de Água PCJ (n.d.), www.agenciapcj.org.br/novo/institucional/o-que-e-a-agencia; CBH PCJ (n.d), Apresentação: Histórico da implantação da Fundação Agência das Bacias PCJ "Agência das Bacias PCJ", http://www.agenciapcj.org.br/novo/images/stories/FABH_Hist-Implantacao.pdf.
8. AguasParaná (n.d.), Câmara Técnica de Cobrança pelo Uso dos Recursos Hídricos – COALIAR,www.aguasparana.pr.gov.br/modules/conteudo/conteudo.php?conteudo=154 (accessed August 2017).
9. AguasParaná (n.d.), Cobrança pelo direito de uso de recursos hídricos, www.meioambiente.pr.gov.br/modules/conteudo/conteudo.php?conteudo=162 (accessed August 2017).
10. AguasParaná (2013), Paraná vai cobrar água usada por indústrias e grandes usuários, www.aguasparana.pr.gov.br/modules/noticias/article.php?storyid=235 (accessed August 2017).
11. AESA (n.d.) www.aesa.pb.gov.br (accessed August 2017).
12. Tariff K1: usage rate or amortisation of the investment of common use irrigation infrastructure and production support infrastructure; Tariff K2: tariff for the administration, operation, conservation and maintenance costs of irrigation infrastructure for common use.

13. Estimation provided during interviews with stakeholders as part of the OECD case study mission (accessed February 2017).

14. ANA (n.d.), Cobrança pelo Uso de Recursos Hídricos de domínio da União na Bacia Hidrográfica do Rio Paranaíba, http://www2.ana.gov.br/Paginas/servicos/cobrancaearrecadacao/BaciaRP_Inicial.aspx (accessed August 2017).

References

Abers R.N. and M.E. Keck (2013), *Practical Authority: Agency and Institutional Change in Brazilian Water Politics*, Oxford University Press, Oxford.

Acselrad M. et al. (2015), "Dez Anos de cobrança pelo uso das aguas do Estado do Rio de Janeiro: situação atual e proposta de aperfeiçoamento, XXI Simpósio Brasileiro de Recursos Hídricos", 22-27 November, Brazil.

Agência de Água PCJ (n.d.), www.agenciapcj.org.br/novo/institucional/o-que-e-a-agencia (accessed August 2017).

CBH PCJ (n.d), Apresentação: Histórico da implantação da Fundação Fundação Agência das Bacias PCJ "Agência das Bacias PCJ", www.agenciapcj.org.br/novo/images/stories/FABH_Hist-Implantacao.pdf (accessed August 2017).

AguasParaná (n.d.), Câmara Técnica de Cobrança pelo Uso dos Recursos Hídricos – COALIAR,www.aguasparana.pr.gov.br/modules/conteudo/conteudo.php?conteudo=154 (accessed August 2017).

AguasParaná (n.d.), Cobrança pelo direito de uso de recursos hídricos, www.meioambiente.pr.gov.br/modules/conteudo/conteudo.php?conteudo=162 (accessed August 2017).

AguasParaná (2013), Paraná vai cobrar água usada por indústrias e grandes usuárioswww.aguasparana.pr.gov.br/modules/noticias/article.php?storyid=235 (accessed August 2017)

ANA (n.d.), Cobrança pelo Uso de Recursos Hídricos de domínio da União na Bacia Hidrográfica do Rio Paranaíba, www2.ana.gov.br/Paginas/servicos/cobrancaearrecadacao/BaciaRP_Inicial.aspx (accessed August 2017).

ANA (2017), Database, Cobrança pelo Uso de Recursos Hídricos, www2.ana.gov.br/Paginas/servicos/cobrancaearrecadacao/cobrancaearrecadacao.aspx.

ANA (2016), "Background report on setting and governing economic instruments for water policy in Brazil", Brazil.

ANA (2015), "Governança dos Recursos hídricos no Brasil", Balanço da Década da Água 15 de dezembro de 2015 Vitória/ES, Gisela Forattini, Diretora da Agência Nacional de Águas, http://projetos.gazetaonline.com.br/agua/pdf/Palestra%20Gisela%20Forattini.pdf

ANA (2014), "Cobrança pelo Uso de Recursos Hídricos", *Cadernos de capacitação em recursos hídricos*, Vol. 7, Brazil.

Bernardes F. S. and Broch S.O. (2015), "Historico de cobrance pelo uso de agua em bacias hidrográficas de domínio da união", *XXI Simpósio Brasileiro de Recursos Hídricos*, 22-27 November, Brazil, www.evolvedoc.com.br/sbrh/.

Braga B.P.F., C. Strauss and Paiva F. (2005), "Water Charges: Paying for the Commons in Brazil", *International Journal of Water Resources Development*, Vol. 21/1, pp. 119-132, http://dx.doi.org/10.1080/0790062042000316848.

Bronzatto L.A. and Amorim M.A.M (2012), "A Cobrança pelo Uso de Recursos Hídricos e seu impacto no setor agropecuário da bacia hidrográfica do rio Verde Grande", in Proceedings Sociedade Brasileira de Economia, Administração e Sociologia Rural, Vitória, 22-25 July, http://arquivos.ana.gov.br/institucional/sag/cobrancauso/baciaverdegrande/sober_2012_cobranca_verde_grande.pdf.

Canali G.V. (2010), "Considerações sobra a natureza jurídica da cobrança pelo uso de recursos hídricos e sua relação com a sustentabilidade econômico financeira da gestão dos recursos hídrico no Brasil", Nota Técnica.

Comité national de l'eau (n.d.), Le rôle du Comité national de l'eau, www.comitenationaldeleau.fr/role (accessed August 2017).

COPETTEC (Fundação Coordenação de Projetos, Pesquisas e Estudos Tecnológicos) (2007), "Plano de Recursos Hídricos Consolidado Resumo", Relatório Contratual R-10.

Formiga-Johnsson R. M. and Kemper K. (2005), "Institutional and Policy Analysis of River Basin Management: The Jaguaribe River Basin, Ceara, Brazil" (June 2005). World Bank Policy Research Working Paper No. 3649. Available at SSRN: https://ssrn.com/abstract=757424.

Hispagua Sistema Español de Información sobre el Agua (n.d.), Consejo Nacional del Agua, http://hispagua.cedex.es/instituciones/consejo_nacional_agua (accessed August 2017);

IGAM (n.d.), Cobrança pelo uso de Recursos Hídricos, http://www.igam.mg.gov.br/gestao-das-aguas/cobranca-pelo-uso-de-recursos-hidricos, (accessed August 2017)

OECD (forthcoming, 2017), "The Social Consequences of Water Pricing", *OECD Environment Working Papers*, OECD Publishing, Paris.

OECD (2015), *Water Resources Governance in Brazil*, OECD Publishing, Paris, http://dx.doi.org/10.1787/9789264238121-en.

Pompeu C.T. (2000), "Fundamentos jurídicos do anteprojeto de lei da cobrança pelo uso das águas do domínio do Estado de São Paulo", in *A cobrança pelo uso da água*, Thame, A.C.M et al., Instituto de Qualificação e Editoração, São Paulo, pp. 41-53.

SigRH (2017a), Agência de Bacia, http://www.sigrh.sp.gov.br/agenciadebacia, (accessed August 2017).

SigRH (2017b), "Cobrança pelo uso da água", www.sigrh.sp.gov.br/cobrancapelousodaagua (accessed August 2017).

Chapter 3

Practical issues for setting and managing water charges in Brazil

This chapter discusses a series of practical issues related to the design and effective implementation of charges to manage water resources in Brazil. Each section states the economic principle, reviews international good practice and discusses the situation in Brazil. Drawing from international experiences, it concludes with sketching some policy recommendations.

The statistical data for Israel are supplied by and under the responsibility of the relevant Israeli authorities. The use of such data by the OECD is without prejudice to the status of the Golan Heights, East Jerusalem and Israeli settlements in the West Bank under the terms of international law.

A review of international experience on abstraction and pollution charges

Abstraction charges

A review of international experience in setting and governing economic instruments for water resources management shows common features to the Brazilian system, but also differences which can provide useful lessons to guide improvement in the Brazilian system. A first observation is that regardless of the constitutional setting (federal or unitary), in the most advanced systems, water abstraction charges are commonly managed at sub-national levels. Among other examples, water charges are administered at the regional level in Belgium, at the hydrographic basin level in France (with a national price ceiling set by law), and at the state (*Bundesländer*) level in Germany. In the United Kingdom, charges are administered by the four devolved administrations.

Another striking feature is that the level of the water charge is usually differentiated by water source (groundwater or surface water) and by the type of user (residential, industry, agriculture). Specific rates are sometimes applied to special zones (e.g. Water Distribution Areas in France – Zones de Répartition des Eaux, ZRE)[1] or specific aquifers or rivers (e.g. aquifer-specific abstraction charges are applied in the Flanders region in Belgium and in Estonia). Abstraction charges are relatively low and higher charges are often imposed on groundwater than on surface water (one exception is the Czech Republic[2]). Abstraction charges primarily target water companies and industries, while the agricultural sector commonly benefits from lower rates or from exemptions. Table 3.1 illustrates water charge differentiation in France.

Table 3.1. Differentiation of water abstraction charges in France

	Drinking water supply (EUR/1 000 m3)			Non-gravitational irrigation (EUR/1 000 m3)			
	Groundwater	Surface water		Groundwater		Surface water	
		Outside ZREs	Witihin ZREs	Outside ZREs	Witihin ZREs	Outside ZREs	Witihin ZREs
Rhin-Meuse	52.0	33.2	144.0	4.7	72.0	4.7	72.0
Loire-Bretagne	34.0	34.0	43.3	12.6	19.0	12.6	19.0
Rhône-Méd. Corse	46.6	30.0	68.3	6.8	12.9	6.3	12.5
Adour-Garonne	42.0	42.0	56.0	8.8	11.7	8.8	11.7
Seine-Normandy*	B: 60.0 Q: 67.0	B: 38.0 Q: 46.0	82.0	B: 21.0 Q: 27.0	34.0	B: 17.0 Q: 20.0	34.0

Notes: * In Seine-Normandy, three zones have been defined: basic zone, zone of quantitative pressure, and ZRE. Here, B refers to basic zone while Q indicates zone of quantitative pressure.

Source: Rhin-Meuse Water Agency, « Les différentes redevances », (www.eau-rhin-meuse.fr/differentes_redevances); Loire-Bretagne Water Agency, « Taux des redevances pour prélèvement sur la ressource en eau », (www.eau-loire-bretagne.fr/nos_missions/redevances/tx-ressource-10epgm.pdf); Rhône-Méditerranée- Corse, « Prélèvement d'eau », (www.eaurmc.fr/aides-et-redevances/redevances-et-primes/prelevement-deau.html); Adour-Garonne Water Agency, « Les redevances perçues par l'Agence », (www.eau-adour-garonne.fr/fr/quelle-politique-de-l-eau-en-adour-garonne/un-outil-le-programme-d-intervention-de-l-agence/les-redevances-percues-par-l-agence.html); Seine-Normandy Water Agency, « Formulaires de demande d'aide financière », (www.eau-seine-normandie.fr/index.php?id=7865) (accessed September 2016).

Contrary to Brazil, the objective of the charge is not always stated in other reviewed countries, in particular regarding its expected achievement in environmental terms. One exception is the legal text introducing water abstraction charges in Baden-Württemberg (one of the German states). The text made clear, as in the Brazilian case, that the charge had three main functions: raising awareness through application of the precautionary principle;[3] incentivising users to save water; and re-balancing competitiveness (self-extraction versus supply through networks). In England and Wales, legislation allows the Environment Agency (EA) and Natural Resources Wales (NRW) to levy abstraction charges so as to recover the costs of delivering their water resources functions (Box 3.1). This includes not only the administration of abstraction licences, but also all the hydrometric monitoring, assessment, and water resource management activities (including the operation of multi-use reservoirs) as set out in detail in law.

Charges are volumetric in most cases, with the user paying a unitary rate per cubic metre abstracted. Other structures are, for example, fixed charges per hectare for non-metered agricultural abstraction or a price per megawatt-hour for energy production. In Belgium (Flanders region), the level of the charge varies with the quantity of water abstracted. For groundwater abstraction, water abstracted is sometimes paid for through Increasing Block Tariff (IBT); the volumetric price is higher for larger volumes. By contrast, the volumetric price sometimes decreases for larger volumes in the case of surface water, the so-called decreasing block tariff (DBT). One issue is that the market signal sent to consumers about the value of the resource might become misleading. Some countries (such as the Netherlands and Denmark) apply a water consumption tax, which is not directly based on abstraction. In Denmark the tax is equivalent to EUR 823 per 1 000 m3.

The tax on water abstraction is the main tool used for water quantity management in France. Under normal conditions, France has enough water resources to satisfy the demand of all users and to maintain the environment in good (ecological) condition. However, because some areas may occasionally suffer from scarcity issues and conflicts of use, a tax on water abstraction has been implemented in order to make users internalise scarcity costs. Scarcity costs have to be covered by water users through the implementation of an incentive-based tariff in accordance with the European Water Framework Directive 2000/60/EC which has been transposed into the French law in 2004. In periods of acute scarcity, it can be complemented by regulatory instruments such as restrictions that apply to specific water uses (Box 3.1).

A low natural level of water supply causes water stress in Israel, an absolute water scarce country according to the Falkenmark indicator. This stress has been mitigated by active policies like the recycling of water (75% of wastewater being treated and used for agriculture, industry, etc., replacing the use of drinking water) and the investments in water infrastructure like desalination plants (expected to provide one third of total water demand in Israel by 2020). Water abstraction is regulated by the volume that can be abstracted and by whom, and the basis for the charge is the volume abstracted. The principle for the water abstraction charge is cost recovery, i.e. tariffs should reflect the total cost of providing water, including capital expenses, energy expenses, and expenses related to operation and maintenance. The means to include a component that reflects scarcity in the tariffs is to add the expenses related to the purchasing of desalinated water on top of the other expenses. Water desalination is the costliest form of providing water in Israel and therefore reflects the marginal cost of producing water.

Box 3.1. Setting national guidelines for water abstraction charge in France

The law sets principles regarding the basis for taxation as well as exemptions to the tax. The tax is a component of the price of water that is paid by all users: households, industries, and farmers. It is collected by water agencies within each hydrographic basin. The rate of the water abstraction tax is defined at the hydrographic basin level but cannot be set above the (national) ceiling defined by French national law for major uses (see below for greater details).

Water tax limits in France

Type of use	Category 1 resources Outside ZREs (EUR/1 000m3)	Category 2 resources Within ZREs (EUR/1 000m3)
Irrigation (except for gravitational irrigation)	36	72
Gravitational irrigation	5	10
Drinking water supply	72	144
Water cooling (more than 99% of the volume abstracted is returned to the environment)	5	10

Principles are set by the national law:

- Basis: the water charge is based on the volume abstracted over a year. Anyone using a well or borehole is required to install a water meter. If abstracted water is not measured, a fee applies. The latter is based on estimates of volumes abstracted or measures from representative samples. For example, water used for gravitational irrigation is taxed on the basis of 10 000 m3 per irrigated hectare.
- The water agency in each hydrographic basin sets abstracted volumes below which users are exempted from the tax. These volumes cannot be larger than 10 000 m3 per year for abstraction from Category 1 resources and 7 000 m3 for abstraction from Category 2 resources. Category 1 resources are those situated outside Water Distribution Areas (Zones de Répartition des Eaux, ZREs) which are zones characterised by a chronic water deficit.
- Exemptions: water abstracted from the sea; water used for mines which are no longer active; water used for aquaculture; water used for geothermic activities; water used for restoring the environment (if those volumes are abstracted outside the period of low water flows); water abstracted to protect perennial crops against frost.
- French legal documents provide justification neither for the level of the tax limit nor for the factor 2-difference between Category 1 and Category 2 resources. As far as we know, these limits were not based on any scientific evidence assessing the costs induced by water abstraction.
- Regarding abstracted volumes for irrigation purposes: when abstraction is made by a Single Collective Management Body (Organismes Uniques de Gestion Collective, OUGC, which gathers several individual irrigators) within a Category 2 resource (ZRE), then the tax rate of Category 1 resources applies. The geographical/spatial distinction between Category 1 and Category 2 resources, and the lower ceiling for those abstracting water from Category 2 sources, reflect the higher scarcity cost in ZREs where there is a serious imbalance between water demand and water availability. There is no adjustment of the tax across seasons, even if the pressure on the resource is usually higher during the summer.

Source: Arnaud Reynaud, Expert, Toulouse School of Economics (France).

In Japan, water pricing arrangements basically do not reflect water scarcity. A legal and authoritative instrument such as use restriction is implemented during episodes of scarcity to co-ordinate water use among stakeholders (OECD, 2015). However, abstraction charges vary according to each prefecture and its ordinance, and thus it is observed that some prefectures (Kanagawa-ken, Okayama-ken, Tottori-ken, Akita-ken, Kumamoto-ken, Yamaguchi-ken, Shimane-ken, Toyama-ken, among 47 prefectures) have collected local level "Water Conservation Tax" (Lee, 2009).[4] This tax is set to cover environmental costs, mainly cost generated from groundwater abstraction and pollution.

In England and Wales there is a well-established system of abstraction charges, which has been in place since abstractions were brought under structured control in 1965. It is designed to ensure that there is full cost recovery to fund the water resources activities of the environmental regulator: that is, all the hydrometric monitoring (rainfall, river flows and groundwater levels), hydrological assessment, hydro-ecological monitoring and assessment, regulation and enforcement of abstraction licences, operation of major resources used for river flow augmentation, and strategic water resources planning (Box. 3.2).

Box 3.2. Abstraction charges in England and Wales

Charges are based upon the authorised volumes (V) on the licence, and are calculated with reference to a number of factors. These are:

- The type of source (A): Unsupported rivers lakes and groundwater; or Tidal; or Supported – where river flows are deliberately enhanced by releases from reservoirs or groundwater pumping.
- The season (B): Summer, Winter or All Year
- The assumed loss (C): High (irrigation, evaporative cooling, dust suppression etc.); Medium (public water supply, most industrial and commercial uses etc.); Low (mineral washing, non-evaporative cooling etc.); Very Low (hydroelectric power, fish farming, transfers of water etc.)

The charge is then calculated as Charge = V x A x B x C x Unit Charge (a factor which is set for each river basin to ensure that the costs of managing water resources in that basin are recovered). The Unit Charge is broadly related to water scarcity, on the basis that as scarcity increases, so do the management costs.

Spray and trickle irrigators pay some of the highest unit costs for their water: they typically abstract in summer, which is the highest seasonal rate, and they are assigned to the High loss category on the basis that all the water is lost through evapotranspiration. In addition, most irrigation licences have 'Hand-Off Flow' conditions on them, which mean that abstraction must cease when river flows drop below a predetermined level. This is to protect the ecology and the rights of other users. The charges, and the flow restrictions, have had the effect of improving irrigation efficiency, and incentivising farmers to look for cheaper, and more reliable, sources of water: many have excavated storage reservoirs to store cheap and reliable winter flows for use during the next growing season. Large farming businesses develop these for their own estates, but increasingly farmers are establishing cooperatives to fund and operate storage reservoirs on a collaborative basis.

The charging scheme does recognise that the volumes of water needed for irrigation are weather and crop dependent, so irrigators are (the only sector) able to take account of a 'two part tariff' arrangement. This allows them to pay a standing charge of 50% of the total, with the remainder pro rata according to the amount used during the growing season.

Box 3.2. Abstraction charges in England and Wales *(cont.)*

All abstractors must measure the volumes of water they use, and they are required to submit returns at least annually of how much they have taken. Large abstractors (e.g. water companies, energy sector) maintain daily records, submitted at least monthly, and in some cases in real time. All meters and other measurement devices must be calibrated regularly, and all sites are visited on a risk basis in order to ensure compliance with the terms of the licence. This is particularly important for irrigators where charges relate to the volumes abstracted, rather than authorised.

Source: Ian Barker, Peer-Reviewer, Water Policy International Ltd (England and Wales).

In Spain the water use fee is either collected by the river basin authority or the tax administration. This fee also includes the use of the public water domain as a whole, including gravel extraction, water sports facilities, etc. In the country, the emphasis is on financial cost recovery, although economic costs are also considered to a greater or lesser extent. Different competent authorities, according to the principle of cost recovery and on the basis on long-term economic projections, establish a wide range of mechanisms to recover from end users accrued costs, including environmental (third-party effects, externalities) and resource costs (scarcity rents). Cost recovery should be made compatible with water use efficiency. Hence it should thus contribute to meeting pre-determined environmental targets (i.e. the good ecological status of water bodies, according to the EU Water Framework Directive). These levies are set up for all water users, with main payments coming from domestic water supply, agriculture, and manufacturing in an accountable way. Finally, affordability concerns and disproportionate costs should be addressed. Other economic instruments in place in Spain are reported in Box 3.3.

Box 3.3. Economic instruments for water management in Spain

In Spain, according to the Spanish Water Law (1/2001, amended on December 26th, 2013), which translates the EU Water Framework Directive (WFD) into the Spanish legal Acquis, there are several financial instruments for water resources management.

There is an ad hoc water use fee for the non-consumptive use of freshwater for hydropower generation (measured at bus bars). This fee is also, in principle, earmarked to the protection and enhancement of water resources. The accrual of the fee is when the license is granted too. The tax base is on the basis of the market value of hydropower output (measured in bus bars). Hydropower plant operators thus pay 22% of the value of that tax base. Plants operated by the river basin authorities themselves do not pay for this fee and is reduced up to 90% for plants with an installed capacity equal to or less than 50MW and for pumped-storage hydropower over 50MW. The collection of revenues is as in the general levy. 2% of those funds become part of the revenue stream of the river basin authority; the remainder 98% goes to the Treasury.

The so-called regulation fee and the tariff for water use are linked to the use of regulation infrastructures for surface (mainly storage reservoirs), groundwater use and other water works. This is a cost recovery mechanism for public works, either partially or totally funded by the State. The tariff mainly refers to publicly operated conveyance systems. They both account for operational and maintenance costs of those infrastructures. Beyond opex, other items are included in the calculation of the tax base: administrative costs of the public body managing those works (only those eligible costs that can be directly attributed to the management of those

Box 3.3. Economic instruments for water management in Spain (*cont.*)

infrastructures); 4% of the value of upfront capital investment, duly discounted, and having into account depreciation and inflation. The allocation of the total cost to be recovered amongst all beneficiaries of water infrastructures is made on the basis of rationalisation of water use, equity, and financial self-sufficiency. There is a correction factor, depending on whether the water user is consuming less or more water than the allocated endowments in the river basin management plan. Sometimes, though, the final charge to be paid is also adjusted on the basis of sectoral policy considerations (especially for irrigation agriculture). The coefficient cannot be higher than 2 or lower than 0.5.

Source: Gonzalo Delacámara, Peer-Reviewer, IMDEA Water Institute (Spain).

In Portugal, a water resources tax was set by a law approved in 2008 (see Box 3.4). The water charging system that goes much beyond water abstraction: it includes charges for pollution; for occupation of the surface, beds and margins of water bodies; for the extraction of sand and gravel from river beds and margins; and also a compensation for administrative costs of planning and management of water resources (see Chapter 5). The components of the tax reflect the varied shortage of water resources in different parts of the territory (Souza d'Alte, 2010). At the beginning of the implementation process, water utilities, hydropower generators, paper industries and irrigators emerged as the largest contributors.

Box 3.4. Water resources charges in Portugal

In Portugal the Water Resources Tax (Taxa de Recursos Hídricos – TRH) implements the basic idea that the user of water resources must compensate the cost generated to the community and/or restore the benefit the community grants (Polluter-Pays and User-Pays Principles). The TRH is due on a yearly basis, and the debtor entity is the user of water resources. The TRH compensates: 1) the advantage resulting from the privative use of public water, 2) the environmental costs related to the activities likely to cause a significant impact on water resources, and 3) the administrative costs regarding planning, management, supervision and water quality and quantity assurance.

The structure of the Water Resources Charges (TRH – Taxa de Recursos Hídricos) is the following:

$$TRH = A + E + I + O + U$$

in which:

- A is the amount paid for the abstracted water in m3;
- E is the amount paid for the discharged effluent, including COD and BOD expressed in kg;
- I is the amount paid for the gravel and sand (inertes) taken from the bed and margins of the river course expressed in m3;
- O is the amount paid for the occupation of the "public water domain" by any sort of infrastructure or construction, expressed in m2; and
- U is the amount paid for the use of water, expressed in m3, subject to public planning and management.

Box 3.4. Water resources charges in Portugal (*cont.*)

Although the parcels A and U relate both to abstracted water (in cubic meters), A corresponds to the appropriation for a privative use of the water itself as a public asset, while U compensates for the planning and management of the river basin. This distinction has an interesting consequence: if the source of water is private (basically groundwater) only TRH = U is considered, because there is no appropriation of public water; if the source of water is public (basically all surface water, except spring water occurring in private land while it stays inside that private property), the water charge is given by TRH = A+U, which pays for the public water (A) and for planning and management activities (U).

This approach circumvented the need of declaring all water as public, because it was found out that such a measure would cause an enormous reaction from farmers that are used to look at water in wells as part of their properties that actually determines to a large extent the value of the land. However, the fact that groundwater is considered "private" does not mean that it is not subject to a "public discipline", namely because the use that is made in one property may interfere with the availability in neighbouring properties. Therefore, although it is considered "private" water, it is subject to licensing procedures but there is no reason to pay the parcel "A" corresponding to the appropriation of a public asset.

Recently, a new parcel "S" was added to the water charges, aiming at promoting the sustainability of water services in the hinterland and in mountainous areas where the cost of water services is much higher than in the more flat and more affluent coastal areas.

According to the original Decree-Law No. 97/2008, revised in 2017 (Decree-law No. 46/2017), typical values per cubic meter for the component A are EUR 0.0032 of water used for irrigation and fish farming, EUR 0.00002 for hydropower production, 0.0027 for cooling thermoelectric stations, and 0.015 for domestic supply. These values can be aggravated up to 20% in scarcity affected areas of southern Portugal. The discharge of one kg of BOD is charged 0.37 euros, and one kg of total nitrogen and total phosphorus are charged EUR 0.17 and EUR 0.21, respectively. The extraction of one cubic meter of gravel or sand is charged EUR 2.5. The occupation of the public domain varies from 0.002 EUR/m2 (hydropower production and fish farming) to 10 euros/m2 (permanent beach occupation for commercial uses). The new parcel S was introduced in 2017 with a value of 0.004 EUR/m3. These values may seem quite low but it should be taken into account that they are applied to hundreds of millions of cubic meters or thousands of square meters.

These values may be multiplied by some aggravating or dis-aggravating factors, including a scarcity factor. Indeed, the water charge for abstraction of public water for private uses includes use of a shortage coefficient which varies across river basin region. It is calculated by multiplying the base value of the respective use by the volume of water drawn, diverted or used expressed in cubic meters, and by the applicable shortage coefficient. The coefficient of shortage is applied differently by river basin region:

- 1 for PTRH1, PTRH2 and PTRH3 (comprehending Minho, Lima, Cávado, Ave, Leça, and Douro basins)
- 1.1 for PTRH4 and PTRH5 (comprehending Vouga, Mondego, Lis, Oeste creeks, and Tejo basins)
- 1.2 for PTRH6, PTRH7 and PTRH8 (comprehending Sado, Mira, Algarve creeks, and Guadiana basins)

This component is applicable to the following sectors: agriculture, fish farming, aquaculture, hydraulic energy production, thermal energy production, public water supply systems and other case. Although it cannot be claimed that the shortage coefficients used in Portugal measure in an accurate way the water resource cost, they constitute a first attempt for charging water scarcity.

Box 3.4. Water resources charges in Portugal (*cont.*)

Of note: since 2008, water supply and sanitation service providers include abstraction charges in the retail tariffs, dependent on the actual use and the type of user. The proceedings are earmarked to a water protection fund (50%), or finance Basin Water Authorities (ABH; 40%), and the National Water Authority in charge of water resources management (INAG; 10%).

Source: Francisco Nunes Correa, Peer-reviewer, Technical University of Lisbon (Portugal), adapted from the European Commission (2015), "Report on the implementation of the Water Framework Directive River Basin Management Plans for Portugal".

In most cases, due to data limitations and practical issues, public authorities are not able to measure environmental and opportunity costs of using water in an accurate way. Still, it is important that water users get an accurate signal about relative water availability and quality across time and space. The above examples show that, however, it is possible to differentiate the level of the charge depending on the water source (groundwater versus surface water), the location (by region or river basin or for special zones such as Water Apportionment Areas in France), and the time of the year (winter versus summer).

The Netherlands implemented a national groundwater abstraction tax in 1995, which was then repealed in 2012 due to competitiveness concerns in the context of the economic crisis and pressures from the water industry. The tax was applied to the abstraction of groundwater by water works and other entities, such as industry and agriculture. Water companies then passed the tax on to their customers' bills. However, exemptions were included, such as sprinkling and irrigating land if less than 40 000 m3 per year were extracted, and pumps with a capacity lower than 10 m3 per hour. These implied that in practice agriculture was more or less completely exempted. Only groundwater abstraction was charged since the goal of the policy was to increase the price of groundwater so that surface water would be used as a substitute. The tax was administered by the Ministry of Finance and the Central Environmental Tax Unit. The exemption system had unintended (and negative) consequences: the pumping capacity exemption created an incentive for farmers to use several smaller pumps to avoid paying the tax, which was said to result in an overexploitation of groundwater. The system also raised complaints from water-intensive industries since the groundwater tax differed between industries which were supplied by water companies and for those with self-extraction, hence raising competitiveness issues (Reynaud, 2015).

If abstraction charges become too high, or incentivise the use of some sources over others, some users could develop alternatives which would not only affect the cost recovery for the collective water service investments, but which might also lead to a less efficient use of water resources. These options could include, for instance, drilling their own boreholes (legally or illegally) where groundwater is charged at a lower rate. In the case of wastewater treatment, building and operating their own private treatment plants to improve their effluent discharge quality could reduce discharge charges, and be a cheaper alternative than making discharges to the sewerage network. These private treatment plants may not be a problem, provided that the effluent quality is carefully monitored. It follows that any reform of water charges should be accompanied by a capacity to monitor and regulate water uses from different sources, and to monitor effluent discharges. A robust water permitting regime is also essential.

Table 3.2. Water abstraction charges in selected OECD countries

Country	Bases for charge			Level of the tax	Authority in charge / Levied by
	Groundwater (GW) or Surface Water (SW)	Other	Units (m3, ha, MWh)	(EUR /1 000m3)	
Australia (Australia Capital Territory)	Not differentiated		m3	Urban water supply: EUR 360 (2013) Others: EUR 175 (2013)	Australia Capital Territory Government
Belgium (Flanders)	GW	Varies by aquifer	m3 + IBT	500 – 30 000 m3: EUR 50 above 30 000 m3: EUR 62	Regional authority
Belgium (Flanders)	SW		m3 + DBT	<1Mm3: EUR 63	Regional authority
Belgium (Wallonia)	GW only		m3 + IBT	3 000-20 000 m³: EUR 25 20 000 – 100 000 m³: EUR 50 > 100 000 m³: EUR 74	Regional authority
Czech Republic	SW	Varies by river basin	m3	country average: EUR 155 (2014)	River boards
Czech Republic	GW		m3	< 6 000 m3 per year: exempted country average: EUR 35 (2013)	
Estonia	GW, SW and mineral water	Varies by aquifer	m3	GW: EUR 60 –160a SW: EUR 2 – 38	
France	Differentiated between GW and SW	Water Distribution Area (ZRE)	m3 if metered; proxied or fixed fee if not metered	Drinking water supply: EUR 33-51 (2009) Irrigation: EUR 2-16 (2009)b Hydropower: EUR 0.17-0.64 (2009)	Water agencies (hydrographic basin level)
Germany (Baden-Württemberg)	GW			Public water supply, heat production and others (incl. irrigation): EUR 51	State government
Germany (Baden-Württemberg)	SW			Public water supply: EUR 51 Heat production and others (not incl. irrigation): EUR 10	State government
Hungary	Differentiated according to the type of water (e.g. surface water, thermal water)		m3 or self-estimation for irrigation	EUR 0-100	Regional Water Directorate
Poland	GW		m3	EUR 15-25/1 000m3 (2011)	
	SW		m3	EUR 9-13/1 000m3 (2011)	

Table 3.2. Water abstraction charges in selected OECD countries *(cont.)*

Country	Bases for charge			Level of the tax	Authority in charge / Levied by
	Groundwater (GW) or Surface Water (SW)	Other	Units (m3, ha, MWh)	(EUR /1 000m3)	
Portugal	GW, SW, but different charges because GW is considered private water	Unit values vary a lot for different uses and vary for different regions reflecting water scarcity	m3	Agriculture and fish farming: EUR 0.003/m3 Hydropower: EUR 0.00002/m3 Cooling thermal energy: EUR 0.0027/m3 Municipal supply: EUR 0.013/m3 Other uses: EUR 0.015/m3 Some coefficients may apply reflecting specific circumstances established in the law	Collected by the river basin administration. 40% necessarily used at the river basin where collected, 50% can be redistributed by all river basins according to their needs, 10% can be used by the central agency
Slovenia			m3 except for energy production and hydropower (MWh)	Drinking water supply: EUR 55c Irrigation of agricultural land: EUR 1 Cooling: EUR 4 Hydropower plants above 10 MW: EUR 1 500 Hydropower plants below 10 MW: EUR 190	

Notes: a. OECD database on economic instruments (n.d.); b. Tax applied to non-gravitational irrigation; c. OECD database on economic instruments (n.d.).

Pollution charges

When discussing pollution charges, it is useful to make the distinction between the type of pollution, as either point source or diffuse source (Box 3.5).

In principle, the aim of the pollution charges is to make polluters internalise the pollution externality. In reality, the levels of the pollution charges are sometimes used to recover the costs related to water management, i.e. the charges do not reflect the social cost of pollution. For instance, in England and Wales the revenues raised related to industrial water pollution only covered the cost of the regulation (EUR 79.2 million compared to EUR 78.8 million) (EEA, 2013). It should be noted that charges come in combination with command and control regulation, which sets environmental quality standards that ensure that the total pollution load (from all sources, including diffuse) does not breach ecological or human health limits.

Box 3.5. Water pollutants

Water pollutants are commonly characterised as point or diffuse, according to their source and pathway to the receiving environment. This distinction is an important function of water quality policy and pollution regulation:

- **Point sources of pollution** are directly discharged to receiving water bodies at a discrete location, such as pipes and channels from sewage treatment plants, industrial sites and confined intensive livestock operations. The most severe water quality impacts from point source pollution typically occur during summer or dry periods, when river flows are low and the capacity for dilution is reduced, and during storm periods when combined sewer overflows operate more frequently.
- **Diffuse sources of pollution** are indirectly discharged to receiving water bodies, via overland and subsurface flow and atmospheric deposition to surface waters and leaching through the soil structure to groundwater during periods of rainfall and irrigation. The most severe water quality impacts from diffuse source pollution occur during storm periods (particularly after a dry spell) when rainfall induces hillslope hydrological processes and runoff of pollutants from the land surface.

Point sources of pollution are largely under control in OECD countries because they are easier to identify and more cost-effective to quantify, manage and regulate. In comparison, diffuse source pollution and their impacts on human and ecosystem health largely remain under-reported and under-regulated. This is because they are challenging to monitor and regulate due to:

- Their high variability, spatially and temporally, making attribution of sources of pollution complex
- The high transaction costs associated with dealing with large numbers of heterogeneous polluters (e.g. farmers, homeowners)
- Because pollution control may require co-operation and agreement within catchments, and across sub-national jurisdictions and countries.

There are also ecological and social response time delays. For instance: different ecosystems will respond differently to pollution, and pollution detection, social awareness, policy development and remediation actions will cause further delays depending on local resources and existing institutional and policy mechanisms.

Source: OECD (2017), *Diffuse Pollution, Degraded Waters: Emerging Policy Solutions*, OECD Publishing, Paris, http://dx.doi.org/10.1787/9789264269064-en.

Pollution charges are usually calculated based on volume and pollution content, and differentiated according to the sector (e.g. industries or agriculture) (Acteon, 2010). More countries have adopted pollution charges compared with abstraction charges (OECD, 2012a). However, examples of pollution charges for diffuse source pollution remain limited (OECD, 2017). The heterogeneous impacts and damage costs of diffuse water pollution make their management more difficult than point source pollution. Additional reasons for the slow uptake of pollution charges in the management of diffuse water pollution may include: political resistance from polluters; limited data on the costs of environmental degradation; difficulties in measuring diffuse sources of pollution and attributing them to landowners; and the complexities of ambient pollution concentrations, which are a function of both point and diffuse pollution sources, natural background levels, watershed characteristics, fate and transport parameters, and stochastic environmental variables (OECD, 2017; Shortle and Horan, 2001).

Because it is not economical to observe individual diffuse water pollution sources directly (i.e. fixing a water quality meter to a discharge pipe), the design of pollution charges must build upon one of three alternative management options:

- ***Attach charges to certain land use practices and inputs as proxies to pollution***. For example, intensive livestock farming, extensive non-permeable pavements, excessive fertiliser use and unsustainable tillage practices can lead to diffuse water pollution. However, such an approach can limit land use practices and innovation, and can be less effective at reducing pollution in some instances[5] (OECD, 2010).
- ***Charge polluters collectively*** for their jointly determined impacts on ambient pollution levels at particular receptors. However, this approach transfers the burden of asymmetric information and the difficulties of the measurement of ambient diffuse pollution and predictions under certain management scenarios from regulators to individual polluters.
- ***Attach charges to estimated diffuse emissions via modelling***. Computer modelling offers an opportunity for individual land parcels to be managed as part of a wider catchment to achieve water quality objectives. Pollution charges to incentivise diffuse pollution can be set at a level directly proportional to the amount of estimated pollution generated or reduced. It allows land managers to innovate farm and land management practices within a pollution limit without being restricted by the inputs and land use practices they use. However, the approach relies on a robust calibrated and validated model and reliable input data.

Pollution charges are typically collected at the local level (OECD, 2010), and since charges are often earmarked for environmental funds and water protection (treatment, monitoring, enforcement, etc.) the money usually remains at the local level (Acteon, 2009; 2010). There is a large variation in how and for which pollutants water pollution charges are implemented in different countries or regions. Table 3.3 provides a few examples.

The EEA (2013) reports that most European countries examined do indeed, in accordance with the WFD, consider also the environmental costs for untreated wastewater discharges, when charging water polluters for the purification of their wastewater, and other activities that affect the quality of aquatic ecosystems. For instance, Spain's water levy is designed with the objective of guaranteeing both water supply and quality. Hence, it aims to tackle both resource and environmental costs. Households and industries face different charging schemes with households facing a three-block increasing eco-tax and industries an eco-tax which is the sum of a use- and a pollution-tax component (EEA, 2013). Water use for agricultural purposes is exempt, but the exemption can be revoked if after inspection water is found be contaminated due to the use of pesticides, fertilisers, or organic material, or due to pollution discharges in relation to livestock farming.

In France, instruments are designed and levels are set taking into account not only environmental but also organisational issues, such as the density of consumers in a specific area and the type and size of a water service (private or public) (EEA, 2013). Charges are differentiated according to water users, such as households, agriculture, and industry (Box 3.6). Charges for domestic wastewater services are based on water consumption of the household (allowing for local variation as described). If agricultural activities only incur pollution with domestic origin (i.e. no pollution from non-domestic origin), then charges are the same for households and agriculture. These charges contrast with those for livestock and pollution with non-domestic origin in agriculture and industry, which are based respectively on number of livestock (above a certain level) and inputs such as plant protection products, and discharged pollutants.

Table 3.3. Pollution charges in selected countries

Country	Levied by	Tax name	Specific tax base	Tax structure
Australia	State	Water effluent charge	Volume, pollution content (types of polluants)	per kg assessable load
Canada	Province	Charge on discharge	Volume and pollution content	per litre or per tonne
Denmark		Nonpoint source	Chemical deterrents of insects and mammals	tax on retail price
France		Nonpoint source	Pesticides	per kg
France		Water effluent charges	Households	per m3
Netherlands		Nonpoint source	Surplus nitrogen and phosphate	per kg per hectare
Netherlands		Tax on the pollution of surface waters	BOD, COD and heavy metals, for large polluters	per pollution unit
Portugal	River basin administration	Component "E" of the Water Resources Tax	BOD5, COD Some coefficients may apply reflecting specific circumstances established in the law	per kg EUR 0.10 per kg of COD and EUR 0.20 per kg of BOD5
Sweden	Municipality	Wastewater user charges	Wastewater and drinking water	varies by municipality; full cost charging
Sweden		Nonpoint source	Pesticides	per whole kg active constituent

Source: The OECD database on Policy Instruments for the Environment, www2.oecd.org/ecoinst/queries/Default.aspx (accessed March 2016).

In Spain, the wastewater effluent discharge fee (or water pollution fee) is aimed at raising revenues to fund the assessment, monitoring, control, protection, and enhancement of water quality in each river basin district. The tax base is calculated on the basis of the discharged volume of wastewater and the unit price of controlling that discharge. That unit price is calculated multiplying the base price per cubic meter times a factor that is established according to the nature, characteristics and degree of contamination of each effluent, as well as considering parameters of the physical environment. The base price was fixed at 0.01683 EUR /m3 in urban wastewater and 0.04207 EUR /m3 in industrial wastewater (2.5 times higher) but they are subject to price review every year in the Central Government Budget Law. The factor that can be used to increase this base price cannot be higher than 4. It is important to note that this fee is independent from other fees or taxes either regional or local Governments may levy to fund sewerage and wastewater treatment facilities. These generally combine fixed and variable charges (based on volume) for industrial wastewater. In some cases, they consider pollution load factors in the calculation. The way these charges are applied widely varies across regions.

Box 3.6. Differentiating pollution charges per user and pollutants in France

In France, water pollution charges are differentiated according to water users, such as households, agriculture, and industry – although they can be the same between users. Charges for pollution with domestic origin are based on the water consumption of the household. The following table compiles the pollution charge for domestic users for the Adour-Garonne river basin (one of the 6 river basins in France).

Pollution charge for domestic users in the Adour Garonne River Basin (France)

Year	2013	2014	2015	2016	2017	2018	Maximum limit set by law
Pollution charge (EUR /m3)	0.3	0.305	0.31	0.315	0.32	0.33	0.5

These charges contrast with those for livestock and pollution with non-domestic origin in agriculture and industry, which are based respectively on number of livestock (above a certain level) and discharged pollutants. In the following table, we report the pollution charge for non-domestic users for the Adour-Garonne river basin.

Pollution charge for non-domestic users in the Adour Garonne River Basin (France)

Main pollution elements	Pollution charge (in euros per unit)						Maximum limit set by law
	2013	2014	2015	2016	2017	2018	
Total dissolved solids (per Kg)	0.119	0.122	0.124	0.127	0.129	0.132	0.3
Chemical oxygen demand (COD) per Kg)	0.074	0.076	0. 77	0.079	0.081	0.082	0.2
Biochemical oxygen demand in 5 days (per Kg)	0.149	0.152	0.155	0.158	0.161	0.164	0.4
Nitrogen (per kg)	0.3	0.305	0.31	0.315	0.32	0.33	0.7
Nitrates, nitrites (per kg)	0	0	0	0	0	0	0.3
Phosphorus (per kg)	0.4	0.41	0.42	0.43	0.44	0.44	0.2
Metox (per kg)	0.7	0.71	0.73	0.74	0.76	0.77	3.6
Metox for groundwater (per kg)	6	6	6	6	6	6	6
Toxicity high (per kiloequitox)	6.7	6.8	7	7.1	7.2	7.4	18
Toxicity high in groundwater (per kiloequitox)	30	30	30	30	30	30	30
Dangerous substances for environment in surface water (per kg)				3	4	5	10
Dangerous substances for environment in groundwater (per kg)				3	4	5	16.6
Dissolved salts (m3 [siemens/centimetre])	0	0	0	0	0	0	0.15
Heated water in sea, except in winter (per megathermie)	1.26	1.29	1.31	1.34	1.37	1.4	8.5
Heated water in river except in winter(per megathermie)	1.26	1.29	1.31	1.34	1.37	1.4	8.5

Source: Arnaud Reynaud, Expert, Toulouse School of Economics (France).

Lessons learnt

- ***Focus attention on the small group of users who abstract the vast majority of water in Brazil***. These include large water utilities, large manufacturing units in water-intensive industries, hydropower generating plants, and large farms growing water-intensive crops. The idea that water charges should be universal for fairness and equity is a trap: currently, a very large proportion of water is used by a very low percentage of water use. Transaction costs to cover smaller users can be high compared to the benefits in terms of water resources management and revenues raised. However, the aggregate impacts of concentrations of small users can be significant in small river catchments, or where there are large numbers of boreholes in an aquifer unit; in these circumstances both regulation and charging may be appropriate. To avoid huge transaction costs and set a fair water charge system, it is important to take account of the impact on other abstractors, as well as to have a good inventory of water users and very clear rules for exemption. As for abstraction charges, lessons from international experience suggest to focus attention on the small group of polluters who discharge the vast majority of (treated and untreated) effluents. In Brazil, these include large water utilities, large manufacturing units in water-polluting industries, mining and farms using large quantities of fertilisers and pesticides. Transaction costs to cover smaller polluters can be high compared to the benefits in terms of water quality and revenues raised. Where they exist, the aggregate impacts of concentrations of small polluters should also be analysed.

- ***Provide national guidance and incentives for setting water charges and spending related revenues***. Guidance should focus on the level of charges, their structure and the water charging process. Clear guidelines on how to set and implement economic instruments would be useful given the large number of stakeholders involved in river basin governance in Brazil. Federal authorities (ANA or the CNRH) could consider setting general rules, for instance lower bounds for abstraction or pollution charges, list of pollutants to be controlled and monitored (mandatory and river-specific), rules for expenditure spending and publishing of accounts. The decentralised nature of the system would however need to be preserved, with river basin committees then deciding on the specific modalities for adapting these guidelines to their context.

- ***Carry out economic analyses to support decision making in water charges***. This could relate to measuring the opportunity cost of water; the cost of pollution and of poor river flow or groundwater management; affordability issues; impact of water charges on competitiveness of water users; etc. In addition, the ANA could design targeted support for clusters of states, based on capabilities, pressures on water management, needs, or progress towards setting up well-designed water charges.

- ***Consider a menu of options to overcome the exemptions for the irrigation sector***. They can include, for instance, incentives in the form of discounts linked to best practices, or recycling of revenues collected to support transition towards efficient water practices.

- ***Move toward a uniform charge for all users extracting the same water body***. This means slowly increasing the charge paid by exempted users (e.g. farmers); preserving their competitiveness by earmarking the extra charge, e.g. through redistributing revenues by subsidising sanitation and water saving technologies or through lump-sum transfers. Hydropower producers should also be charged the same rate on water stored or diverted during drought period. The shift can be budget neutral for hydropower producers by reducing the tax they pay on production.

Keep it simple

Assessing the distinct values, costs and benefits associated with water (both quantity and quality) can assist policy makers in prioritising investments and determining policy options that provide the greatest welfare. However, choosing the level of an abstraction or pollution charge such that it covers exactly the cost of the environmental and opportunity costs is an almost impossible task for public authorities. First, assessing environmental costs implies valuing the cost of the damage caused by abstraction or pollution of water on the ecosystem. Some of these costs may be visible only in the long run (for instance, the impact on the fish population or biodiversity) and are difficult to monetise because several environmental benefits are not currently priced. However, in a well-monitored, well-regulated system the use of controls on abstraction rates and effluent load should ensure that any impact on ecosystems is prevented. Second, measuring some costs faces acute methodological issues. For instance, diffuse pollution (Box 3.6) is difficult to measure independently of the inputs that produced it; it is also difficult to attribute to individual polluters; improved water quality can be difficult to attribute to the uptake of abatement practices; stock pollutants (with time delays in abatement measures spanning over more than one generation) and historic pollution (with those responsible no longer around) both pose problems in terms of who should pay. Finally, measuring the opportunity cost of using water in a scarce environment requires measuring the benefit induced by water for all types of use (agriculture using irrigation water, drinking water supply, hydropower etc.), with benefits that commonly vary from one season to another (opportunity costs are usually higher when rainfall and runoff are low).

Economics can provide estimates of (use and non-use) values attributed to a water resource. How practical such estimates are remains an empirical question. There are likely to be conflicting values, missing values and double counting identified during a total economic value study (IUCN, 1998). There are also uncertainties about the underlying environmental responses. The monetary estimates will be context dependent, i.e. they will be contingent on where and when, and under what regulatory system they are estimated. Hence, it is likely that values will vary both in time and space.

There are several techniques to assess environmental and opportunity costs, which can be inspiring for the case of Brazil.

- Bio-economic studies can be employed to estimate the full marginal value of the environmental flow in each watercourse. Such studies are difficult to undertake since they require expertise from various sciences. They are resource-intensive and their findings may not be easily transferable since estimates are going to be site-specific.
- Non-market valuation techniques (e.g. contingent valuation, travel cost method…) are employed since environmental benefits are typically not priced. They can estimate the economic value of environmental benefits of water flows and water of a certain quality. Box 3.7 provides an example of use of non-market valuation technique for environmental flows in Australia. Non-market valuation

techniques can also be used to monetise scarcity but other techniques to value scarcity are either production function approaches or intermediate good (value added) approaches where the production cost and income will be affected by access to water. For instance, if there is a government programme providing water for farmers, income differences between those having access to the programme and those not having access would reflect the benefit of the programme.

- Markets for trading water abstraction and pollution rights, which are outside the scope of this report, can provide a clear indicator of the value of water, but prices would depend on the amount of rights initially provided by the regulator. For instance, in a situation with a too generous regulator the value of water rights would be lower, which would not be a good signal of the value of water in a water scarce context.

Box 3.7. Non-market valuation of environmental flows in the River Murray and the Coorong, Australia

The River Murray and the Coorong and its mouth are a unique ecosystem which provide habitat for breeding birds, fish, and vegetation. However, decreasing environmental flows during an extensive drought contributed to over-extraction and declining inflows mean that the area and its habitat have been in decline. One method of estimating the value of environmental flows is to design a survey which asks people their willingness to pay for improvements in environmental quality, using this as a measure of the value people put on the environmental services provided.

In order to estimate the value of these environmental flows in the Murray River and the Coorong, MacDonald et al. (2011) designed a survey that was sent out to over 3 000 Australian residents. The survey described the impact of low environmental flows on waterbird breeding habitat, native fish populations, and healthy vegetation in the area, and set out ways of improving environmental quality by purchasing water user's rights from willing sellers, investments in irrigation efficiency, and habitat rehabilitation, together with the costs of these policies. The survey then asked respondents to choose between various policy options that had different environmental impacts and different costs.

Through a statistical analysis of the results from the survey, MacDonald et al. (2011) found that Australian residents were willing to pay substantial amounts to improve the quality of the Murray River and Coorong indicating that the value of environmental flows in the area is significant. Specifically, total willingness to pay (in present value terms) to increase the frequency of waterbird breeding from every 10 years to 4 years, to increase native fish populations from 30 to 50% of original levels, to increase the area of healthy native vegetation from 50 to 70%, and to improve waterbird breeding habitat quality in the Coorong was AUD 13 (USD 14) billion. The authors stress that, due to the uniqueness of the Coorong, this value cannot be used to estimate the value of other watercourses in Australia, and further surveys are required.

Source: MacDonald et al. (2011), "Valuing a Multistate River: The Case of the River Murray", *The Australian Journal of Agricultural and Resource Economics*, Vol. 55, pp. 374-392.

Proxies are as effective as and more practical than detailed calculations. The private sector provides a crude illustration. Nestlé introduced an *internal shadow price of water* in countries where it operates and where water is not charged: the absence of a charge should not mean that water has no value, and Nestlé seeks to calculate and reflect that value: it sets shadow prices for internal decisions (e.g. investment decision on the location of a new factory, or on the introduction of water saving technologies), based on water availability in the region. In agricultural areas where water is abundant, a price of USD 1/m3 was used; in water scarce areas, the price was USD 5/m3. That shadow price directly affects decisions, as it helps make the economic case for investment in water efficiency. An important message is that the basis of the calculation does not need to be sophisticated: a rough proxy can be used, which sends the right signal to decision makers.

Lessons from international experiences to measure costs

1. Methodological issues should not be taken as an excuse to postpone implementation or reform of water charges. Costs can be difficult to measure. Sophisticated methods exist but implementation can be challenging. Crude proxies are practical ways to send consistent messages to water users.
2. Monitor the effectiveness of abstraction and pollution charges and whether they are helping to deliver the policy objectives, or whether there are unintended consequences. Reforms should be accompanied with proper monitoring and regulatory capacities.

Combining water charges with other policy instruments

Water charges do not operate in a vacuum. In Brazil, other policy instruments are already in place, at federal and state levels. The question is how to introduce water abstraction and pollution charges or how to reform them where they exist in combination with existing instruments. For instance, one way of tackling inefficient water use is to allocate water against benchmark efficient use for the crop or manufacturing process: increasing charges would provide some incentive, but must be accompanied by a more proactive attitude by the regulator and by awareness raising and education vis-à-vis end users. In this case, an abstraction charge would deliver better in combination with an incentivising water allocation regime.

A good justification for combining several types of policy instrument comes from the fact that public authorities in charge of water management usually have simultaneous – at times conflicting – objectives, including: i) achieving cost recovery (of environmental and resource costs), ii) sending adequate incentives to water users and iii) ensuring water affordability. Achieving a good balance is difficult, and the outcome may depend on preferences and considerations that vary in time and space. Water charges alone cannot realise the three objectives simultaneously. The water sector is not immune to the Tinbergen (1952) rule, whereby for each and every policy target there must be at least one policy tool. Therefore, three different purposes cannot be accomplished with one instrument alone; a combination of different instruments is needed.

While a water charge has a role to play in this policy mix, it may well be a modest one in the short term. As Massarutto (2007) argues, using prices as a tool for water allocation only makes sense if two conditions are met: short run marginal costs are high and price elasticity of demand for water is high. Both conditions are the exception rather than the rule in water markets. Despite this limited allocative role, water charges are important in conveying the message that water is scarce and that one should look for options to use it efficiently. Charges also play a useful role in implementing the Beneficiary Pays principle and contributing to cost recovery (including environmental and resource costs). Cost recovery, however, is unlikely to be achieved through water charges alone – a mix of regulatory, economic and voluntary or information-based instruments is often required for an effective policy response to improve water-use efficiency, reduce pollution, and restore and maintain freshwater ecosystems (Table 3.4). Coupling water charges with regulatory and voluntary instruments can help foster acceptability of charges.

Table 3.4. Examples of water policy instruments to address selected water-related risks

Water-related risk	Regulatory	Economic	Voluntary or information-based
Water scarcity (including drought)	Restriction on water use Administrative allocation of water Abstraction limits Non-compliance penalties – non-renewal of resource permits or greater restriction on current permits Non-compliance fines	Abstraction charges Tradable rights to use water Payments for ecosystem services (PES) Microfinance schemes	Information and awareness campaigns Drought warning and information Farm advisory services for improved farming techniques (to increase water efficiency and reduce water demand) Contracts/bonds (e.g. land retirement contracts) Best environmental practices (or good management practices) Environmental labelling – products that meet certain environmental standards can be marketed and sold at a premium and/or subsidised
Water pollution	Water quality standards Bans on the manufacture/ use of certain chemicals Mandatory best environmental practices and restrictions on inputs Pollution discharge permits Non-compliance penalties – non-renewal of resource permits or greater restriction on current permits Non-compliance fines	Pollution taxes (on inputs) Pollution charges (on outputs) Tradable pollution permits PES	Information and awareness campaigns Farm advisory services for improved farming techniques (to minimise negative impacts on water quality) Contracts/bonds (e.g. land retirement contracts) Best environmental practices (or good management practices) Environmental labelling – products that meet certain environmental standards can be marketed and sold at a premium and/or subsidised
Risk to the resilience of freshwater ecosystems	Minimum environmental flows (also for pollution dilution) Specification obligations relating to return flows and discharges in resource consents in drought conditions	"Buy-backs" of water entitlements (quantity or quality) to ensure adequate environmental flows and water quality	Information and awareness campaigns Voluntary surrender of water entitlements and pollution discharge allowances Data sharing arrangements Environmental reporting

Source: OECD (2015), *Water Resources Allocation: Sharing Risks and Opportunities*, OECD Publishing, Paris, http://dx.doi.org/10.1787/9789264229631-en; OECD (2017), *Diffuse Pollution, Degraded Waters: Emerging Policy Solutions*, OECD Publishing, Paris, http://dx.doi.org/10.1787/9789264269064-en.

Command-and-control regulations are good complements to abstraction or pollution charges for two reasons:

- Setting caps on pollutant emissions ensures that ambient pollution never exceeds a threshold. This is particularly important when pollution has dramatic and irreversible impacts on biodiversity or health above some threshold. At the extreme, banning some chemicals (e.g. pesticides) for high toxicity makes sure that no one will be poisoned. Adding a water pollution charge in the policy mix can help create incentives for polluters to minimise emissions in a dynamic way. Without a charge, polluters align with the threshold or standard at best, and only consider minimising pollution when the threshold is revised.

- Similarly, restriction on water consumption in cases of drought can be used to guarantee a minimal flow of water in watersheds to preserve biodiversity. Adding an abstraction charge to the policy mix provides for a dynamic process and a capacity to adjust to shifting circumstances with minimal transaction costs. When it comes to recovering environmental and opportunity costs, regulatory instruments are more commonly used (EEA, 2013). Capacity limits for groundwater abstraction, bans and limits on the discharge of certain pollutants (based on best available techniques), and obligations to restore or compensate wetlands degraded by human activities are examples of such regulatory instruments that make the polluters pay by forcing them to invest in pollution prevention and abatement or to neutralise environmental damage. Another example of regulation aiming at cost recovery by making users pay is a "connection obligation": when an infrastructure for water supply or sewage is built, all dwellings and other buildings in the area can be obliged to connect to this infrastructure, thus preventing overcapacity and ensuring the spread of investment costs over the largest possible number of customers.

Water markets and tradable emission permits are usually seen as substitutes for abstraction and pollution charges. They are both market-based instruments that aim at reducing water consumption or pollution at the lowest cost. The difference relates to the decision choice: whether to fix quantities or prices.

Water quality trading can be an alternative to pollution charges when the latter cannot be implemented for political reasons. It is recognised that there can be inefficiencies associated with regulations, charges and subsidies. Where property or use rights are established, water quality trading requires less control from government and offers a mechanism for achieving a cost-effective allocation of environmental effort across alternative sources, without environmental regulators knowing the abatement costs of individual agents (OECD, 2017). Although they can be complex in nature, water quality markets can also stimulate innovation, potentially enable continued growth in a capped watershed without jeopardising water quality, and water quality goals may be met at a faster pace than without trading. Box 3.8 shows the experience with water quality trading in New Zealand.

Participation by farmers is often voluntary, as they are not subject to pollution caps. Pollution abatement is remunerated with revenues rather than tax savings. Farmers have incentives to reduce pollution to obtain payments for credits. However, one drawback of not capping farmers is that this favours big polluters who get more credit because their baseline emission level is higher. It also induces perverse incentives in terms of choosing the baseline emission level. Importantly, it also opens the door to pollution "leakage" along a water stream because total pollution is not capped: the reduction in pollution of participating farms might be offset by a pollution increase of other unregulated polluters.

Voluntary policies such as environmental certification and nudges can contribute to achieving water policy objectives. However, they work best in combination with water abstraction or pollution charges. When operating in isolation, their impact on water consumption and pollution is limited. For example, policy approaches used to date for the control of diffuse pollution tend to be voluntary and developed at the local level via partnerships, around watersheds or cities, and most often include government's paying farmers to reduce pollution. However, there is evidence that voluntary participation may not reach the major polluters and subsidy-based programmes can have limited impact due to public budget constraints and a lack of environmental regulations on diffuse pollution.

Many green labels and environmental certification programmes induce marginal pollution reduction. More stringent voluntary programmes such as organic farming certification involve only few producers. Also the effect of nudges on resource consumption often turns out to be temporary: after one month consumers go back to their usual consumption level.

Box 3.8. Water quality trading in New Zealand

To date, market-based instruments to address water pollution in OECD countries have been limited (primarily to point-point sources), but there is growing interest in their use. The Lake Taupō nitrogen market, New Zealand, is the first diffuse source nitrogen pollution market in the world, enabled by a national computer model to cap nitrogen emissions at the catchment scale and allocate discharge allowances to individual farmers for trading (OECD, 2017). The target was to reduce manageable nitrogen emissions to 20% below current recorded levels, to restore water quality and clarity to 2001 levels by 2080.

The Waikato Regional Council, Taupō District Council and Ngati Tuwharetoa (the local iwi) implemented an innovative diffuse water quality trading project, comprising three components: i) a cap on nitrogen emission levels within the Lake Taupō catchment by OVERSEER®; ii) establishment of the Taupō nitrogen market; and iii) formation of the Lake Taupō Protection Trust to fund the initiative. The costs were to be spread across local, regional and national communities; the independent Lake Taupō Protection Trust was established in 2007 to use public funds (NZD 79.2 million) to buy back allocated nitrogen allowances to retire land and to reduce the economic and social impacts of the nitrogen cap. The trading scheme was also complemented by the New Zealand Emissions Trading Scheme, which came into force during the early stages of the project and advancing the achievement of nitrogen reductions; the promotion of forestry land-use change from pasture to forestry not only surrendered nitrogen discharge allocations and, but also received carbon sequestration credits for a time.

The policy package has been fully implemented. It is providing the flexibility for land to move to its highest value and best use, and still meet the overall nitrogen load reduction targets. The use of the model OVERSEER® is essential to the cap-and-trade programme, providing incentives for farmers to reduce nitrogen emissions. The Lake Taupō Protection Trust has permanently retired 20% of the original nitrogen discharge allowances. New lower-nitrogen ventures are emerging in the catchment, such as growing olives, farming dairy sheep, and producing and marketing "sustainable" beef. The environmental certainty enables development of added-value products with credible green branding. It also generated positive environmental impacts, particularly carbon sequestration, from the reforestation of more than 5 000 ha of land to pine plantations.

Source: OECD (2017), *Diffuse Pollution, Degraded Waters: Emerging Policy Solutions*, OECD Publishing, Paris, http://dx.doi.org/10.1787/9789264269064-en.

In agriculture, achieving the full outcome from implementing water charges presupposes that efficient risk management policies are in place. In the absence of risk management tools, it is often the case that governments tend to alleviate the effects of crop failures or other natural disasters (flood, drought, etc.) by providing post disaster direct compensation as a relief measure. This poses a "Samaritan's dilemma" whereby post-disaster aid may discourage farmers to react *ex ante* to water scarcity signal transmitted by water charges. By anticipating that they will get post disaster direct compensations, farmers may not take *ex ante* efficient decisions such as switching toward more resilient cropping pattern. In that perspective insurance schemes have some comparative advantages: insurance companies can introduce conditionalities for payment of compensation, requesting farmers or industries to take *ex ante* measures to minimise exposure to risk or enhance resilience capacities.

Lessons from international experiences to combine charges with a broader policy mix

- Consider water charges in combination with other policy instruments: water resources plans, expenditure planning, water allocation regimes, conditions to determine and manage exceptional events and conditions (droughts in particular) are particularly relevant.
- In addition, consider water charges in combination with compliance monitoring and enforcement, awareness raising and nudging, and risk management tools (especially in agriculture); a point that will be reiterated in Chapter 5.
- Facilitate the reform of water allocation regimes, so that they accompany and benefit from well-designed abstraction charges and contribute to improved water management, in normal times and in episodes of scarcity. Similarly, effective controls on discharges, both point sources and diffuse impacts would be needed. For the agricultural sector, collective management of entitlements could be considered.

Raising and spending revenues from water charges

Water charges are not primarily aimed to raise revenue for financing infrastructure investment and maintenance for water supply and sanitation. The main economic rationale is to make users internalise the economic value of the water abstracted from and polluting emissions in water streams. Water charges are thus grounded on behavioural responses from users rather on levying revenue from taxing abstraction and pollution. However, in addition, abstraction and pollution charges do raise revenues from water users and polluters. From that perspective, they deliver best as water policy instruments if the revenues are used to cover expenditures that contribute to water management, possibly in the basin where they originate.

Public finance economists usually do not favour earmarking revenues collected from taxes (i.e. spending revenues from the taxes on specific projects related to the original purpose of the tax) for several reasons. First, they argue that efficiency will be improved if the revenues from the tax are used to cut existing distortionary taxes (for instance, a wage income tax makes labour more expensive and may thus discourage work). This refers to the so-called double-dividend hypothesis: the environmental tax (such as a tax per unit of pollution) addresses the environmental problem by sending signals on the damage caused (first dividend), and the revenues raised by this tax can help reduce the distortions associated with existing taxes (the second dividend). Second, the revenue collected can finance any public spending not related to water management that is considered a priority, e.g. investment in infrastructure or, more generally, the provision of public goods and services such as education, national defence and security. Moreover, earmarking distorts budget allocation decisions since decision makers are not free to allocate spending on the basis of need or the value of public money, but have to accept predetermined allocation rules. Other examples of criticisms of the use of earmarking is that scrutiny and control of governance may be weakened since spending does not have to be justified, there may be fluctuations in programme funding, and no necessary link between the earmarked tax and the provision of the good (ITIC, 2013). For instance, on the one hand, a rise in revenues from earmarked taxes may lead to excessive spending; on the other hand, in case of a decrease, the earmarked taxes may only partly finance the programme; the link between the collected revenues and the cost of the programme is lost, with the effect that people may misperceive the cost of the programmes.

Nevertheless, earmarked taxes can be defended based on political economy arguments. When revenues from the charge are earmarked, individuals "can make "private" choices on the basis of some reasonably accurate comparison of the costs and benefits of the specific public services, one at a time (Buchanan, 1963, p. 458). Moreover, other arguments in favour of earmarking include: the "benefits principle of taxation" (i.e. taxes should be borne by those who benefit from the associated expenditure); weak control and weak internal incentives in bureaucracies; mitigating erratic financing decisions of programmes; and the fact that budgeting with general fund financing (i.e. non-earmarking) may not be periodically reviewed to ensure that spending is allocated according to need and the value for money (Ranjit, 1988).

Several measures can be adopted to compensate the drawbacks mentioned above from earmarking revenues from water charges. Typically, expenditures should be somehow related to revenues. The action plan adopted for public expenditure must be commensurate with the revenue collected. If not, stakeholders would not see the benefit from taxation either because the action plan is not implemented, or because the contribution of water charges to the plan is insignificant. It does not mean that the action plan should be strictly tied to revenues. Additional sources of funding could be considered, such as budget transfers. Moreover, the revenues and expenditures should be of the same magnitude for the water action plan to be realistic. Differences of one or more orders of magnitude – as witnessed in several occasions in Brazil – undermine feasibility and credibility of the programme of action, and the legitimacy of the water charges. The rules for matching revenues to spending should be transparent and effective to improve the 'benefit principle of taxation'.

In Brazil by law, revenues from water charges are earmarked to the basin committee and to water management projects within the basin (see Chapter 2). In practice, rates do not allow to finance actions foreseen in the water resources plans. The ratio of the financial needs for the water plan over the money collected is often about ten to one or more. In addition, the value added by expenditures financed through earmarked funds is invisible to water users in the basin, reinforcing the view that water charges are not returned to, or do not benefit the water users. This is particularly the case when revenues – in the orders of tens of thousands reals – are blended with other sources of funding and spent on the construction of sanitation infrastructure – in the order of hundreds of million reals.

A way to improve the acceptability of water charges is to invest part of the revenue collected directly to industrial users and farmers. This can be done in two ways: feebates and support to water saving or pollution mitigation technologies or practices. Both can rely on a recycling mechanism, whereby revenues collected from the charge are used to support either further performance from the water user (feebates), or adoption of water saving or pollution abating technologies or practices. Both can be considered, on a temporary basis only, to facilitate transition towards compliance.

A feebate is a combined charge and subsidy scheme to address environmental externalities. Polluters are charged for polluting emissions that are exceeding a pre-defined threshold. They obtain subsidies if they manage to emit less than this threshold: they receive a subsidy per unit of emission reduction below this threshold. The feebate is meant to be budget neutral: the charges paid by polluters who are emitting more than the threshold finance subsidies assigned to those who emit less. It has been implemented in Europe for the energy efficiency of cars.

Feebate schemes could be adapted to water abstraction and pollution. Threshold water level per output or per hectare can be defined as a target. Firms can be rewarded with subsidies for each volume of water saved below this target. They will have to pay abstraction charges for water volumes exceeding the target. Of course, defining the target is critical. It would require a good knowledge of the production process, the technology and its potential for improvement. A charging scheme that provides subsidies needs to be very carefully design to prevent existing high performers from subsidising poor performers on their journey to improvement.

When it comes to water pollution, a feebate scheme could be designed by referring to the international experiences on water quality trading mechanisms (OECD 2012b). Under those mechanisms, polluters are usually assigned a cap on their emissions. If they manage to emit less than the cap, they receive credits issued by a regulatory agency or a third-party certification. The cap is computed based on a "business-as-usual" production process: farmers get emission reduction credits on the pollution reduction from adopting cleaner practices as compared to conventional agriculture. Water quality markets have been implemented in Australia to reduce salinity from coal mining and power plants, as well as in Ontario (Canada) to deal with phosphorus. The United States has launched the most important water pollution offset market with the Pennsylvania Nutrient Trading Programme in the Chesapeake Bay for nutrients (nitrogen and/or phosphorus from fertilisers and breeding). California has used a similar cap-and-trade approach to reduce selenium: it imposed a cap on agricultural emissions.

Water markets are quite costly to manage, as they require a lot of information to compute the credits and to enforce regulation. Trade is usually restricted. Several programmes include trading ratios among trading partners to better control the localisation of pollution concentration, which adds another layer of complexity (see EPA, 2009).

Ways forward to unlock the water-related public expenditure bottlenecks in Brazil

- Accompany basin plans with strategic financial plans, tailored to an agreed action plan and affordable timescales for implementation. River basin plans should be integrated with other plans (e.g. for agriculture development or sanitation) as they can contribute to enhance water security.
- Consider redistributing part of the revenue from water charges to users. This can be done through subsidies for reducing water abstraction or pollution below a pre-defined threshold (feebate). Alternatively, part of the revenue can be used to support the adoption of water efficient or cleaner technologies or practices. Such recycling should be time-bound and directly related to clear policy targets. Progress towards those targets should be regularly monitored.
- Change rules so that agencies can effectively spend the money collected through water charges (see Action Plan). At the moment staff in the state or delegated agencies faces difficulties to comply with existing rules. How that can be done in practice requires administrative capacities which are beyond the scope of this report as they are of cross-sectoral nature and relate to public governance dimensions at large.

Integrating behavioural dimensions into water charge design

By relying on water charges, it is implicitly assumed that economic agents (farmers, firms, household) are fully rational. The theory of rational choice assumes that, when making decisions, economic agents take into account all the available information and make self-interested and consistent decisions over time. Yet, behavioural research shows that, among others, most of economic agents are ill-informed and have difficulties in making the most of market opportunities. They have in fact a limited rationality in particular because they may be subject to several cognitive biases; they may face conflict between long-term and short-term preferences; they care about themselves and also about others.

Box 3.9. Behavioural policy initiatives across Europe in the environment domain

In **Spain**, a study by the University of Las Palmas de Gran Canaria used a randomised control trial to test the effect of defaults and framing in the context of a policy for mitigating CO2 emissions. Results showed that framing influenced travellers' willingness to pay EUR 10 extra for a flight ticket to mitigate their CO_2 emissions. That is, 81% paid extra when the question was framed as a rejection (i.e. tick in this box if you would like to deduct the additional amount) vs. 62% when this was framed as an addition (i.e. tick in this box if you would like to include the additional amount). Note however that rejection was also the default option.

In **France**, the bonus-malus scheme for cars (a.k.a. ecological bonus) – an environmental tax applied as a malus in French Registration Documents – incorporates the idea of fairness. Specifically, the higher revenue brought about by the most polluting cars serves to subsidise the least polluting ones. The National Institute for Agronomic Research is carrying out research exploring the extent to which social norms can be used as levers to influence farmers' behaviour related to the use of pesticides, and consumers' behaviour related to recycling and waste reduction.

Source: Lourenço J.S. et al. (2016), "Behavioural insights applied to policy", European Report, http://publications.jrc.ec.europa.eu/repository/bitstream/JRC100146/kjna27726enn_new.pdf.

Thaler and Sunstein (2008) show that individual choices are influenced not only by information about what others in the same social group do, but also by the way the information is formulated and provided, the so-called "framing" of information. They introduce the concept of "nudge" as the use of a specific policy design, type of information and framing of information which influences people's decisions without changing the structure of economic incentives or restricting their available options. Box 3.9 provides some example of behavioural policy initiatives across Europe in the environment domain.

A way to influence producers' and consumers' behaviour related to water use is to provide more information about water stress (transitory or permanently) and water quality. Information can be framed to 'nudge' water users. A nudge can be defined as any aspect in the framing of a decision problem that can affect people's decisions without changing economic incentives (Croson and Treich, 2014). The concept has attracted a lot of attention in recent years, especially in the United States and the United Kingdom, among regulatory authorities. For public policy purposes, the framing is chosen to guide people's decisions in the 'right' direction of protecting the environment by saving natural resources or reducing pollution. For instance, Ferraro et al. (2011) ran a real-controlled experiment in which they tried to nudge households on their water consumption. They modified water bills by providing different kinds of information: messages on the negative impacts of water consumption on ecosystems, and on several ways to effectively reduce water use. They also used social influences to affect individual consumption, typically by providing feedback information about self-consumption and others' consumption. They found that, in the short run, the effect of social comparisons is equivalent to that which would be expected if average prices were to increase by 12-15%.

Lessons learnt to include behavioural insights for more effective water charges

- Consider nudging to accompany the reform of water charges in Brazil. Take stock of recent developments in international best practices in this domain. Nudging can increase the willingness-to-pay and the efficiency of water charges.

Addressing affordability and equity issues for households

If the extra charge implemented to cover the environmental and opportunity costs of using water is passed on through the customer bill, it will increase the average price households pay for each cubic meter. Empirical evidence shows that residential water demand is inelastic to its price in most cases (see above), so it is likely that most households would experience an increase in their water bill if an additional charge were implemented, potentially exacerbating affordability issues for low-income households.

However, since the average level of the water abstraction and pollution charges is low, and the share of the water charge in the total water bill is minimal, implementation of such charges should not create *on average* any major affordability issues in Brazil. Of course low-income households may suffer from the implementation of the water charges. Two main sets of instruments can be used to address affordability issues due to rising water charges: "social tariffs", defined as any intervention that changes the price households are charged for water and wastewater services; these include increasing block tariffs (IBTs), subsidised volumetric rates in the lowest (lifeline) block, or minimum quantity allowances delivered for free; and social assistance. In principle, any social tariff is best avoided since it distorts the price signal sent to consumers and may thus counteract the objectives of cost recovery and economic efficiency (Box 3.10). Moreover, social tariffs usually are poorly targeted and tend to benefit users who could afford to pay the real price for water services. Social tariffs also require some information which may not be available (at places, for legal reasons and issues related to protection of privacy); typically, IBTs require information on the size and the health condition of the family living behind the meter: water companies need to make intrusive and unpopular information requests. This may not be necessary if other government agencies hold such information (e.g. low income, in receipt of some form of means-tested benefits, mobility or other health issues that affect water use), and are able to liaise with the water and sanitation provider regarding the households that would be eligible for a social tariff.

Affordability should be addressed by social measures that are separated from the payment of water and wastewater services and based on criteria (such as means-testing) to identify the most vulnerable households.[6] This approach is in line with recommendations made by the OECD: "[…], it is important that subsidies are provided independently of the level of water consumption. This is because subsidies based on the level of water consumed will cause distortions in water consumption and the allocation of water resources will no longer be efficient. […] better outcomes can be achieved if pricing is set so as to achieve efficiency goals and subsidies are set independently of consumption to achieve equity goals" (OECD, 2011).

When such measures do not exist, or governments are not equipped to deliver targeted social support, social tariffs can be considered as a second best. They do represent a cross-subsidy from better off customers, but, in the United Kingdom, all water companies have found that customers support the idea and consider it a fair thing to do. This may reflect people's attitude to water as an essential good that no one should be without. Increasing block tariffs require knowledge of the number of people in a household, and their state of health.

Box 3.10. IBT: Social tariffs or regressive pricing instruments?

The use of IBTs is becoming more and more widespread in both developing and developed countries. It is commonly said that IBTs are pro-poor: they permit access to a minimum quantity of water at a reduced volumetric price, and rich households cross-subsidise poor households by paying a higher volumetric price. However, the success of IBTs in targeting subsidised prices (in the lowest block) to poor households relies on the assumption that low-income households consume less water than high-income households. This, however, may not be true – in particular if low-income households are large. The rare evidence that exists in the literature indicates a small correlation between household income and water use.

Evidence from industrialised countries mainly comes from the 2008 OECD Environmental Policy and Individual Behaviour Change (EPIC) survey, which includes eight OECD countries (Australia, Canada, France, Italy, South Korea, Netherlands, Norway, and Sweden). Quoting Nauges and Whittington: "In four of the thirteen country data sets, the correlation was not statistically significant. For the remaining nine data sets in which the correlation was statistically significant, it varies between +0.1 and +0.3. The correlation between household water use and income is thus typically (but not always) positive, but surprisingly low. This means that there are many rich households that use small amounts of water, and many poor households that use large quantities of water."

Due to the low correlation between water use and income, one can expect IBTs to deliver a significant share of subsidies to non-poor households. Subsidies targeting has been mostly studied in developing country contexts and there is now a broad consensus that subsidies delivered through the IBTs are poorly targeted (Whittington et al., 2015).

Source: Arnaud Reynaud, Expert, Toulouse School of Economics (France).

Lessons learnt to tack affordability issues in Brazil

- Thoroughly assess the social impact of water charges. While it tends to be overstated, it cannot be ignored.
- Use distinct instruments to address affordability and equity issues. Avoid using subsidies which may have harmful impacts. OECD experience shows that targeted and accompanying social measures are more effective to address vulnerable groups than subsidising the system at large. Complement water charges with non-economic instruments (behavioural economics).

Addressing competiveness issues

When assessing the impacts of water user charges on industrial water consumers, several particular features of water used by industries have to be considered.

Industrial firms use water for several purposes including cooling intermediate inputs, producing high-pressure steam, moving intermediate inputs, sanitation, and as a direct input (e.g. breweries). Although water may be considered as an essential input for some activities, the direct cost of water for industrial firms remains low. As indicated by

Renzetti (2015) for Canada, the cost share of water in the manufacturing industry rarely rises above 1%. For Mexico, Guerrero (2005) reports a slightly higher water cost share, 2.2% on average. There are of course some variations across sectors. In the US, although the average water cost share for the manufacturing industry is found to be 2.4% (Babin et al., 1982), it is larger than 1% in only three of the seven sectors considered (namely, food and kindred products, paper and allied products, chemicals and allied products). This sectoral heterogeneity in terms of water cost shares may drive different firms' behaviours. On average, however, since water user charges represent in practice only a small fraction of the total cost of water expenses to be paid by firms, one may imagine that implementing water user charges (or modifying their level) will only have a marginal impact on a firm's competitiveness.

A well-designed water charge is one that bites; i.e. it is a charge that effectively affects the competitiveness of a corporation, or its capacity to make profit; this is the very rationale of using an economic instrument to drive behaviour. In addition, impacts on competitiveness at firm or industry level are not the issue, from an economic perspective. The real issue is impacts of competitiveness of the Brazilian economy. In principle, water charges (in combination with other policy instruments) can signal inefficiencies in the Brazilian economy (for instance, developing water intensive crops or industries in water scarce regions) and direct water where it creates the most value for the Brazilian society.

A few studies have analysed the impact of implementing water charges (Stöver and Weche, 2015) or of modifying water price on the competitiveness of industrial firms (Féres and Reynaud, 2005; Féres et al., 2008). Different measures of the impact on competitiveness have been considered (such as the direct effect on costs of production, impact on labour productivity or impact on export intensity). Féres et al., 2008 finds that the estimated marginal effluent treatment costs are far above the current values established for the pollution-related component of the water charge. Hence, competitiveness conflicts will not necessarily pervade the political economy of water charges in Brazil. The main insight from this (rather limited) literature is that the impact on the competitiveness of industrial firms is relatively moderate, a result in line with the low cost share of water in the manufacturing industry.

The absence of a significant impact of water user charges on a firm's competitiveness can be driven by their quite low level in practice. Indeed, for acceptability reasons, water user charges may not fully reflect environmental and resource costs. Féres et al. (2008) provide some insights on the acceptability of water charges in the Paraíba do Sul River Basin, Brazil. In 2003-2004, they conducted a survey on a sample of 488 industrial plants asking whether firms approved the charge system. Results indicated that the degree of acceptance was high but varied according to the size of the industrial plant. The approval rate was about 71% among large users but around 45% in small and medium plants. One explanation for the quite high acceptability rate of the water charge is that, due to the consensus process in the river basin committee, water charges were initially set at very low levels with the expectation that they would increase in the following implementation period in 2006.

A second explanation for the absence of a significant impact of water user charges on a firm's competitiveness relates to the way water enters into the production function of industrial firms. Water is usually used by industrial firms in conjunction with other production factors such as energy, labour or capital. When facing a water price increase (due to the implementation of water user charges for instance), industrial firms may reduce their water use while increasing other production factors in order to continue to minimise their production costs. However, this change in input mix is constrained by the substitutability or complementarity relationships existing between water and other production factors. It is, for instance, usually found that water and capital are substitutes for industrial firms (Dupont and Renzetti, 1999; Féres et al., 2008; Angulo et al., 2014). This result means that when the water price increases, firms will reduce water use by increasing capital investment, including water efficiency and water recycling or recirculation technologies. From a policy perspective, any measure aiming at facilitating input substitution (i.e. developing an easy access to capital market) can be viewed as a way of mitigating the impact of implementing water user charges on firms' competitiveness.

A third explanation is that industrial and commercial firms may usually obtain water from several potential sources. Most commercial and small industrial users are usually supplied through municipal water systems whereas large industrial plants, such as oil and gas refineries or steel plants, usually rely on a combination of self-supplied water (pumping directly from surface or groundwater resources) and water supplied through municipal water systems. These large industrial plants then have the possibility of switching from one source to another. For instance, in response to an increase in water user charges set on water supplied through the municipal water system, a large industrial plant may switch towards using a larger amount of self-supplied water. From a policy perspective, this reflects the need for good co-ordination of water user charges across the different sources of water that can be used by industrial firms.

A particular feature of industrial water use, which also explains the moderate impact of implementing water user charges on the competitiveness of industrial firms, is the relatively high price elasticity of the industrial water demand function (in absolute values), compared to other water users (domestic or agricultural users; see above).

Lessons learnt to assess and manage water charges on competitiveness in Brazil

- Document competitiveness impacts of water charges. A fine-grained analysis is required to account for differences across industries, industrial processes, types of firms, capacities to innovate, etc. At the same time, consider the economic benefit of water charges when they accompany the transition of the Brazilian economy towards efficient use of water.
- Where appropriate, mitigate competitiveness impacts by supporting the transition of corporates towards water-wise practices. The support must be targeted and time-bound. It can be financed by the proceeds of water charges.

Notes

1. Water Apportionment Areas are zones that suffer from chronic water scarcity.
2. In the Czech Republic, higher charges are imposed on surface water: almost two to three times higher than for groundwater abstraction. This has led to a significant increase in water abstraction from aquifers as a substitute for surface water (Ministry of Agriculture of the Czech Republic).
3. "Despite the current water abundance in Baden-Württemberg, water shall be seen as a valuable resource by its users, as its current availability may be reduced in the future by competing uses and climate change-related impact on hydrology." (quote from Möller-Gulland and Lago, 2011).
4. The abstraction charges of public projects (national projects, publicly-owned projects, and irrigation projects) are usually free or reduced (OECD, 2015).
5. For example, fertiliser taxes can cause an additional burden on horticulture production while making livestock production more profitable. They may also provide unintended incentives to increase livestock levels, leading to greater manure production through more intensive protein feeding, larger acreages devoted to nitrogen-fixing plants and reorganisation of crops in favour of those with less nitrogen consumption, but not necessarily less nitrogen surplus (OECD, 2010).
6. Here it is not discussed the subsidisation of connections to the piped water network, which is an instrument used primarily in developing countries where piped water access is not universal. For an interesting discussion and experiment of a subsidised interest-free loan to install a water connection in the city of Tangiers (Morocco), see Devoto et al. (2012).

References

Acteon Innovation, policy, environment (2010), "Economic instruments for mobilising financial resources for supporting IWRM", additional information and illustrations for the OECD initiative, https://search.oecd.org/environment/resources/46228724.pdf.

Acteon Innovation, policy, environment (2009), "Which role for economic instruments in the management of water resources in Europe? In search for innovative ideas for application in the Netherland", final report of a study undertaken for the Ministry of Transport, Public Works and Water Management, Colmar, The Netherlands.

Adour-Garonne Water Agency (n.d.), « Les redevances perçues par l'Agence », www.eau-adour-garonne.fr/fr/quelle-politique-de-l-eau-en-adour-garonne/un-outil-le-programme-d-intervention-de-l-agence/les-redevances-percues-par-l-agence.html, (accessed September 2016).

Angulo A. et al. (2014), "Economic analysis of the water demand in the hotels and restaurants sector: shadow prices and elasticities", *Water Resources Research,* Vol. 50/8, pp. 6269-7066, http://agupubs.onlinelibrary.wiley.com/hub/issue/10.1002/wrcr.v50.8/.

Babin F.G., C.E. Willis and P.G. Allen (1982), "Estimation of Substitution Possibilities Between Water and Other Production Inputs", *American Journal of Agricultural Economics*, Vol. 64/1, pp. 148-151, https://doi.org/10.2307/1241187.

Buchanan J.M. (1963), "The Economics of Earmarked Taxes", *Journal of Political Economy*, Vol. 71, pp. 457-469.

Croson R. and N. Treich (2014), "Behavioral Environmental Economics: Promises and Challenges", *Environmental and Resource Economics*, Vol. 58/3, pp. 335-351, https://doi.org/10.1007/s10640-014-9783-y.

Devoto F., Duflo E., Dupas P., Pariente W., and Pons V.(2011). "Hap piness on Tap: Piped Water Adoption in Urban Morocco." National Bureau of Economic Research Working Paper 16933

Dupont D. and S. Renzetti (1999), "An Assessment of the Impact of Charging for Provincial Water Use Permits", *Canadian Public Policy*, Vol. 25/3, pp. 361-378, doi: 10.2307/3551525.

EEA (European Environment Agency) (2013), "Assessment of cost recovery through water pricing", EEA Technical Report, No. 16.

EPA (Environmental Protection Agency) (2009), "Water Quality Trading Toolkit for Permit Writers", Office of Wastewater Management, Water Permits Division, https://www3.epa.gov/npdes/pubs/wqtradingtoolkit_fundamentals.pdf (accessed September 2017).

Féres, J. et al. (2008), "Competitiveness and Effectiveness Concerns in Water Charge Implementation: A Case Study of the Paraíba do Sul River Basin, Brazil", *Water Policy,* Vol. 10/5, pp. 595-612.

Féres J. and A. Reynaud (2005), "Assessing the Impact of Environmental Regulation on Industrial Water Use: Evidence from Brazil", *Land Economics*, Vol. 81/3, pp. 396-411.

Ferraro P.J. and Price M.K. (2011), "Using Non-Pecuniary Strategies to Influence Behavior: Evidence from a Large Scale Field Experiment", NBER WORKING PAPER SERIES

Guerrero H. (2005), "Industrial water demand in Mexico: Econometric analysis and implications for water management policy", PhD dissertation, Université de Toulouse 1, Toulouse, France, https://hal.archives-ouvertes.fr/halshs-00008624/document (accessed September 2017).

ITIC (International Tax and Investment Center) (2013), "Are earmarked taxes on alcohol and tobacco a good idea? Evidence from Asia", special report, www.iticnet.org/images/are%20earmarked%20taxes%20on%20alcohol%20and%20tobacco%20a%20good%20idea%20-%20evidence%20from%20asia.pdf (accessed September 2017).

IUCN (International Union for Conservation of Nature) (1998), "Economic Values of Protected Areas: Guidelines for Protected Area Managers", prepared by the Task Force on Economic Benefits of Protected Areas of the World Commission on Protected Areas (WCPA) of IUCN, in collaboration with the Economics Service Unit of IUCN, IUCN, Gland, Switzerland and Cambridge, United Kingdom.

Lee, S.C. (2009), Water Use Charge System and Basin Management in Korea – Comparative Analysis with the Forest and Water Source Tax in Japan, Research Center for Sustainability and Environment, Shiga University.

Loire-Bretagne Water Agency (n.d.), « Taux des redevances pour prélèvement sur la ressource en eau », www.eau-loire-bretagne.fr/nos_missions/redevances/tx-ressource-10epgm.pdf, (accessed September 2016).

Lourenço J.S. et al. (2016), "Behavioural insights applied to policy", European Report, http://publications.jrc.ec.europa.eu/repository/bitstream/JRC100146/kjna27726enn_new.pdf.

MacDonald et al. (2011), "Valuing a Multistate River: The Case of the River Murray", The Australian Journal of Agricultural and Resource Economics, Vol. 55, pp. 374-392.

Massarutto A. (2007), "Water pricing and full cost recovery of water services: economic incentive or instrument of public finance?", *Water Policy*, Vol. 9/6, pp. 591-613.

Ministry of Agriculture of the Czech Republic (2015), "Report on Water Management in the Czech Republic in 2014, Department of State Administration of Water Management and River Basins", Department of Water Protection, Ministry of the Environment of the Czech Republic, http://eagri.cz/public/web/file/428082/report_on_water_management_in_the_czech_republic_in_2014.pdf (accessed September 2017).

Möller-Gulland J., M. Lago and G. Anzaldua (2015), "Water Abstraction Charges and Compensation Payments in Baden-Württemberg (Germany)", in: Lago M. et al., *Use of Economic Instruments in Water Policy, Global Issues in Water Policy*, Vol. 14, Springer, Cham, https://doi.org/10.1007/978-3-319-18287-2_5 (accessed September 2017).

Nauges C. and D. Whittington (2010), "Estimation of water demand in developing countries: An overview", World Bank Research Observer, Vol. 25/2, pp. 263-294, https://doi.org/10.1093/wbro/lkp016.

OECD (n.d.), Database on Policy Instruments for the Environment, www2.oecd.org/ecoinst/queries/Default.aspx (accessed March 2016).

OECD (2017), *Diffuse Pollution, Degraded Waters: Emerging Policy Solutions*, OECD Publishing, Paris, http://dx.doi.org/10.1787/9789264269064-en.

OECD (2015), *Water Resources Allocation: Sharing Risks and Opportunities*, OECD Publishing, Paris, http://dx.doi.org/10.1787/9789264229631-en.

OECD (2012a), *A Framework for Financing Water Resources Management*, OECD Publishing, Paris, http://dx.doi.org/10.1787/9789264179820-en.

OECD (2012b), *Water Quality and Agriculture: Meeting the Policy Challenge*, OECD Studies on Water, OECD Publishing, Paris, http://dx.doi.org/10.1787/9789264168060-en.

OECD (2011), "Economic instruments for water management", Working Party on Biodiversity, Water and Ecosystems, [ENV/EPOC/WPBWE(2011)13].

OECD (2010), *Pricing Water Resources and Water and Sanitation Services*, OECD Publishing, Paris, http://dx.doi.org/10.1787/9789264083608-en.

Ranjit, S.T. (1988), "The Case for Earmarked Taxes", Staff Papers, International Monetary Fund, Vol. 35/3, pp. 523-533.

Renzetti S. (2015), "Non-household water demand: industrial and commercial sectors", *in* R.Q. Grafton et al. (eds), *Understanding and Managing Urban Water in Transition*, Springer Publishing, pp. 297-310.

Reynaud A. (2015), "Revisiting the incentive properties of water charges: the case of the Czech Republic", Mimeo, Toulouse School of Economics.

Rhin-Meuse Water Agency (n.d.), « Les différentes redevances », www.eau-rhin-meuse.fr/differentes_redevances, (accessed September 2016).

Rhône-Méditerranée- Corse (n.d.), « Prélèvement d'eau », www.eaurmc.fr/aides-et-redevances/redevances-et-primes/prelevement-deau.html, (accessed September 2016).

Rodrik D. (2014), "Green Industrial Policy", Oxford Review of Economic Policy, Vol. 30/3, pp. 469-491.

Seine-Normandy Water Agency (n.d.), « Formulaires de demande d'aide financière », www.eau-seine-normandie.fr/index.php?id=7865 (accessed September 2016).

Shortle, J. S. and R.D. Horan (2001), The economics of nonpoint pollution control, Journal of Economic Surveys, Vol. 15 (3), pp. 255 – 289.

Souza d'Alte T. (2010), "Report on Portuguese Environmental Economic Instruments", Agencia Portuguesa do Ambiente.

Stöver J. and J.P. Weche (2015), "Environmental regulation and sustainable competitiveness: Evaluating the role of firm-level green investments in the context of the Porter hypothesis", Hamburg Institute of International Economics (HWWI).

Thaler R.H. and C.R. Sunstein (2008), *Nudge: Improving Decisions about Health, Wealth, and Happiness*, Yale University Press, New Haven, CT.

Tinbergen J. (1952), "On the theory of economic policy, North Holland", Amsterdam.

Whittington D. et al. (2015), "A diagnostic tool for estimating the incidence of subsidies delivered by water utilities in low- and medium-income countries, with illustrative simulations", *Utilities Policy,* Vol. 34, pp. 70-81, doi: 10.1016/j.jup.2014.12.007.

Chapter 4

Sector-specific issues for setting and managing water charges

The chapter analyses challenges and opportunities related to the design and implementation of water abstraction and pollution charges for the main water users in Brazil, namely hydropower, water supply and sanitation, industry and agriculture. For each user, the chapter provides the key underlying economic principles, selected examples from international experience, a specific zoom on the issues for Brazil and some ways forward.

Hydropower and multipurpose dams

Economic principles

Hydropower production does not extract water per se since all water that is used to produce electricity is returned to the river stream. Yet it often modifies water flows over time and space. Typically, water is stored in reservoirs and is released later to produce electricity when demand is high. Water is sometimes diverted from its main stream to increase power through pipes. Furthermore, hydropower plants require dams on the river stream, which create negative externalities for biodiversity by retaining nutrients and sediment and by creating obstacles to fish migration. However, the dams can also provide positive externalities for the local population by storing water for consumption during dry seasons (e.g. for irrigation), protecting against flooding and providing some recreational services. Dams are often built for multiple purposes, not only hydropower but also flood protection and water supply for irrigation.

Charges for hydropower should reflect water scarcity and the externalities faced by other water uses. Fees applied to water should mitigate conflicts on water use such as the seasonal conflict between hydropower and irrigation. For instance, when electricity is used for heating, hydropower producers tend to release water in winter when it is not valued by agriculture. Every cubic meter of water released in winter is no longer available for irrigation in summer when farmers need water to be stored in reservoirs to irrigate their crops. This has an economic value that should be reflected in the water charges. Similarly, charges on dams and hydropower infrastructures should reflect the externalities generated on society in order to induce efficient investment in dams and hydropower plants. The capital, maintenance and operating costs should be shared among stakeholders (such as electricity producers and farmers using water for irrigation) in a fair way; for instance, costs could be proportional to the benefits.

Charges on hydropower generation should be analysed in conjunction with climate and energy policies. Today, hydropower is the main source of renewable and low carbon energy in many countries. In Brazil, the energy mix has one of the highest shares of renewable energy in the world, with 41% of TEPS coming from renewable energy sources in 2014, more than five times the OECD average. A total of 87.1% of electricity generation comes from renewables (OECD, 2015). Public policies have been launched recently to enhance investment in renewables, not only hydropower but also biomass, wind and solar. Some countries such as the United States have opted for renewable portfolio standards programmes, which generally require a minimum fraction of electricity demand to be met by renewable sources (including hydropower). These programmes are usually implemented on the basis of renewable energy certificates issued by state-certified renewable generators. Most European countries have implemented feed-in tariffs: they have committed to purchasing renewable generated electricity at a price fixed well above the wholesale price. The increased penetration of solar and wind powered energy in the electricity mix driven by those policies introduces new challenges for its management. One is the intermittency of solar and wind power which are available only when the weather conditions are met. With more intermittency in electricity production, hydropower becomes more valuable as energy can be pumped and stored in reservoirs to supply electricity when windmills are not spinning.

International experience

Most of the charges on hydropower are corporate and real estate taxes like those for any other production activity. Yet several countries have implemented charges specific to hydropower production related to water release. There are three types of water charge for hydropower generation:

- Fee per volume of water release, which reflects water use. France charges a fee for water released by hydropower plants. The rate in 2016 is EUR 0.93/Mm3. This is multiplied by the water head to evaluate the electricity generation or by 1.5 for run-of-river power stations. The rate per MWh of electricity generation is estimated at EUR 0.455/MWh (Adour Garonne Water Agency, n.d.).
- Fee per kWh of electricity production is a good proxy for water used. Norway and Finland tax each kWh of electricity generated by hydropower production plants. In Norway, production tax is applied to the value of production net of operating costs and adjusted for the lifetime of the plant (see Amundsen et al., 1992, for details). Acteon (2010) reports a rate of EUR 1.6/MWh in Norway. China also charges electricity production at a rate decided at the provincial level.
- Fee per kW of generation capacity. Swiss hydropower producers pay a fixed fee per kW capacity. The fee is set and levied by the cantons with a cap fixed by federal law. The maximum level was EUR 54/kW gross capacity in 2010. It amounted on average to about Euro cent 0.73/kWh electricity produced. It is an important source of revenue for cantons as it can make up to 25% of total fiscal income (see Banfi and Filippini, 2010; Acteon, 2010). Sweden has a similar capacity-based taxation plan for electricity production including hydropower.

When it comes to water charges for dams, the European Water Framework Directive prescribes not only covering scarcity costs and environmental costs but also investment (or capital recovery cost) as well as maintenance and operating costs. These costs are sometimes difficult to disentangle – in particular for dams serving multiple purposes. Costs allocation requires robust governance arrangements (see Chapter 5). For instance, Berbel et al. (2007) report that in Spain, the sharing of costs between different uses is made by a 'stakeholders agreement' at the basin level considering flood control (20% in most dams in Spain), urban use, irrigation, electricity production (hydropower and refrigeration) and environmental uses. They evaluate that only 71% of costs are recovered. In European countries, water charges do not cover all costs and dams are partly subsidised by tax payers (Berbel et al., 2007).

Dam water charges for irrigation are levied and managed by irrigation districts. Irrigation districts are non-profit associations with legal status in many countries, for instance France, Spain, Italy or Mexico. In some cases, such as Austria or Greece, they are controlled by public authorities. They usually charge water abstraction by volume or by surface irrigated (see the previous discussion on abstraction charge).

To fully reflect opportunity costs of using water, the charge should depend on local conditions (scarcity and local uses) as well as vary with season (e.g. winter versus summer): in the Northern hemisphere, water has typically lower value when released in winter than in summer (when irrigators need it).

The situation in Brazil

According to the Law 7990/89 and 9648/98 (modified by Law 13360/2016), hydropower plants with power generation capacity above 30MW pay a financial compensation for the use of water for hydropower generation, established at 6.25 % of the value of energy output. The National Electric Energy Agency (ANEEL) defines and collects the financial compensation. Funds are distributed as follows: 45% to the municipalities affected by reservoirs (it is also a major source of revenue for some municipalities); 45% to the states affected by reservoirs; 4% to the FNDCT; 3% to the Ministry of Energy; 3% to the Ministry of the Environment. The distribution criterion among affected municipalities and states is determined by the ANEEL based on the area flooded by the reservoirs. However, fiscal revenues are not earmarked for water expenditures: only a few states take actions related to water resources with this revenue; this is rarely the case for municipalities. According to the Law, the share allocated to the Ministry of Environment is intended for the implementation of the National Water Resources Policy and the management of the national hydro-meteorological network. However, this quota often suffers expenditures limitations.

After the creation of the ANA in 2000, in addition to the financial compensation for the use of water for hydropower, hydropower plants were charged for the non-consumptive use of water: an additional amount of 0.75% of the value of the energy output, for each hydropower plant with an installed capacity above 30MW. Revenues are collected by ANEEL and allocated to the ANA. From 2001 to 2016 revenues increased from BRL 48 million to BRL 208 million (Figure 4.1). This can be considered a crude but convenient proxy for the use of water resources. The charge for the hydropower sector (7% of the value of the energy produced, including the share of 0.75% that is considered payment for the use of water resources) is updated annually for inflation and revised every four years by the ANEEL.

Figure 4.1. Total amount collected from hydroelectric power plans subject to water use charges

BRL million; 2001-2015

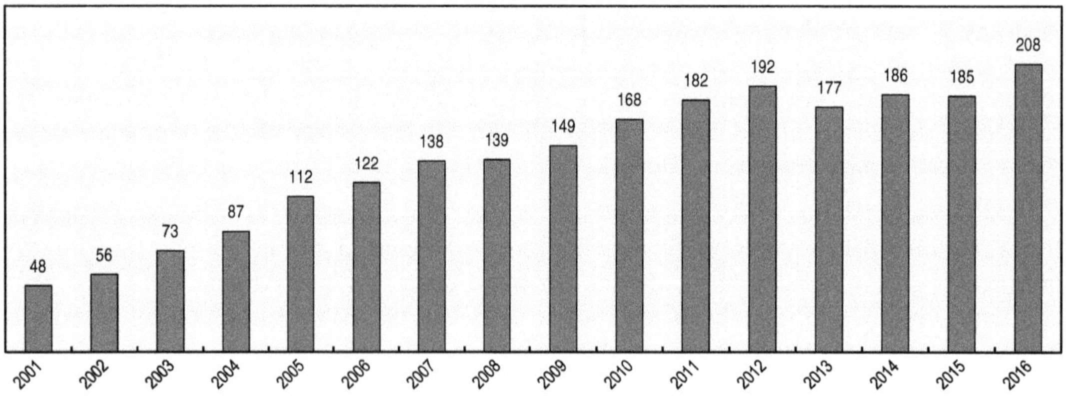

Notes: Law No. 7990 / 1989, together with Law No. 9427 / 1996, exempts small hydropower plants from the payment of financial compensation. The figure represents data concerning the payment for the use of water resources (0.75% of the value of the energy output, for each hydropower plant with an installed capacity above 30 MW).

Source: ANA (2016), "Valores Cobrados e Arrecadados", http://www2.ana.gov.br/Paginas/servicos/cobrancaearrecadacao/cobrancaearrecadacao.aspx (accessed August 2017).

It follows that the compensation is the same across the country and does not reflect local conditions (the opportunity cost of using or storing water, which varies across space and time). The charge provides no incentive to generate hydropower in basins where water is abundant and opportunity costs are low. This is a missed opportunity to make the best use of available water resources, in a country which benefit from a national power grid. It should be noted that a similar objective is meant to be achieved via the operating rules of hydropower plants set by ONS: ONS may require minimising power generation where water is scarce; affected plants are compensated by other plants operating in where water is abundant. It remains to be seen how such transactions operate in practice, the costs (negotiations) associated to them, and delays in adjusting to unstable conditions.

It would be beneficial to move towards a system that reflected water use and impact. High head, (relatively) low volume schemes may have different impacts from low head, high volume schemes. And the operation of the impoundment is also critical, in terms of beneficial or adverse effects on other water users downstream. As other charging schemes are introduced, or become more sophisticated (towards their use as economic instruments) there may be a case for reviewing the hydropower charging arrangements.

Figure 4.1 indicates that the charges paid on hydropower generation are quite significant. As such it can be used as an instrument to incentivise energy companies for preserving water. However, a main drawback of the charge on hydropower production is that it is not tailored on the specificity of the water basin where plants are operating. The charge on electricity production is the same for all water basins regardless on scarcity or conflicts of uses. Water charges or electricity taxes on hydropower should be basin-specific to take that into account. Moreover, charges and taxes could vary with the season to reflect seasonal water scarcity. One way to better adjust taxes on hydropower on water stress and uses could be to involve agencies – where they exist – in its design.

Another drawback of the hydropower charges is that they are assigned in the general budget of several administrative units (municipalities, states, ministries). Only 0.75% is directly devoted to water management. As a consequence, the taxed companies do not see any direct benefit of their contribution to the river basin. Assigning a higher share of the 6.75% production taxed to tangible investments within the river basin would improve acceptability of the water charge system. Earmarking the revenue collected is difficult when part of the water flow is transferred to another river basin. This is indeed the case in the Paraíba do Sul River Basin described below.

In addition, attention should be paid in revisiting the 30MW threshold for hydropower plants contributing paying a charge for water use and financial compensation. In fact, in some rivers or under certain conditions, small hydropower plants can have a massive effect. Another option could be to implement seasonal charges (higher during the dry or irrigation seasons). A good example is the system of tariff flags in the electricity sector, which distinguishes charges according to power generation conditions for the four subsystems. The system uses the green, the yellow and the red flag, to indicate progressively favourable conditions in place which do not require tariff increases, to less favourable/critical conditions requiring established tariff increases per kWh consumed.

Suggestions to consider

- Adjust water charge for hydropower to reflect scarcity and impact in the main basins. This would signal the cost of scarcity and simplify ONS decisions about generation requirements per plant or area. Consider involving river basin agency for setting water charges for hydropower and for agreeing an operating regime which takes account of multiple interests downstream, including the environment.

- Revisit the 30MW threshold for hydropower plants contributing a charge for water use and financial compensation, as in some rivers or under certain conditions, small hydropower plants can have a massive effect. Administrative costs should be factored in and kept minimal.
- Allocate revenues from the 6.25% charge to expenditure that produces tangible results in basins. Alignment with (or reference to) water resources plans should be encouraged.
- In the long term, consider shifting the basis of charges for hydropower to a measure that takes account of the impact on downstream flows, ecology and other abstractors.

Water supply and sanitation

Economic principles

Changes in abstraction or pollution charges are likely to the transferred to final users by the utilities operating water supply and sanitation services. This argument is often used to claim that higher water charges will affect the poor and trigger affordability issues. These objections to reflecting environmental and opportunity costs in water charges for domestic users are misdirected. In the United Kingdom, charges are typically 1-2% of a water companies' operating costs. In France (in the Seine Normandie basin), the abstraction charge only represents around 12% of the final water price paid by households (French Ministry of Ecology, Sustainable Development, and Energy, 2012). Therefore, while any increase in the rate or structure of the charge is likely to affect final users, it is unlikely to raise distinct affordability issues, compared to other features of the water bill.

The question is whether abstraction and pollution charges can affect the behaviour of final users. Domestic users are commonly found to be sensitive to prices but the elasticity of water use to price[1] changes is usually rather small (in the range -0.1 to -0.4). In Brazil, André and Carvalho (2014) estimate that the residential water demand function for the city of Fortaleza, with the price elasticity of the household water demand between -0.35 and -0.40, depending upon the price specification (average or marginal price) (Table 4.1). Gómez (1987) provides a value of -0.60 for household water price elasticity in Brazil (based on a sample of 400 families in Brazilian cities of approximately 1.5 million inhabitants).

Because water use is relatively inelastic to its price, the charge increase needs to be substantial to induce a change in water users' behaviour. If the abstraction charge represents 2% of the water bill, doubling the water charge will increase the bill by 2%, which is unlikely to drive any significant response.

Table 4.1. Empirical evidence on household water price elasticities in Europe

Country	Study	Price elasticity
Belgium	Vanhille (2012)	-0.62
Czech Republic	Grafton et al. (2009)	-0.42
	Hortova and Kristoufek (2014)	-0.20;-0.54
Denmark	Hansen (1996)	-0.10

Table 4.1. Empirical evidence on household water price elasticities in Europe (*cont.*)

Country	Study	Price elasticity
France	Nauges and Reynaud (2001)	-0.22; -0.08
	Nauges and Thomas (2003)	-0.40; 0.40
	Garcia and Reynaud (2004)	-0.25
	Grafton et al. (2009)	-0.41
	Rinaudo et al. (2013)	-0.18
Germany	Frondel and Messner (2008)	-0.49
	Schleich and Hillenbrand (2009)	-0.24
	Muller (2012)	-0.46; 0.26
Greece	Athanasiadis et al. (2005)	-0.34
	Bithas and Chrysostomos (2003)	-0.10
	Vagiona and Mylopoulos (2009)	-0.95
Italy	Mazzanti and Montini (2006)	-1.33; -0.99
	Statzu and Stazzera (2007)	-0.25
	Musolesi and Nosvelli (2007)	-0.47; 0.27
	Grafton et al. (2009)	-0.59
	Di Cosmo (2011)	-0.36; -0.14
Luxembourg	MECE (2012)	-0.33
Malta	Delia (2004)	-0.37; -0.28
Netherlands	Kooreman (1993)	-0.19; -0.09
	Linderhof (2001)	-0.07
	Grafton et al. (2009)	-0.40
Poland	Bartczak et al. (2009)	-0.20
Portugal	Martins and Fortunato (2007)	-0.56
	Monteiro and Roseta-Palma (2011)	-0.13; -0.05
	Monteiro et al. (2014)	-0.48
Romania	Ciomos et al. (2012)	-0.70
Slovakia	Dalmas and Reynaud (2005)	-0.50; -0.35
Spain	Martinez-Espineira (2002)	-0.16; -0.12
	Martinez-Espineira (2003)	-0.67; -0.37
	Arbues (2004)	-0.06; -0.03
	Martinez-Espineira and Nauges (2004)	-0.10
	Garc a-Valinas (2005)	-0.55; -0.46
	Martinez-Espineira (2007)	-0.50; -0.10
	Martinez-Espineira and Garcia- Valinas (2010)	-0.06
	Arbues et al. (2012)	-1.31; -0.26
Sweden	Hanke-de Maré (1982)	-0.15
	Hoglund (1999)	-0.20; -0.10
	Grafton et al. (2009)	-0.41
United Kingdom	Gardner (2010)	-0.29

Source: Adapted from Reynaud A. (2015), Modelling Household Water Demand in Europe, Insights from a Cross-Country Econometric Analysis of EU-28, http://publications.jrc.ec.europa.eu/repository/bitstream/JRC96268/reportresidentialwatereu28reportjrc_v5_final_correctedforjrcstyle.pdf.

Most published studies provide single price elasticity for the household water demand function; however, some authors have investigated the heterogeneity of price elasticity.

- *Price elasticity varies depending on the type of water use*. Essential uses such as water for human consumption or for cooking are found to be very price inelastic, whereas water-related leisure activities (watering the garden or making use of swimming pools) are usually much more price reactive.

- *Price elasticity also varies over time*. Demand studies using summer data appear to exhibit higher price elasticity in absolute value (Arbués, Garcia-Valinas, and Martinez-Espineira 2003).
- *Price elasticity is found to depend upon some characteristics of households*. For instance, elasticity varies with household size (Arbués, Villanua, and Barberan 2010, Vanhille 2012). In developed countries, price elasticity varies with household income, lower income groups being more price-responsive than higher income groups.

Box 4.1. Evidence of water pricing schemes providing incentives to reduce household water use

Although establishing a causality link remains difficult, there are examples showing that household water consumption may react to change in water price.

Since 1992, urban water prices in Denmark have been based on cost recovery so that prices cover both economic (through user charges) and environmental (through taxes) costs. All urban water users are metered, and water prices are charged according to the volume consumed. Since the policy's introduction, water prices have risen substantially; during the period from 1993 to 2004, the real price of water (including environmental taxes) increased by 54%. The rise in prices has led to a substantial decrease in urban water demand, from 155 litres to 125 litres per person per day, one of the lowest levels in the OECD.

In the Czech Republic, between 1990 and 2004, the water and wastewater tariff for households increased from 0.8 to 48 CZK/m3, covering an increasing fraction of the extraction, treatment and distribution costs related to water provision. The reform also increased the fees for the extraction of both surface and groundwater, as well as for the discharge of wastewater. The volume of household consumption decreased by 40 %, from 171 litres per capita per day in 1989 to 103 litres in 2002.

Source: EEA (2013), "Assessment of cost recovery through water pricing", EEA Technical Report, No. 16.

International experience: A focus on EU countries[2]

Across European member countries, the Drinking Water Directive sets quality standards for drinking water to protect public health. There are no EU-wide environmental licensing obligations relating to the establishment of drinking water treatment plants. Abstraction licenses for raw water abstraction are however required under the Water Framework Directive as part of the basic measures in river basin management plans. The Water Framework Directive requires that water abstraction and discharges of urban waste water are subject to discharge permits or regulation.

European counties apply the Polluter and User Pay principles so that revenues from service provision cover all capital expenditure, operational and maintenance expenditure. France and Germany provide good illustrations of how revenues from water abstraction or pollution charges are recycled to co-finance expenditures that contribute to improved water management. In France, service provision by municipalities is self-financed, although national or EU subsidies may be provided in the framework of regional policies in some regions which are in economic decline or transition. In addition, subsidies may be provided, e.g. for innovative or specially demanding measures by river basin agencies financed by recycling revenues from water and pollution charges which are collected from all water users and polluters in the basin. In Germany, financial assistance to municipalities is today limited mainly to those where the conditions are such that special measures are needed to ensure implementation of legislation and to municipalities that innovate, e.g. by implementing expensive measures to remove micro-pollutants from urban waste water. This assistance is normally provided through special funds from revenues from water related charges such as the federal waste water charge where revenues are earmarked for use in water management.

Water charges should incentivise utilities to improve their efficiency in freshwater use. For instance, well-designed abstraction charges can deter a company from abstracting from sensitive rivers, particularly during drought events and set at a level that has a meaningful impact on operational costs, thus potentially driving behaviour. A well-managed company would then operate its sources on a least cost basis. Otherwise, the company would just stand the charges and try to pass the costs through end users. A regulator should reduce the risk of this happening. In Brazil, water charges represent only a small share of the costs of water service providers and therefore have little impact on utilities' operation and visibility for end users.

The structure of water charges needs to be adapted to the objective towards which they must contribute. An obvious example of this need is charging with a view not only to provide water consumers with an incentive to save water, but also to limit the losses from the water distribution networks. A charge on water abstraction on its own will normally not provide an incentive for network operators to reduce losses as the operator will pass on the cost to consumers connected to the network. If the charge is to provide an incentive to the network operator, additional measures are needed to do so. An example of how this can be done is Denmark's adoption in the late 1990s of a law introducing a tax on all water delivered to consumers through piped systems. The objective of the law was to reflect the value of water and thus provide incentives, especially for households, to save water and for water distributors to reduce losses in the form of non-revenue water (Box 4.2).

Box 4.2. Incentives for water distributors to limit losses: The case of Denmark

The current (2017) value of the water tax is 5.86 DKK/m3 (0.79 EUR / m3), which amounts to 1 EUR /m3 when Value Added Tax (VAT) is included. The taxes are calculated on the basis of hydrometer readings (meters are required by law at the entry into the distribution system and at the entry points into households) and are collected by water distribution companies and paid to the State. The proportion of the water taxes in relation to the total price of water (including sewage collection and treatment) was 9.9% in 2015.

Private companies that are registered as paying VAT can deduct the water tax paid from their VAT payments and are thus in practice exempt from the tax. Other instruments are used to incentivise these companies to save water. The water tax is therefore mainly a tax on households' use of water.

In 2013-14, water bills accounted for 1.4% of total household consumption in Denmark. The total weight of taxes in the 2015 Danish water prices was 30.8%, with about 20 % accounting for the VAT and about 1 % accounting for waste water taxes in addition to the 9.9% water tax.

The law contains provisions that limit the ability of water distributors to pass on tax on water losses from the distribution network to consumers. Water distributors can only pass on water taxes to households corresponding to a maximum of 10% of the total volume of water entering the distribution system. Any tax in excess of this amount has to be paid out of the water distributors' own funds. The organisation of water distributors in private law companies prevents passing the tax on losses exceeding 10% being passed on to taxpayers through subsidies from the public authorities.

Box 4.2. Incentives for water distributors to limit losses: The case of Denmark (*cont.*)

The effect of the water tax can be seen on household water consumption and on the development of network losses:

- Household water consumption has in the period 2005-2015 fallen by 10% from 44 m3/person/year (121 l/person/day) to 40 m3/person/year (110 l/person/day)
- Network losses are still decreasing (in spite of decreasing overall consumption). Benchmarking data for 52 companies show losses falling from 9.5% in 2011 to 7.8% (2015) of the total water entering the distribution network. The average of the IWA's Infrastructure Leakage Index (ILI) for 24 selected Danish water distributors was 0.70 in 2015.

Source: Contribution from Peter Gammeltoft (2016), Expert, former Head of Unit for Water at European Commission, Directorate General for the Environment based on "Water in figures 2016", DANVA, Skanderborg, Denmark, www.e-pages.dk/danva/200/.

The situation in Brazil

Universal access to improved safe drinking water and sanitation is yet to be achieved in Brazil especially in peri-urban areas, small cities and rural areas. Today, more than 36 million people still do not have improved access to drinking water in Brazil; less than half of Brazilians have improved access to sewage collection and only 38% of the country's sewage is treated (Instituto Trata Brazil in Casa Civil, 2016). Solely in the State of Rio de Janeiro, investment needs in the sanitation sector amount BRL 60 billion. Although sanitation projects are included in river basin plans, revenues collected from water charges are not commensurate with investment needs, nor should they be used to cover them. Urban water infrastructure can be subsidised by the Growth Acceleration Programme (Programa de Aceleração do Crescimento, PAC).

Despite progress in the legal framework on sanitation during the last decade, implementation is lagging behind. The Law 11445/2007 represented a first step towards better integration between the sanitation sector and water resources management. It established the hydrographic basin as a reference unit for the elaboration of basic sanitation plans, which should be set in accordance with the river basin plans. This is relevant for the discussion, as the river basin plan provides guidance to prioritise investment and expenditure programmes. The Decree 7217/ 2010 detailed the minimum content of basic sanitation plans to be defined by municipalities or service providers, which became a condition for access to federal funding (ANA, 2016a).

Suggestions to consider

- Charge water utilities for water abstracted from rivers and groundwater and treated water discharged back to the environment, where it is not yet the case. The charge on effluents should come in addition to, or should include, the charge on BOD. Revenues could be used to co-finance expenditures that contribute to priorities in river basin management plans (in terms of water quality or quality). There should be no discharge of untreated effluent. Ensure that the water regulation regime works in parallel with the water charging schemes.
- Use water charges to incentivise the utilities to limit non-revenue water and improve the efficiency of wastewater treatment, while ensuring that the charge is

not simply passed on to water users through tariffs, by defining clear limits for the right of utilities to do so.

- Strengthen the link between water supply and sanitation and water resources management, especially in areas where water resources are considered to be at risk, or may become so within the lifetime of existing or proposed sanitation infrastructure. One way to achieve this is to require that municipal sanitation plans be compatible with regional and river basin needs for protection of water resources. Revenues from abstraction and pollution charges could be recycled to co-finance expenditure programmes which are well-aligned with the needs of the basin (as they should be for all income from abstractors and polluters). Relevant river basin agency or delegated water agency (or, in the absence of such an agency, the ANA) certify that the conditions especially with respect to impact of water abstractions and polluting discharge from treated sewage, are satisfied before the municipality can adopt the Sanitation Plan.

Industry

Economic principles

The relevance of abstraction charges to manage industrial water demand depends on the elasticity of industrial water use to price. Although most industrial water demand studies find that water demands are inelastic (Renzetti, 1992; Guerrero, 2005; Arbués et al., 2010; Angulo et al., 2014), some of them indicate that industrial water demand may exhibit some significant elasticity (Dupont and Renzetti, 2001; Wang and Lall, 2002; Féres and Reynaud, 2005; Strzepek et al., 2006; Tobarra-González, 2015).

Two aspects regarding the industrial price elasticities should be pointed out. First, price elasticities differ greatly from one sector to another. Renzetti (1992) reports significant price elasticities for four of the seven Canadian industries considered: plastics and rubber -0.15; textile -0.33; paper and pulp -0.59; and minerals -0.32. In France, Reynaud (2003) reports a price elasticity of -0.74 for extractive industries and of -0.30 for the food and beverages industries. As a result, all industrial firms will not react in the same way to a water price increase or to the implementation of water user charges. Second, firms have different price elasticities for water supplied though municipal water systems (network water) and for self-supplied water (Renzetti, 1992; Reynaud, 2003). The same water price increase will then have a different impact on industrial use of network water and self-supplied water.

Table 4.2. Empirical evidence on industrial water price elasticities

Study	Sector / country	Water price elasticity
Renzetti (1992)	Manufacturing / Canada	Intake: -0.153 to -0.588
Dupont and Renzetti (2001)	Manufacturing / Canada	Intake: -0.79 to -0.81 Recirculation: -0.51 to -1.48
Wang and Lall (2002)	Manufacturing / China	Water use: -1.03
Reynaud (2003)	Manufacturing & Services / France	Intake (network): -0.10 to -0.79 Intake (self-supply): -0.90 to -2.10
Féres and Reynaud (2005)	Manufacturing / Brazil	Intake: -1.09

Table 4.2. Empirical evidence on industrial water price elasticities (*cont.*)

Study	Sector / country	Water price elasticity
Guerrero (2005)	Manufacturing / Mexico	Intake:-0.30
Strzepek et al. (2006)	All / World	Intake:-1.27
Arbués et al. (2010)	Manufacturing & Services / Spain	Intake (network): -0.25
Angulo et al. (2014)	Touristic / Spain	Intake (network): 0.08
Tobarra-González (2015)	Manufacturing / Chile	Intake: -1.10

Source: Renzetti, S. (1992), "Estimating the structure of industrial water demands: The case of Canadian manufacturing", *Land Economics*, Vol. 68/1, pp. 396-404; Dupont, D. and S. Renzetti (2001), "The role of water in manufacturing", *Environmental and Resource Economics*, Vol. 18/4, pp. 411-432, https://doi.org/10.1023/A:1011117319932; Wang, H. and S. Lall (2002), "Valuing water for Chinese industries: a marginal productivity analysis", *Applied Economics*, Vol. 34/6, pp. 759-765; Reynaud, A. (2003), "An econometric estimation of industrial water demand in France", *Environmental and Resource Economics*, Vol. 25/2, pp. 213-232; Féres, J. and A. Reynaud (2005), "Assessing the Impact of Environmental Regulation on Industrial Water Use: Evidence from Brazil", *Land Economics*, Vol. 81/3, pp. 396-411; Guerrero, H. (2005), "Industrial water demand in Mexico: Econometric analysis and implications for water management policy", PhD dissertation, Université de Toulouse 1, Toulouse, https://hal.archives-ouvertes.fr/halshs-00008624/document (accessed September 2017); Strzepek, K., J. Juana and J.F. Kirsten (2006), "Marginal Productivity Analysis of Global Inter-sectoral Water Demand Marginal productivity analysis of global inter-sectoral water demand", poster paper prepared for presentation at the 26th International Association of Agricultural Economists Conference, Gold Coast, Australia, 12-18 August; Arbués, F., I. Villanua and R. Barberan (2010), "Household size and residential water demand: an empirical approach", *Australian Journal of Agricultural and Resource Economics*, Vol. 54/1, pp. 61-80, http://onlinelibrary.wiley.com/doi/10.1111/j.1467-8489.2009.00479.x/full; Angulo, A. et al. (2014), "Economic analysis of the water demand in the hotels and restaurants sector: shadow prices and elasticities", *Water Resources Research*, Vol. 50/8, pp. 6269-7066, http://agupubs.onlinelibrary.wiley.com/hub/issue/10.1002/wrcr.v50.8/; Tobarra-González, M.Á. (2015), "Value of water in the manufacture industry: The case of Chile", paper presented at the European Association of Environmental and Resource Economists 21st Annual Conference 24-27 June, Helsinki.

The higher price elasticity of industrial water demand means that over time industrial water users can more easily adjust their water consumption to changes in the water price, compared to other water users. The higher price elasticity (in absolute values) for commercial and industrial users can be related to the potential for in-plant recirculation of water. Indeed, in a number of industrial production processes, firms may choose to recirculate used water, either in order to limit the amount of water discharged (which may be subject to environmental regulation) or to reduce the amount of water intake (which may be costly for the firm). The empirical literature provides evidence concerning the link between water user charges set on intake water and the decision by firms to invest in recirculation technologies. For instance, working on manufacturing firms in Brazil, Féres et al. (2012) show that water charges act as an effective mechanism in inducing firms to undertake water recirculation investment and reducing freshwater demand.

As a result, water recirculation and freshwater intake are usually found to be substitutes. In Canada, Bruneau et al. (2010) demonstrate that the marginal costs of water intake (which can be directly affected by water user charges) play a significant role in influencing a firm's optimal volume of water recirculation once the decision to recirculate has been taken. One important policy implication is that any change in water user charge can be expected to have a strong impact on the water recirculation decisions of firms.

These different options can explain that responses of industrial users to changes in abstraction and pollution charges will depend on industries, the initial source of water (municipal or self-supplied), and time (as it takes time to consider alternative means of using water, shifting to alternative sources, or recirculating water).

Combining water charges with energy and industrial policy

Industrial policy has ambivalent impacts on water management. On the one hand, industrial policy can support compliance with water regulation, such as subsidies to green technologies e.g.wastewater treatment and recycling, which can reduce the cost of meeting water quality standards. Similarly, policies that support the development of water saving devices can reduce the bill for abstraction charges. On the other hand, industrial policy can increase water use and, therefore, intensify water conflicts. For instance the support to renewables through feed-in tariffs and renewable portfolio standards makes hydropower or biofuels more attractive for investors, driving water demand up. It also fosters the development of intermittent sources of energy such as wind and solar power, which in turn creates additional demand for energy storage in hydropower dams. Biofuel mandates and tax cuts on energy in the agricultural sector favour water intensive crops such as maize.

It follows that industrial and water policy should be co-ordinated. For instance, well-designed industrial policy to support green technologies can complement water abstraction or pollution charges as it aims to bring new opportunities to reduce the water bill and contribute to enhanced water management.

The situation in Brazil

The industrial sector generally claims that water charges change behaviour and that rates should not be revised, although a cause-effect relationship is hard to prove. Throughout recent years, several companies have made technological choices to save and re-use reclaimed wastewater: the steel industry, the textile and the chemical sector for example progressively reduced the use of water in manufacturing, while more than 60% of companies use reclaimed water and 65% of them have programmes to reduce demand. According to CNI (2015) since the beginning of the charge in the PCJ River Basin, water withdrawal for industrial uses has been reduced by half; in the Paraíba do Sul River Basin water demand was reduced by 18% and the discharge of organic load by 23%. However, observed water savings may result from a combination of factors. For instance, companies report saving water to comply with international best practices (when competing on global markets), or to minimise the cost of treating polluted water.

The current level of charges is far from correcting externalities. Water charges should incentivise the manufacturing sector to internalise the cost of pollution. The inefficiency of the current charging regime is demonstrated by the fact that, due to untreated pollution, the cost of treating abstracted water to make it suitable for industrial use is higher than the charges currently imposed (sometimes by two orders of magnitude, according to selected interviews). A related issue is to understand how diffuse pollution from nutrients, pesticides, herbicides, sediment pass costs to other sectors including industry.

The manufacturing sector reckons some challenges concerning the implementation of water charges. The CNI argues first that water charges cannot solve all the problems, especially those related to water pollution and that water use and discharge permits should be properly implemented. Second, all sectors should be subject to water charges. Third, there is a need for legal certainty about the charge, including on the definition of objective criteria for unit prices, correction of distortions and procedures for revision. Among others, solutions could be based on allowing the sectors to receive funds for investments in actions and initiatives focused on the optimisation and conservation of water resources and applying funds on a repayable basis (CNI, 2015).

Suggestions to consider

Two issues require particular attention in the case of industry. One relates to the implementation of an abstraction charge: as noted above, all industries should be covered. At the same time, opportunities for using alternative sources of water should be monitored, as an abstraction charge can incentivise corporates to use alternative sources of water (e.g. drilling their own wells). Incentives to use reclaimed water contribute to conservation objectives. Incentives to use groundwater may be misdirected. This confirms that a reform of abstraction charges should be coupled with a review of the capacity to monitor and control abstraction from surface and groundwater.

The other issue relates to pollution charges. They are currently based on BOD, which is a poor proxy of the externalities generated by industrial discharges, in a country which has benefitted from rapid industrialisation and diversification. Action should focus on the monitoring of the harmful consequences of a wide range of pollutants in industrial discharges, including from mining activities, with attempts to monitor them and to monetise them. Pollution charges would be reformed to better reflect the costs for society of these discharges, and to support more stringent standards in discharge permits. Similar attention should be paid to the economic consequences of such adjustments. Some industries may win, while others may lose. The proceeds of the revised pollution charge could be used to support a transition towards less polluting processes (although this could have the effect of subsidising the least efficient operators), at least for a set period of time.

These actions would benefit from economic analyses on the impact of a charge on the competitiveness of firms, the benefits for other users and the community, the cost of adaptation to new charges, and the measures that can minimise these costs. In the case of industries, economic analyses are often limited to the costs incurred by (selected) industries. It does not account for other social, economic, and environmental consequences, some of which are likely to be beneficial. As stressed above, decisions can be based on proxies, pending robust analyses, and additional revenues can be used to support adaptation to the new charging regimes, and to the benefits of water users, preferably in the basin. Charging schemes and expenditure programmes can be refined as more information is available about the cost and the benefits for industries and for the wider community.

Agriculture

Economic principles

Facing a water pollution or abstraction charge increase, farmers might be expected to react in two ways. First, they may shift from relatively water-intensive crops (i.e. corn) towards relatively water-saving crops. This type of crop adjustment is called change in *extensive margin*.[3] Second, they may decrease the irrigation rate of individual crops. This is called change in *intensive margin*. The price elasticity of agricultural water demand is then a combination of these two effects.

Various methods have been used by economists to measure agricultural water price elasticities. Elasticity estimates are sensitive to the method used to estimate them, depending on whether they are econometric studies, mathematical programming, or field studies. It is usually found that agricultural water demand is *less inelastic* than residential water demand, in particular due to the possibility to adjust extensive and intensive margins. Most of the literature on irrigator water values tends to be derived from programming models. Scheierling, Loomis, and Young (2006) reviewed 24 studies of price elasticity of demand for irrigation water and report estimates ranging from -0.001 to -1.97, with a mean of -0.48 (Table 4.3).

Table 4.3. Empirical evidence on agricultural water price elasticities

Study	Country	Method	Water price elasticity
Howitt et al. (1980)	USA	MP	-0.97
Ellis et al. (1983)	USA	MP	-0.13 to -0.35
Bernardo et al. (1987)	USA	MP	-0.12
Hooker and Alexander (1998)	USA	MP	-0.22
Scheierling et al. (2004)	USA	MP	-0.02 to -0.16
Ayer and Hoyt (1981)	USA	FE	-0.06 to -1.45
Hoyt (1982)	USA	FE	-0.05 to -0.16
Kelley and Ayer (1982)	USA	FE	-0.04 to -0.21
Ayer et al. (1983a)	USA	FE	-0.01 to -0.03
Ayer et al. (1983b)	USA	FE	-0.001 to -0.07
Hoyt (1984)	USA	FE	-0.03 to -0.16
Nieswiadomy (1985)	USA	EC	-0.80
Ogg and Gollehon (1989)	USA	EC	-0.26
Moore et al. (1994)	USA	EC	-0.03 to -0.10
Schoengold, Sunding, and Moreno (2006)	USA	EC	-0.79
Hendricks and Peterson (2012)	USA	EC	-0.10
Wheeler et al. (2008)	Australia	EC	-0.50 to -1.90
Zuo et al. (2016)	Australia	EC	-0.57

Notes: Method: MP for mathematical programming; FE for field experiment; EC for econometric analysis.

Source: Adapted from Scheierling M., J.B. Loomis and R.A. Young (2006), "Irrigiation water demand: A meta-analysis of price elasticities", *Water Resources Research*, Vol. 42, www.soil.tu-bs.de/lehre/Master.Irrigation/2011/Lit-Weber/Scheierling-etal-2006.WRR.Irrigation_water_demand.pdf and based on author work.

Two issues that may be of interest for the Brazilian context: i) the weight of the intensive margin compared to the extensive margin; and ii) the measure of elasticity in a context of tradeable water entitlement (which is not the case in Brazil).

Concerning the first issue, Hendricks and Peterson (2012) report in the USA a price elasticity for irrigation from groundwater in the High Plains equal to -0.10. Most of the adjustment occurs at the intensive margin (changes in the water applied per unit of area), which is limited by prevailing levels of efficiency and technical progress. Possibly, the reason for such an inelastic estimate is because the number of wells is constrained due to water rights. A new water right can only be issued if it does not impair on existing ones. If the number of wells were unconstrained, the extensive margin effect would certainly be larger and increase the total elasticity estimate. One important policy message is that since most of the response is at the intensive margin, policies that target per-unit-area irrigation rates will be nearly as cost-effective as a first-best pricing policy.

Concerning the second issue, water permits or entitlements in Brazil, can be issued to both public and private parties. The water permit does not transfer the ownership of water, but allows the use of water for a specific period of time, under specific conditions.

In a different context where water entitlements can be traded (Australia), some scholars have investigated how water entitlements vary with price. Using water market trade data for the Goulburn Murray Irrigated District in Australia, Wheeler et al. (2008) estimated price elasticities using bid demand and supply data for seasonal water from 2001 to 2007, and actual prices paid from 1997 to 2007. These authors found a bid price elasticity of demand of -1.51; while using actual prices paid, the study found a short-run demand elasticity of -0.52, which was very similar to that found in Scheierling, Loomis, and Young (2006). Zuo et al. (2016) have extended this analysis to different levels of security (high security and low/general security) for permanent water entitlement. Their estimate for demand for high security water entitlements is around -0.57, which is at the lower end of the range from the literature on price elasticity of demand for water allocations.

Combining water charges with agricultural policy

Policy coherence between agriculture and water is required to avoid conflicting signals and incentives, in particular to farmers in achieving sustainable water management. Abstraction and pollution charges have an important role to play.

Some government non-environmental programmes and subsidies inadvertently lead to degradation of water quality and increased scarcity. For example, policies that support agriculture production encourage greater land use change and intensive use of inputs, such as fertilisers, pesticides, irrigation, and fossil fuel use (Shortle et al., 2011). Input subsidies can also encourage more intensive use of potentially environmentally harmful inputs. The reform of such policies will make water abstraction or pollution charges even more effective in driving cropping patterns and farming practices in directions that contribute to water security and sustainable growth.

Voluntary programmes such as agro-environmental schemes aim to reduce the negative impact of agriculture in exchange for some payment. Farmers are paid for adopting greener practices and for providing ecosystem services such as protecting biodiversity, increasing water quality, and providing flood protection. Agro-environmental programmes are increasingly important components of agricultural policy both in Europe and the United States (e.g. subsidies for converting to organic farming, for crop rotation). Farmers are paid for planting cover crops during the winter, which curb erosion and prevent nitrogen leaching into groundwater. They also get some compensation for establishing grass buffer strips along rivers and streams, which filter nonpoint source pollution from fertilisers and pesticides. In England, payment for ecosystem services schemes is gaining traction with water utilities, with improved outcomes not only for water quality and reduced water treatment costs, but also for biodiversity, flood management and environmental flows (Box 4.3). The scheme was more environmentally effective and cost-efficient than upgrades in water treatment to remove nutrients and pesticides.

Box 4.3. Collaboration with farmers and Payment for Ecosystem Services schemes in England

Former problems of water pollution from point sources such as factories and other industrial activity have declined through both structural change in the economy and effective regulation. Although some legacy water quality problems from industrialisation (e.g. old mine workings, now managed through public investment in the absence of historic polluters), and morphological alteration to waterbodies as a result of human activity (e.g. navigation, hydropower, flood

Box 4.3. Collaboration with farmers and Payment for Ecosystem Services schemes in England (*cont.*)

defence activity), the most significant modern water quality problem is diffuse pollution, particularly from agriculture. Policies such as agricultural subsidy frameworks and land use planning systems, and under-reported and under-regulated diffuse pollution, have contributed to water quality pressures.

The primary pollutants which water utilities have to deal with are nitrates, phosphates, sediments and pesticides. It is estimated that since the 1989 privatisation of the water sector (supervised by three regulators and national government), water utilities have invested around GBP 1.7billion in traditional drinking water treatment approaches to reduce the levels of pesticides and nitrates. The scale of these costs has been a key driver for the industry to pursue new ways of working with land managers to reduce pollution at the catchment scale. In recognition that, in a wider social sense, it is not efficient to pollute at source through sub-optimal land management practices and then have to consume resources downstream to remove pollution, water utilities began considering diverting investment from traditional water treatment into land management as payment for ecosystem services (PES).

"Upstream Thinking" is South West Water utility's catchment management scheme which has been applying natural landscape-scale solutions to water quality issues since 2008. The PES scheme draws upon the knowledge and expertise of a number of partners including South West Water, the Devon Wildlife Trust, the Cornwall Wildlife Trust, the Westcountry Rivers Trust, the Exmoor National Park Authority, and local farmers to improve raw water quality at source. Over the 2015-20 period, the latest GBP 11.8m programme is focussing on 11 catchments across Devon and Cornwall. The target for the programme is 750 farms and 1 300 ha of moorland and other semi-natural land under revised management.

Upstream Thinking targets priority pollutants associated with different catchments – typically nutrients, pesticides, and sediments. Upstream Thinking Farm advisers visit farms and carry out an assessment resulting in a whole-farm plan to reduce nutrients, pesticides and sediments. This includes a water management plan and future capital investment proposals targeted at water quality improvements. Up to 50% of capital investment proposals are funded by Upstream Thinking. These can include improvements to slurry storage, fencing to keep livestock out of rivers, providing alternative water sources for livestock, and improved pesticide management including investment in new equipment such as weed wipers which deliver targeted doses of herbicide.

The Upstream Thinking programme has also successfully investigated and restored over 2 000 hectares of sensitive upstream land on Exmoor in 2010-15 to improve peatland, and reduce sediment loads and flood risk downstream. The overall programme is fully endorsed by the Environment Agency, Natural England and the Drinking Water Inspectorate (DWI). The work is targeted to benefit 15 water treatment works supplying 72% of the total daily water to customers.

Although physical evidence is emerging on the water quality benefits of working with land managers in catchments, through water companies making investments to pay for ecosystems services, the economic evidence on the costs and benefits of the approach has been slower to emerge. In its 2011 report, From Catchment to Customer, Ofwat (the economic regulator) acknowledged a lack of hard economic evidence on the net benefits of land management PES approaches. It also highlighted the role for polluter-pays mechanisms alongside the beneficiary-pays approach which characterises the water company schemes. To avoid concerns about equity that can arise if PES payments are seen to "reward polluters", while neglecting producers already demonstrating best practice, there is a need for collective compliance by farmers with baseline regulation so as to achieve "additionality" in response to PES incentives (OECD, 2013b). Nevertheless, Ofwat does see a role for PES schemes, saying "Water customers could

Box 4.3. Collaboration with farmers and Payment for Ecosystem Services schemes in England (*cont.*)

legitimately expect to pay for those elements of catchment management that bring direct and measurable benefits to them, under the principle of paying for ecosystem services" (Ofwat, 2011). In 2009, Ofwat approved ultilities' proposals to spend GBP 60m on water quality investigations and PES schemes throughout England and Wales, representing something of a departure for Ofwat.

Source: OECD (2017), *Diffuse Pollution, Degraded Waters: Emerging Policy Solutions*, OECD Publishing, Paris, http://dx.doi.org/10.1787/9789264269064-en.

Agro-environmental schemes have been criticised for generating windfall profits: subsidies sometimes more than offset the cost of implementing the greener production process (Chabé-Ferret and Subervie, 2013). Concerns about equity can arise if payment for ecosystem services (PES) are seen to "reward polluters" while neglecting producers already demonstrating best practice. To address these concerns, PES should only be considered when farmers collectively comply with baseline regulation so as to achieve "additionality" in response to PES incentives (OECD, 2013).

Charges for water management should be linked with agricultural policy since the cost for the farmer of paying those charges, or of reducing water abstraction and pollution, is partly determined by restrictions and charges on inputs, subsidies on equipment, or for environmental practices such as agro-environmental programmes.

The situation in Brazil

The irrigation sector abstracts more than 50% of water, but is almost exempt from paying water charges (Figure 4.2). There are total exemptions in the states of Paraná and São Paulo. In other cases, the contribution of the sector is lower than in others: in the Paraíba do Sul River Basin and the Piracicaba, Capivari and Jundiaí (PCJ) river basins, the agricultural sector pays from 2 to 20 times less than other water users. In the São Francisco and the Doce River Basin, the volumetric charge for agricultural users is 40 times lower than for other sectors. However in the São Francisco this will not be longer applied from 2018 onwards, if the new resolution of water charges issued by the Committee is approved by the National Water Resources Council (CNRH) (ANA, 2016b).

Irrigators claim that water charges would significantly affect their competitiveness and put them at risk, given the low value of their products and the international competition. Such claims can be challenged in the absence of solid evidence. For instance, if the agricultural sector in the State of Rio Grande do Sul paid a charge of 0.01 BRL per cubic meter (i.e. the same charge as other water users) this would represent 2% of farmers' overall costs (less than average inflation, or fluctuations in currency rates). If agricultural users were to pay 5% of the 0.01 BRL per cubic meter, the impact of charging on overall costs would only be 0.1%. Given that in many cases farmers pays only 2-5% of what other users pay on a volumetric basis, the affordability issue stemming from paying the full water charge is not self-evident.

Figure 4.2. Water abstracted and consumed by sector in Brazil

2015

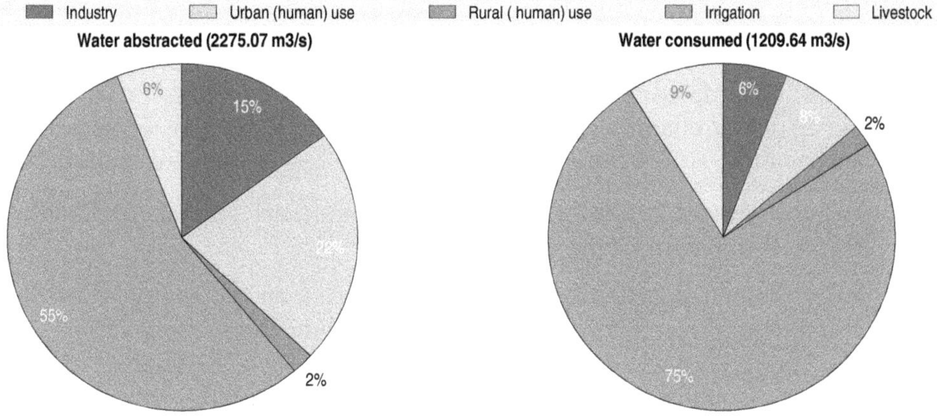

Source: ANA (2016), "Conjuntura dos recursos Hidricos no Brazil", *Informe 2016.*

Moreover, supplying artificially cheap water to grow low value crops comes at an economic cost. It deprives other users from using water for more valuable uses. The experience of England and Wales and France is reported in Box 4.4. Finally, a fine-grained analysis is required. Large farming sector may be better equipped to invest and change cropping patterns and farming practices, than subsistence agriculture and poor farmers. Distinctive and targeted policies and accompanying measures may be required.

Box 4.4. Water charges for the agriculture sector in England and Wales, and France

In England and Wales, the same level of charges applies to agriculture as to other sectors. The only special feature is to acknowledge that for irrigation the demand will fluctuate from year to year depending on rainfall. Consequently, irrigators are subject to a two-part tariff, where there us a standing charge of 50% of the full amount, and the remainder is variable according to actual usage. In order to be eligible for this, they must have a well-maintained, calibrated meter on the pump, and submit data on usage to the Environment Agency. They are also subject to more rigorous inspection, particularly in dry years.

In France, farmers are due to pay an abstraction charge, based on the volume of water taken from a water body. The charge varies by basins. In the Seine River Basin, the abstraction charge for irrigation is 1.8 cents per cubic meter for surface water and 2.3 cents for groundwater. The charge goes up to 3.45 cents per cubic meter in parts of the basin where water is chronically scarce (Zone de répartition des eaux, ZRE). When farmers agree to collectively manage an entitlement in a water scarce area, they benefit from a reduced rate (2.3 cents for surface water and 3.4 for groundwater): this serves as an incentive for farmers to create users associations (Organismes uniques de gestion collective, OUCG).

Source: Ian Barker, Peer-Reviewer, Water Policy International Ltd (England and Wales); Data provided by the Agence de l'Eau Seine Normandie, visited in May 2017.

Suggestions to consider

- Set or increase water charges for farmers to reflect environmental and opportunity costs. While all farmers should be charged in principle, start with and focus attention on the ones who have the more severe impacts on water quantity and quality. Consider a distinctive approach for small subsistence farming than for large industrial farming.

- Strengthen the policy mix to ensure that agriculture policy and water charges reinforce (and do not undermine) each other.
- Consider other instruments, such as charges on pesticides, to accompany the reform of water charges and to address issues such as diffused water pollution from agriculture which cannot be addressed by charges on water pollution.
- Ensure that permit conditions control environmental impacts and that farmers would see the benefits of the charge collection.

These actions would benefit from economic analyses on the impact of a charge on different agriculture sub-sectors. A distinction should be drawn between subsistence agriculture and poor farmers, and agro-industry, which have distinctive capacities to invest and adjust production patterns. Economic analyses should factor in the benefits for other users and the community, the cost of adaptation to the charging system, and the measures that can minimise these costs. As stressed above, decisions can be based on proxies, pending robust analyses, and additional revenues can be used to support adaptation to the new charging regimes, and to the benefits of water users, preferably in the basin. Charging schemes and expenditure programmes can be refined as more information is available about the cost and the benefits for farmers and for the wider community.

Notes

1. The elasticity of water demand to price measures the percentage change in demand that results from a 1% increase in price.
2. This section draws from Gammetltoft P. (2017).
3. A shift from irrigated towards rain-fed agriculture can also be observed (super-extensive margin).

References

Acteon (2010), "Economic instruments for mobilising financial resources for supporting IWRM – Additional information and illustrations for the OECD initiative", https://search.oecd.org/environment/resources/46228724.pdf.

Adour Garonne Water Agency (n.d.), www.eau-adour-garonne.fr/fr/eau-et-activites-economiques/l-hydroelectricite/redevance-pour-l-hydroelectricite.html.

ANA (Agência National de Agua) (2016a), "Subsidies for formulating an approach for the sanitation sector in the context of water resources in Brazil", Note prepared by the National Water Agency (ANA) within the OECD/ ANA Policy Dialogue, Brasilia, March.

ANA (2016b), "Background report on setting and governing economic instruments for water policy in Brazil", Brasilia.

Angulo, A. et al. (2014), "Economic analysis of the water demand in the hotels and restaurants sector: shadow prices and elasticities", *Water Resources Research*, Vol. 50/8, pp. 6269-7066, http://agupubs.onlinelibrary.wiley.com/hub/issue/10.1002/wrcr.v50.8/.

Arbués, F., I. Villanua and R. Barberan (2010), "Household size and residential water demand: an empirical approach", *Australian Journal of Agricultural and Resource Economics*, Vol. 54/1, pp. 61-80, http://onlinelibrary.wiley.com/doi/10.1111/j.1467-8489.2009.00479.x/full.

Arbués, F., M.A. García-Valiñas and R. Martínez-Espiñeira (2003), "Estimation of Residential Water Demand: A State-of-the-art Review", *The Journal of Socio-Economics*, Vol. 32/1, pp. 81-102, https://doi.org/10.1016/S1053-5357(03)00005-2.

Banfi, S. and M. Filippini (2010), "Resource rent taxation and benchmarking – A new perspective for the Swiss hydropower sector", *Energy Policy*, Vol. 38/5, pp. 2302-2308.

Berbel, J., J. Calatrava and A. Garrido (2007), "Water pricing and irrigation: a review of the European Experience", in F. Molle, J. Berkkoff and R. Barker (eds), *Irrigation Water Pricing Policy in Context: exploring the Gap between Theory and Practice*, Wallingford, CABI, Chapter 13, pp. 295-327, United Kingdom.

Bruneau, J., S. Renzetti and M. Villeneuve (2010), "Manufacturing Firms' Demand for Water Recirculation", *Canadian Journal of Agricultural Economics*, Vol. 58, pp. 515-530, doi:10.1111/j.1744-7976.2010.01196.x.

Chabé-Ferret, S. and J. Subervie (2013), "How much green for the buck? Estimating additional and windfall effects of French agro-environmental schemes by DID-matching", *Journal of Environmental Economics and Management*, Vol. 65, pp. 12-27.

CNI (Confederação Nacional da indûstria) (2015), "Cobranca pelo uso dos recursos hídricos no Brasil: a visão da indústria", Percy Soares Neto Coordenador da Rede de Recursos Hídricos da Indústria, Seminario CTOB, 5 August.

De Maria André, D. and J.R. Carvalho (2014), "Spatial Determinants of Urban Residential Water Demand in Fortaleza, Brazil", *Water Resources Management*, Vol. 28/9, pp. 2401-2414, https://link.springer.com/article/10.1007%2fs11269-014-0551-0.

DANVA (2016), "Water in figures 2016", Skanderborg, Denmark, www.e-pages.dk/danva/200/.

Dupont, D. and S. Renzetti (2001), "The role of water in manufacturing", *Environmental and Resource Economics*, Vol. 18/4, pp. 411-432, https://doi.org/10.1023/A:1011117319932.

EEA (European Environment Agency) (2013), "Assessment of cost recovery through water pricing", EEA Technical Report, No 16.

Féres, J. and A. Reynaud (2005), "Assessing the Impact of Environmental Regulation on Industrial Water Use: Evidence from Brazil", *Land Economics*, Vol. 81/3, pp. 396-411.

Féres, J., A. Reynaud and A. Thomas (2012), "Water Reuse in Brazilian Manufacturing Firms", *Applied Economics*, Vol. 44/11, pp. 1417-1427.

French Ministry of Ecology, Sustainable Development and Energy (2012), "Tax on water abstraction: how can it be used in the quantity management of the resource?", Department of the Commissioner General for Sustainable Development, No. 127, Paris, http://temis.documentation.developpement-durable.gouv.fr/docs/Temis/0076/Temis-0076146/Point_127_ENG.pdf (accessed September 2017).

Gammettoft, P. (2017), "Governance of water and sanitation infrastructure in Brazil", Working Paper prepared for the National Water Agency (ANA), Unpublished.

Goméz, C. (1987), "Experience in predicting willingness to pay on water projects in Latin America", in Monatanari FW (ed), *Resource mobilization for drinking water and sanitation in developing nations*, *American Society of Civil Engineers*, New York, pp 242–254.

Guerrero, H. (2005), "Industrial water demand in Mexico: Econometric analysis and implications for water management policy", PhD dissertation, Université de Toulouse 1, Toulouse, https://hal.archives-ouvertes.fr/halshs-00008624/document (accessed September 2017).

Hendricks, N.P. and J.M. Peterson (2012), "Fixed effects estimation of the intensive and extensive margins of irrigation water demand", *Journal of Agricultural and Resource Economics*, Vol. 37/1, pp. 1–19.

OECD (2017), *Diffuse Pollution, Degraded Waters: Emerging Policy Solutions*, OECD Publishing, Paris, http://dx.doi.org/10.1787/9789264269064-en.

OECD (2015), *Water Resources Governance in Brazil*, OECD Publishing, Paris, http://dx.doi.org/10.1787/9789264238121-en.

OECD (2013), *Providing Agri-environmental Public Goods through Collective Action*, OECD Publishing, Paris, http://dx.doi.org/10.1787/9789264197213-en.

Renzetti, S. (1992), "Estimating the structure of industrial water demands: The case of Canadian manufacturing", *Land Economics*, Vol. 68/1, pp. 396-404.

Reynaud, A. (2015), "Revisiting the incentive properties of water charges: the case of the Czech Republic", Mimeo, Toulouse School of Economics.

Reynaud, A. (2003), "An econometric estimation of industrial water demand in France", *Environmental and Resource Economics*, Vol. 25/2, pp. 213-232.

Scheierling, S., J. Loomis and R. Young (2006), "Irrigation Water Demand: A Meta-analysis of Price Elasticities", *Water Resources Research*, Vol. 42; W01411.

Shortle, J. S. and R.D. Horan (2001), The economics of nonpoint pollution control, Journal of Economic Surveys, Vol. 15 (3), pp. 255 – 289.

Strzepek, K., J. Juana and J.F. Kirsten (2006), "Marginal Productivity Analysis of Global Inter-sectoral Water Demand Marginal productivity analysis of global inter-sectoral water demand", poster paper prepared for presentation at the 26th International Association of Agricultural Economists Conference, Gold Coast, Australia, 12-18 August.

Tinbergen, J. (1952), "On the theory of economic policy, North Holland", Amsterdam.

Tobarra-González, M.Á. (2015), "Value of water in the manufacture industry: The case of Chile", paper presented at the European Association of Environmental and Resource Economists 21st Annual Conference 24-27 June, Helsinki.

Vanhille, J. (2012), "A Social Gradient in Households' Environmental Policy Responsiveness? The Case of Water Pricing in Flanders", paper prepared for the 32nd General Conference of The International Association for Research in Income and Wealth, Boston, 5-11 August, www.iariw.org/papers/2012/VanhilleAbstract.pdf (accessed September 2017).

Wang, H. and S. Lall (2002), "Valuing water for Chinese industries: a marginal productivity analysis", *Applied Economics*, Vol. 34/6, pp. 759-765.

Wheeler, S. et al. (2008), "Price Elasticity of Allocations Water Demand in the Goulburn-Murray Irrigation District of Victoria, Australia", *The Australian Journal of Agricultural and Resource Economics*, Vol. 52/1, pp. 37–55.

Whittington, D. et al. (2015), "A diagnostic tool for estimating the incidence of subsidies delivered by water utilities in low- and medium-income countries, with illustrative simulations", *Utilities Policy*, Vol. 34, pp. 70-81, doi: 10.1016/j.jup.2014.12.007.

Zuo, A. et al. (2016), "Measuring price elasticities of demand and supply of water entitlements based on stated and revealed preference data", *American Journal of Agricultural Economics*, Vol. 98/1, pp. 314-322, https://doi.org/10.1093/ajae/aav022.

Chapter 5

Governing water charges design and implementation

This chapter analyses three sets of issues that affect the governance of economic instruments for water management in Brazil: the role of information for supporting decision-making in water charges; the issue of scale for managing water charges; and planning as a tool that drives both the design of water charges and the allocation of revenues from water charges.

Key principles

A perfect model does not exist for setting and governing water abstraction and pollution charges. International experiences show a great variety of governance models, which reflect different institutional organisations, local circumstances, historical and cultural choices. But regardless of the place-based considerations to get water charges right, a number of common and overarching governance principles should be followed to set the needed framework conditions for economic instruments to deliver.

Setting and governing water charges is a highly sensitive and daunting task, which requires effective multi-level governance (OECD, 2011). For water charges to deliver, it is crucial to address not only the question of "what to do?" but also "who does what?", "why?", "at which level of government?" and "how?" The *OECD Principles on Water Governance* (OECD, 2015a) offers an overview of the governance system for water charges, which were developed on the premise that there is no one-size-fits-all solution to water challenges worldwide, but a menu of options building on the diversity of legal, administrative and organisational systems within and across countries (Box 5.1).

According to the OECD Principles, water charges will only be viable if responsible authorities are clearly in charge and endowed with the needed capacity: if they are designed, collected and disbursed at the right scale; if they are documented with robust information-based systems to guide decisions; if they are drive by solid, realistic and policy coherent planning; if they are properly regulated, with effective enforcement and compliance; if stakeholders are engaged well upstream to raise their awareness and secure their buy-in; if their design implementation is transparent; and if they are properly monitored and evaluated.

Box 5.1. The OECD Principles on Water Governance

On 4 June 2015, the OECD Principles on Water Governance were endorsed by OECD ministers as standards for more effective, efficient and inclusive design and implementation of water policies. The Principles were developed and discussed through a bottom-up and multi-stakeholder approach within the OECD Water Governance Initiative, an international network of 120+ policy makers and stakeholders gathering twice a year in a Policy Forum.

The Principles were developed on the premise that there is no one-size-fits-all solution to water challenges worldwide, but a menu of options building on the diversity of legal, administrative and organisational systems within and across countries. The OECD Principles on Water Governance recognise that governance is highly contextual, that water policies need to be tailored to different water resources and places, and that governance responses have to adapt to changing circumstances. They acknowledge that water governance is a shared responsibility between levels of government, public, private and non-profit stakeholders.

The Principles aim to enhance water governance systems that help manage "too much", "too little" and "too polluted" water in a sustainable, integrated and inclusive way, at an acceptable cost, and in a reasonable time-frame. They consider that governance is good if it can help to solve key water challenges, using a combination of bottom-up and top-down processes while fostering constructive state-society relations. It is bad if it generates undue transaction costs and does not respond to place-based needs. The Principles consider that water governance systems (more or less formal, complex, and costly) should be designed according to the challenges they are required to address. This problem-solving approach means that "forms" of water governance should follow "functions" of water governance. Structuring, institutionalising, and/or formalising institutions should not detract from the ultimate objective of delivering sufficient water of good quality, while maintaining or improving the ecological integrity of water bodies.

Box 5.1. The OECD Principles on Water Governance (*cont.*)

The *OECD Principles on Water Governance* intend to contribute to tangible and outcome-oriented public policies, based on three mutually reinforcing and complementary dimensions of water governance (Figure: OECD Principles on Water Governance):

- **Effectiveness** relates to the contribution of governance to define clear sustainable water policy goals and targets at all levels of government, to implement those policy goals, and to meet expected targets.
- **Efficiency** relates to the contribution of governance to maximise the benefits of sustainable water management and welfare at the least cost to society.
- **Trust and Engagement** relate to the contribution of governance to building public confidence and ensuring inclusiveness of stakeholders through democratic legitimacy and fairness for society at large.

OECD Principles on Water Governance

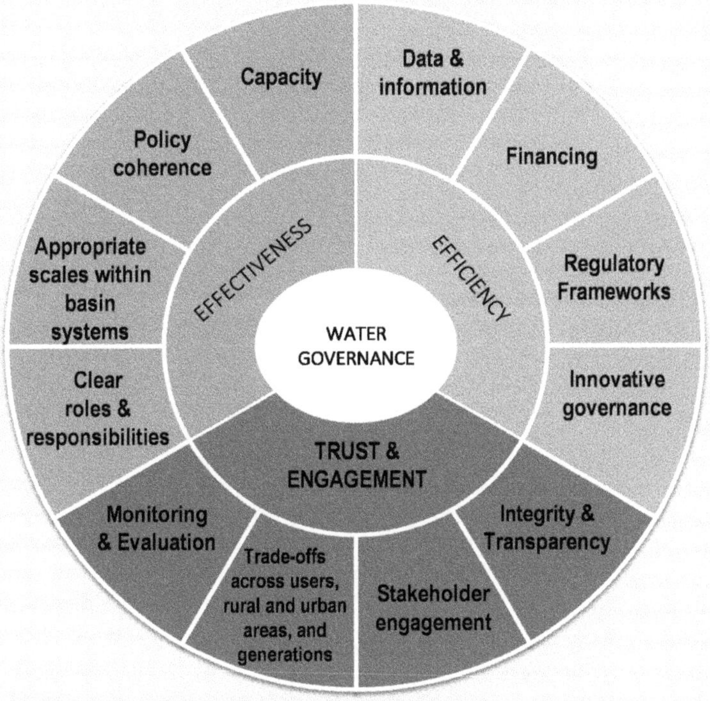

Source: OECD (2015a), "OECD Principles on Water Governance", welcomed by Ministers at the OECD Ministerial Council Meeting on 4 June, www.oecd.org/cfe/regional-policy/OECD-Principles-on-Water-Governance-brochure.pdf.

Table 5.1. OECD Principles on Water Governance applied to water charges in Brazil

OECD Principles	Tailored guidance for water abstraction and pollution charges in Brazil
1. Clear roles and responsibilities	• Clearly allocate and distinguish roles and responsibilities amongst federal, state and basin authorities for setting, implementing and regulating water charges, and adjust where need be based on results • Identify and address duplications, overlaps, gaps or grey areas across levels of government, given the multiplicity of state and federal agencies involved. Overcome the legal gap concerning water agencies, in charge of allocating revenues from water charges • Ensure the consultative and deliberative functions of state/interstate river basin committees, and state/national water councils are outcome-driven
2. Appropriate scales within basin systems	• Design, collect and disburse water charges at the appropriate scale to reflect distinctive local capacity, hydrographic situations and water-related risks • Foster co-ordination between hydrographic and administrative scales, which often do not correspond, with due attention to the higher complexity and multiplicity of stakeholders involved in federal rivers and the double dominion • Foster co-ordination between local, state and federal levels of government
3. Policy coherence	• Ensure that decisions taken in agriculture, energy, spatial planning, land use, and environmental licensing do not undermine the water use efficiency rationale of charges • Foster planning tools that drive water charges decisions and policy complementarity between water-related domains
4. Capacity	• Identify and address capacity gaps to design and implement water charges in state/interstate river basin committees, agencies and councils.
5.Data & Information	• Produce, update and share consistent and comparable data and information to guide, assess and improve the design and implementation of water charges • Ground the level of charges on sound technical criteria, building on economic analysis to support decision -making, and impacts on affordability and competitiveness
6. Financing	• Ensuring that governance arrangements help raise and spend revenues from water charges in an efficient, transparent and timely manner • Ensure that Polluter-Pays Principle and User-pays Principle are properly taken into account when designing charges • Consider pros and cons of earmarking to show the benefits of water charges to end users (e.g. allowing them to access to some funds for water conservation measures)
7. Regulatory framework	• Ensure that regulatory frameworks support the efficiency, effectiveness and inclusiveness of water charges and are effectively implemented and enforced. • Ensure sound inspection and control mechanisms as well as sanctions and penalties in case of non-enforcement and compliance
8. Innovative governance	• Promote innovative practices for the design and implementation of water charges, for example integrating behavioural dimensions into water charge design • Enhance pilots and experimentation, building on the proposed OECD typology of states, to test some ways forward before upscaling
9. Integrity & transparency	• Mainstream integrity and transparency practices in the water charge cycle, in particular • who pays for what across water users • how revenues collected are spent and according to which criteria
10. Stakeholder engagement	• Raise the awareness of stakeholders on water risks to secure the political/social buy in for water charges • Build capacity and share information for outcome-oriented debates and actions to charges in committees, councils and agencies • Manage the risks of consultation capture, vested interests and low representativeness in deliberative and consultative fora
11. Trade-offs across users, rural and urban areas, and generations	• Use water charges as a contribution to managing trade-offs across users, rural and urban areas, current and future generations. • Evaluate the possibility of cross-subsidies and solidarity mechanisms across users in period of droughts
12. Monitoring & evaluation	• Promote regular monitoring and evaluation of the adequacy, implementation and results of water charges to assess to what extent they fulfil the intended outcomes and adapt where necessary

Source: Adapted from OECD (2015a), "OECD Principles on Water Governance", welcomed by Ministers at the OECD Ministerial Council Meeting on 4 June, www.oecd.org/cfe/regional-policy/OECD-Principles-on-Water-Governance-brochure.pdf.

International experiences

When looking at the main steps of the water charges cycle, design, use of revenues and enforcement, some features from international experiences can be highlighted and be relevant for the implementation of water charges in Brazil:

- Water abstraction charges are usually designed and managed at subnational level. Central government authorities should also play a role, for instance, in ensuring coherence across national and basin plans (e.g. the case of Spain, Box 5.3); setting guidelines for river basin committees for water charges design (e.g. France).
- Revenues should be used to improve water quality and quantity in the basins. While there is an important financial component in the implementation of water charges, more and more the economic goals are of increasing relevance, due to the need of enhancing water security. In Spain, as many other countries, water charges are considered neither the panacea nor the main drawback in any water management system. However, the discussion is progressively moving away from the level (or the methodology of calculation) of the charge towards the different elements to be reflected in it and the necessary investments.
- While being recognised as key steps in the proper implementation of water charges, monitoring and enforcement show room for improvement. In Europe, measures such as fines and sanctions for illegal abstraction and pollution do not yet represent a strong incentive for complying with / avoiding these activities: e.g. in Spain to prosecute illegal water abstractions is difficult due to the complexity of administrative procedure; in France sanctions are very low and do not incentivise changes in polluters behaviour, since revenues from those polluting activities are greater (EEA, 2013). As enforcement implies substantial transaction costs due to the inspections, it is key to define *how* it is carried out, *when, towards* whom and what are the consequences in terms of bringing additional revenues and taking the water quantity and quality situation under control.

In depth description of the implementation of water charges in England and Wales, Spain, France Portugal, and Germany is provided in the following sections, as they are deemed relevant references to inspire some Brazilian states.

England and Wales

In England and Wales, the Environment Agency (EA) designs the charging schemes and proposes values for the different charging factors for the annual (subsistence) charge. It also recommends the level of charge for the administration and determination of new applications for, or variations to existing, licences and permits.[1] The EA is a single unified environment agency, responsible for operation, water management and regulation in England. Charges are approved by the relevant government minister in the Department for Environment Food and Rural Affairs (Defra). The Treasury takes an interest in the costs imposed. The EA sets up and operates the billing system, and is responsible for the collection of all charges. Every abstraction licence and discharge permit is monitored for compliance. Inspections are carried out on a risk basis: if it is a large abstraction or discharge, or if the abstractor has cheated in the past, he will be subject to more inspections. Non payers are pursued and licences can be revoked in case of refusal to pay.

Charges are levied annually. Some (above a threshold) can be paid quarterly. Each year the EA, as part of the five year work plan, proposes its work activities for the following year and consult on the abstraction and discharges charges which need to be raised on in order to be able to deliver that plan. The main charge schemes (abstraction and discharge) are only reviewed when a major change is needed (e.g. to include previously exempt uses, or to raise funds to compensate for compulsory changes to unsustainable licences). New schemes of charges, major changes, and the annual review of charges are approved by Defra. Ministers expect to see efficient use of funds by the EA. Since the financial crisis of 2008-09 there have been no increases in the charges, which have generally remained static in the face of inflation; the result has been increasing efficiency of operations, which has become an increasing challenge.

Major changes to charging schemes are subject to widespread consultation. If very complex or contentious, there is first a consultation on options, followed by consultation on the preferred option. The consultation responses are summarised and published. Major changes would have a Regulatory Impact Assessment, which sets out how the proposals would affect different classes or sectors of water users. Consultations are approved by Defra before release. Stakeholders are understandably interested in how the income is spent. All the money raised from charges is spent by the EA in the delivery of its statutory water management functions, and it publishes high level accounts in the interests of transparency.

Charges for abstraction are set by the EA on a regional basis, which broadly reflects river basins. The level of charges is designed to fund the water resource management activities in that region, and so are a proxy for water scarcity (less water implies more work to manage it) (see Chapter 3). Pollution charges are set nationally for England, and for an individual permit holder they reflect the conditions in the permit which are tailored to Environmental Quality Standards in each river basin.

The right to charge is set out in legislation, and allows the EA to recover the full costs of its water resource management activities (monitoring, assessment and modelling, permitting and regulation, compliance monitoring, operational management of assets, capital works, strategic planning). Discharge charges cover the costs of regulation, modelling and compliance monitoring.

The National Audit Office (NAO – the body responsible for ensuring the efficient use of public funds) can review and challenge the levels of charges and the efficiency of operational activities. It has only done this once in the past 30 years, when it reported that the EA provided a 'professional and well-managed service'. The Parliamentary Public Accounts Committee (PAC), which is comprised of members of Parliament from all parties, can also hold the EA and ministers to account.

Charges do not pay for flood defence works, which are usually funded from general taxation. Nor do they pay for actions within a river basin in order to improve water quality (e.g. from discharges from abandoned mine workings) or remove obstructions to flow. In the United Kingdom, abstraction licences are deemed to be property rights. If the EA needs to change a licence which is creating an unsustainable flow regime and damaging the environment, it has to pay compensation to the licence holder. This is funded by a separate charge on abstractors within that river basin. Ideally, the abstraction licence would be a permit that did not confer property rights, so that it could be varied without compensation. Ideally, the charges would also cover routine environmental monitoring costs (water quality, ecology and fisheries) to understand the state of and pressures on the environment.

France

In France, there are six water agencies for six river basins (Adour-Garonne, Artois-Picardie, Loire-Bretagne, Rhin-Meuse, Rhône-Mediterranée and Corse and Seine-Normandie) in charge of managing all water resources. They were created by the Water Law in 1964. River basin committees were created in 1964 and are deliberating bodies that unite all stakeholders from each river basin district. Their composition is as follows: elected government officials (40%), water users (40%), and state representatives (20%). RBCs determine the strategy for the protection of water and aquatic environments for each river basin (the management plans for river basin districts – Schémas Directeurs d'Aménagement et de Gestion des Eaux, SDAGE). They vote on the water agency's action programme and the rate of fees within the limit of the rates set by law. The implementation of the intervention programme of the water agency (vote of the annual budget, fees, financial support) is administrated by the Administration Board within each water agency. The Administration Board, whose President is appointed by decree, is composed of administrators designated by and from the members of the river basin committee (elected officials and users), state representatives, and water agency staff representatives.

The budget of the financially autonomous water agencies is directly related to charges on water abstractions and discharges from all the users. On average, 90% of revenues collected by the water agencies are redistributed to water users of the river basin based on the water agency Action Plans, which is a legal document and is mandatory. The remaining 10% is used to fund the river agencies. There are three important principles implemented by the water agencies: "Polluter-Pays" and "User Pays" principles and "Water pays for water" principle, which implies that all the money collected should be used for water-related topics. There are rules to subsidise water users applied by the water agency: if the water user will invest in equipment, the rule foresees that the water agency will pay a certain percentage of the investment. So the water agency should check the eligibility, that the rules are met to provide the subsidy to the water users.

The framework and modalities of charges are defined at national level by the Parliament and modulated by the basin committees according to local priorities. Rates are defined for each agency with the agreement of the river basin committee. Charges are collected through the payment of the water service invoice. The water service operator transfers the amount of the charge to the basin agency. In the seventies, when the depollution investments were too high compared to the low amount of water charges for implementing the Polluter Pay principle, the Ministry of Environment engaged some industry sectors through contracts (*contrats de branche*) to distribute collected revenues from the industry sector, as subsidies to be used for investment in wastewater treatment plants or depollution systems. In the nineties water charges for the industry sector were tripled to comply with the Rhine Action Programme (1987). Most recent years were devoted to the compliance with the EU WFD and Urban Wastewater Directive.

In France, there are at least seven different water charges established by Law of 30 December 2006: water pollution charge, charge on non-point agricultural pollution, charge on water abstraction, charge or water storage in low flow periods (paid by the hydropower sector), charge on obstacle on rivers, charge for the protection of aquatic environments, charge for modernisation of the wastewater drainage systems. Water charges are decided by each water agency (river basin committee and water agency board) but they cannot be set above the (national) ceiling defined by French National Law.

Water users are required to hold a water entitlement to abstract water except for small scale domestic water abstractions (under 1 000 m3/ year). Entitlements are defined through a process of impact assessment and public inquiry. Abstraction authorisations are granted by local representatives of state administration. According to the abstracted volumes (above or under local thresholds), they can be submitted either to declaration or to authorisation (with a public inquiry). The Water Distribution Areas (Zones de Répartition des Eaux, ZRE) thresholds are lower than in other areas. Entitlements should be issued in conformity with the SDAGE and the national framework (respect of minimum thresholds for the ecosystem use of water). Water entitlements are unbundled from property titles and are granted for a few years to several decades for permanent use like drinking water abstraction. Six month entitlements can be granted for temporary uses (considered as uses without dramatic environmental impacts).

There are several long-term planning instruments at the hydrographic basin level (SAGE/SDAGE): Water Development and Management Plans are aimed at preventing crisis situations by planning offer (i.e. volumes that can be abstracted) and use (demand) over the long-term, and defining priorities in terms of water use. Limits on consumptive use through the volumes that can be abstracted are defined within SDAGEs and SAGEs. They are statutory instruments that must be followed, as all decisions (on water entitlements, etc.) are driven by the plans. Abstractable volumes have to be redefined after a few years to consider the latest available scientific data (Water Management Plans are re-defined every six years).

Water agencies are currently operating under the 10th programme which covers the years 2013 to 2018. Over these six years, the six water agencies plan to manage a budget of around EUR 13 billion (around EUR 2.2 billion/year). The agencies plan to collect about EUR 11.5 billion out of 13 in the form of water charges paid by the domestic sector, while the industrial sector should contribute around EUR 1 billion and the agricultural sector the rest. The domestic sector is thus the major contributor to the charges (80% to 90% of revenues come from this sector only).

In case of shortage, an "exceptional circumstances status" can be declared by a crisis unit, called the "Drought Unit". This unit is convened by the Prefect (the local representative of the State) and involves stakeholders. It is mandated to suspend prevailing entitlements and to allocate water according to a set list of priority uses, as defined in the decrees.

The Water Police (local representatives of central government administration) is responsible for monitoring and enforcement. For those not complying with the rules, there are two kinds of sanctions: administrative sanctions (from the formal notice to the suspension of the authorisation) and penalties, with fines (the fine can amount to EUR 1 500).

While the French system of water charges is often considered an international best practice, some of its limitations can inform water charging reforms in Brazil:

- The incentive power of the abstraction tax remains limited (for households in particular) since it represents a small share of the average price of water (around 12%). In 2013, the average price for water and wastewater sanitation services was 3.85 EUR/m3 while the abstraction tax was around 0.5 EUR/m3.
- There is currently no reference value for the scarcity costs on which charge rates on abstraction could be based. Consequently, it is difficult to judge whether the level of the tax is appropriate. Scarcity costs should be related to the pressure

exerted on the resource by the various users and higher tax rates should be imposed on uses that exert greater pressure. This principle does not seem to apply in general. For example, abstraction tax rates are higher for domestic users while volumes abstracted for drinking water supply are much lower than volumes abstracted for irrigation purposes. The pressure exerted on the resource can also be assessed through the difference between the volumes of water that are abstracted and the volumes that are returned to the environment. For example, it is estimated that around 90% of the volume used for cooling thermal and nuclear power plants is returned to the watercourse, while irrigation returns a small portion of its abstracted volume to the environment. The latter explains why rates for cooling purposes are quite low compared to other uses, but does not explain why rates for irrigation are lower than rates applied to drinking water supply knowing that almost all volumes used by households are returned to the environment after treatment.

- Users from the industrial and agricultural sectors are commonly over-represented in river basin committees compared to households, which may explain higher rates applied to drinking water supply.
- Ceiling (maximum rates) are set by the national law. It could be appropriate to also set minimum rates to avoid some uses to be charged close to zero.
- Exemptions could be better justified. It is unclear why activities such as aquaculture, which use a lot of water, are exempted and why the Single Collective Management Body (Organismes Uniques de Gestion Collective, OUGC) benefits from reduced tax rates even if abstracting water from ZREs. It is not known whether impact assessments were performed to justify these decisions.

Table 5.2. Governing water charges in England & Wales and France

	Setting water charges		Approval		Collection		Management	
	England & Wales	France	England & Wales	France	England & Wales	France	England & Wales	France
Who does what	The Environment Agency (EA): • designs the charging schemes and levels • can modify licences and permits	Water charges are decided by each water agency(river basin committee and water agency board) The charge rate follows guidelines set at national level in the Loi sur l'Eau et les Milieux Aquatiques [Law on Water and Aquatic Environments] (or LEMA) of 30/12/ 2006	Charges are approved by the relevant government minister in the Department for Environment Food and Rural Affairs (Defra)	Charge-rate can be re-modulated by the basin committees according to local priorities	The EA is responsible for the collection of all charges	Water agencies are in charge of the collection	The EA manages water resources and quality and the charges scheme	RBCs are in charge of the management plans for river basin districts The Administration Board within each water agency administers the action plan of the water agency

Table 5.2. Governing water charges in England & Wales and France (*cont.*)

	Setting water charges		Approval		Collection		Management	
	England & Wales	France	England & Wales	France	England & Wales	France	England & Wales	France
When	The main charge schemes are only reviewed when a major change is needed *The level of the charges is reviewed annually	Water charges have been operating under the 10h intervention programme of water agencies which covers 2013-18	Defra approves New schemes of charges, major changes, and the annual review of charge	Water charges are initially set for a period of 6 year. A formal vote from the water agency board is required for changing water charge rates	Charges are levied annually. Some can be paid quarterly	Foreseen budget management per year is EUR 2.2 million. Charges are levied in general annually	The EA proposes the need for reviews when necessary.	Water charges are redistributed through the Action Plan of each water agency
How (scale, co-ordination, laws, regulations, etc.)	Charges for abstraction are set by the EA on a regional basis to fund the water resource management activities in that region. Discharge charges are set nationally	The rates applied for calculating charges are defined for each agency with the agreement of the river basin committee. France complies with the EU WFD The System is regulated by Law of December 2006 (LEMA)	The National Audit Office can review and challenge the levels of charges and the efficiency of operational activities. The Parliamentary Public Accounts Committee (PAC) can also hold the EA and ministers to account	Basin committees can modulate levels of charges	The right to charge is set out in legislation, and allows the EA to recover the full costs of its water resource management activities	Water agencies financial autonomous is explained by their collection water charges		90% of revenues collected by the Water agencies are redistributed to water users of the river basin The remaining 10% is used to fund the river agencies. Water police is responsible for monitoring and enforcement

Source: Author's elaboration.

Spain

In Spain there are 17 River Basin Authorities (RBAs). Those dealing with trans-regional boundaries are closely linked to the Ministry of Agriculture, Fisheries and Environment, otherwise to Regional governments. There are three levels of management: central, regional and municipal. An important feature of the Spanish system is that RBAs were created before the regions, in 1926, avoiding possible conflicts over water management in the country. Municipalities are legally responsible for sanitation. There are more than 8 000 municipalities and 25 000 operators. This model is very fragmented, creating problems with nation-wide regulation (e.g. in terms of prices for water).

Water use in Spain like in many other countries is considered a public good and use is granted by the government. Licences are granted and managed by the RBAs, including decisions on any amendments (temporal or permanent). The 1999 water law reform paved the way for more flexible water allocation regimes including trading (Santato et al. 2016). The reform requires license or permit holders to pay a fee, determined by the RBA, for water use. As per interregional watersheds, this fee is either collected by the river basin authority or the tax administration. It also includes the use of the public water domain as a whole, including gravel extraction, water sports facilities, etc. Revenues from water charges are earmarked to protect and enhance the public water domain. When there is a formal agreement between the central and the regional governments, the latter may collect water pollution fees and transfer revenues to the RBAs.

As a European member country, Spain must comply with the overarching cost recovery principle included in the art. 9 of the EU Water Framework Directive. The Directive seeks to incorporate environmental and resources costs and provide adequate incentives for water users. The approach, however, is based on the recovery of incurred costs (all or part of them), and does not focus of water charges as a method to raise revenue, The implementation of water charges would help to tackle future water challenges such as an economic crisis or fiscal consolidation efforts that generate severe restrictions on public expenditure, and climate change related impacts, i.e. maintain water infrastructure efficiency and adapt water supply system to potentially decreasing bulk water resources. In other words, it is desirable to move towards a pricing scheme that is able to consider medium- and long-term objectives for enhancing water security and resilience, placing emphasis on long-term sustainable water availability levels, rather than on consumption levels.

Portugal

The 2005 Portuguese Water Law (Law No. 58/2005) established for the first time a very comprehensive system of water charges: the Water Resources Tax *(*Taxa de Recursos Hídricos). This framework law was complemented and detailed by the Decree-Law No. 97/2008 on the "Economic and Financial Regime of Water Resources."

In political terms, the process to establish the system of water charges in Portugal was not an easy one. The Polluter-Pays principle and the Beneficiary-Pays principle were established for the first time in the 1987 Framework Law for the Environment, but remained merely "ink in the paper". Six years later, in 1993, an attempt to approve the necessary regulations and implementation procedures failed to a large extent because of the resistance of the agriculture sector. It was necessary to wait for another 12 years and count on the strong incentive of the European Union Water Framework Directive (Directive 2000/60/EC) to make it possible and approve and implement those important pieces of legislation.

Meanwhile, a forceful and arduous negotiation with all water users was necessary, showing them the advantages of giving this financial "muscle" to the water resources administration and explaining to them that the largest share of the financial resources collected by water charges would be given back to water users through "programme-contracts" and other measures aiming at improving water management at the basin scale. The implementation of river basin councils (*Conselhos de Região Hidrográfica)*, with the participation of representatives of all water uses that would be effected by the charge collection, helped to pave the way and build consensus for a water abstraction charge. The idea that EU funds were coming to an end and that it was necessary to build on the sustainability of the water sector was underscored during discussions.

The system that was finally approved is very comprehensive and includes charges for water abstraction (volume) and all uses of the so called "public water domain," which includes any occupation of the bed and margins of a water body (including reservoirs) and the extraction of gravel and sand for construction. The tax promotes the idea that privative uses (both public and private) of water resources should compensate the cost generated to the community or restore the benefits to the community (User-Pays and Polluter-Pays principles). The tax aims at collecting funds for water management and guiding users towards a more efficient use of water and to allocate water where it creates most value.

A total of 50% of the amount collected in each one of the five hydrographic regions stays in that hydrographic region and is used in the implementation of the river basin plans or in other initiatives approved by the Hydrographic Region Council. While 10% goes to the National Water Authority (role currently played by the National Environmental Agency) to cover expenses at the national level, the remaining 40% goes to a National Environmental Fund and is used on a competitive basis to finance project proposals submitted by the hydrographic regions. This means that the hydrographic regions are guaranteed use at least 50% of the funds they collect. They can also apply for additional funds on a competitive basis and receive more revenue than what they collected. This is an effective way of promoting a national redistribution of resources, because those that need more funds are not necessarily those that are able of collecting them. This redistribution among regions, made through the National Environmental Fund, seems to be well accepted and is made on behalf of a sense of national solidarity among regions. The unit values of the water charges are approved by the Government and can only be changed by the Government through a Decree-Law that has to follow the general principles established by the Water Law (Law No. 58/2005).

Germany

In Germany, water abstraction charges have two main objectives: reduce abstraction and use revenues for environmental protection measures. Charges are volumetric and require the installation of meters for all water abstractors. Their introduction dates back the eighties and currently are in place in 11 out of the 16 federal states but they are not foreseen by the Federal Water Act.[2] Therefore, Landers are not obliged to use them and their design and application may vary from one Lander to another. Revenues are collected by regional administrations and go to state budget where they are earmarked for expenditure (with the exception of two Federal States). They can be used for nature conservation, protection of ground and surface water, reforestation, soil protection and decontamination. In seven Lander (e.g. in Berlin), part of the revenue is earmarked for groundwater protection (OECD, 2010). In North Rhine-Westphalia, the revenues are used for the administration and for supporting the implementation of the Water Framework Directive (Acteon 2010).

In Baden-Württemberg, water charges were introduced in 1987 and amended in 2010 through a participative process that saw stakeholders groups (energy industry, manufacturing industry, agriculture, water supply sector, and environmental and user associations) involved in the legislative process. The amendment was a consequence of a public hearing initiated by complaints from the industry, claiming lack of legislative back up of water abstraction charges. Eventually, the industry sector obtained from the negotiation the offset of the water abstraction charge with investments (Möller-Gulland and Lago, 2011).

Water pollution charges are paid for the discharge of wastewater containing certain contaminants into water bodies. The Federal Wastewater Charges Act (Abwasserabgabengesetz, AbwAG, 1976) and supplementary legal acts of the Lander (Federal Ministry for Environment, Nature Conservation, Building and Nuclear Safety, 2016) represent the legal framework in place. Revenues are usually collected by the Lander and used for improving water quality. In 2010, the amount charged corresponded to only 3% of the total water pollution control costs in industry, representing more a penalty tax for non-compliance with standards than an application of the Polluter-Pays principle. These charges can be modified by the parliament (Acteon, 2010).

Key issues in governing water charges in Brazil

Three main issues deserve particular attention for efficiently governing water charges in Brazil. They are sketched schematically below and further developed in the subsequent sections of this chapter:

- *Information*: Producing, updating and sharing consistent and comparable data and information on the state of environment and resources and to carry out the technical and socio-economic assessments, is crucial to guide, assess and improve water charges setting and implementation. However, the availability of good, accessible data and information on water varies across Brazilian states, preventing effective decision making in terms of who gets water, where and when and who pays for what (OECD, 2015b).
- *Scale*: Managing water charges at the appropriate scale implies reflecting local conditions (e.g. opportunity cost of using water, or pollution externalities); reaching across different agencies acting within and across states; as well as a common understanding of the state of the water resources, the pressures, and the actions needed to protect and improve the resource; and co-ordination between the different levels of government In Brazil, as a consequence of the double dominion generated by interstate rivers, water charges, in several cases, are applied and governed at both state and federal levels. This causes some issues with the enforcement of different water quality regulations and abstraction rules within the same interstate basin where two or more water management bodies are in charge of different sections of a river; the difference in terms of rates across federal and state domains and the consequences on water quantity and quality management where charges are not applied, even within the same state; the difference in the levels of expertise, capacity, and knowledge across agencies, with consequences on the ability to set and effectively implement charges.
- *Planning and spending*: River basin plans should drive decisions on what the *cobrança* is for in the basin and how to spend revenues collected through water charges. At the moment, plans do not set clear priorities or criteria that define available water resources and drive allocation decisions for hydropower development, irrigation extension and domestic and industrial use, amongst others. Planning is a responsibility of the river basin committees, which are endowed with strong deliberative powers, but have limited implementation capacity (OECD, 2015b). Their role in setting and governing water charges deserves specific attention for an outcome-oriented process. Revenues from water charges should be allocated to expenditures where they can make a difference, building on river basin plans and needs at hydrographic scale, and users should have information on how they are disbursed.

Information-based decision making and implementation

OECD (2015b) highlighted that effective water management requires a robust set of data to support decision-making. Implementing water charges requires a good understanding of how water is used and valued by competitive users. However, the availability and quality of hydrological, social and economic data varies across states, due to different levels of capacities, resources and expertise to collect, analyse and interpret them. A significant omission, in most of the states, is the lack of compelling information about the state of the ecology in each river. Hydro-ecological monitoring and assessment is essential in order to set discharge limits for pollutants, and to determine a sustainable flow regime.

Without a solid knowledge base any assessment of needs, efficiency and effectiveness of economic instruments will remain subjective. A robust and policy-relevant water information system should help assess the opportunity cost of using water; the cost of pollution and of poor river flow or groundwater management; affordability issues; impact of water charges on competitiveness of water users; as well as impact of abstraction charges on water use, on profits, on the revenue levied compared to financing needs, including infrastructure, amongst others.

The need for economic analysis for the design and implementation of efficient water resources management policies is well documented in the economics literature (see Birol et al., 2006). *Ex ante* economic analysis can help to guide decisions (Box 5.2). It can provide some hard facts and figures to overcome power struggles. For example, discussions at the French Water Agency Seine Normandie confirm that rates for water charges are primarily driven by revenue raising objectives, and differentiation among categories of users reflect political influence. However, economic valuation provides the initial frame within which such discussions take place.

International experience provides useful insights for better economic appraisal of water charges in Brazil. In the United Kingdom, the Environment Agency released a guide in 2013 to assist with the assessment of benefits for economic appraisal of measures which affect the water environment.[3] This can be used for river basin management planning and other disciplines where relevant. The main output from using this guide is a summary statement of the level of expected benefits compared to costs of implementing a bundle of measures at specific geographical scales (in particular, a river basin). In Canada, the Canadian Council for Ministers of the Environment (CCME) released a guidance document for water valuation in 2010.[4] The document concludes that relevant water valuation should account for two further aspects, in addition to practical issues: best practice in economic analysis, and stakeholder engagement.

Box 5.2. Examples of *ex ante* assessment of economic costs associated with water use

An interesting entry point is the report "An economic analysis of water use in the Scotland river basin district" published by the Scottish Environment Protection Agency (SEPA) in the United Kingdom. The report illustrates the links between the environmental effects and the value gained from different water uses and also examines the economic sectors that are associated with point source discharges, diffuse source discharges, abstraction and impoundment and alteration to physical habitat. This report also underlines the difficulties to get accurate data (on water use and non-water costs) at the river basin level to conduct such an assessment.

Brouwer (2004) proposes an assessment of environmental costs of water use in the Netherlands. In this framework, the environmental costs are approximated by looking at the costs of measures whose primary aim is to protect the water environment (cost-based approach).

Box 5.2. Examples of *ex ante* assessment of economic costs associated with water use (*cont.*)

The total environmental costs (mainly wastewater treatment costs) are estimated to be EUR 1.3 billion in 2000 for the Netherlands. The costs are calculated separately for industry, agriculture and the regional water services. This working paper has been used by the Drafting Group ECO2 in charge of the Common Implementation Strategy of the Water Framework Directive (EU Commission). Although this report is "legally non-binding" information sheet on the definition and assessment of environmental and resource costs has been used in the context of the implementation of the WFD by the EU.

More recently Kauffman (2011) has used a global assessment approach to estimate the socioeconomic value of water, natural resources and ecosystems in the Delaware River Basin. The socioeconomic value of water, natural resources and ecosystems in the Delaware River estimated as the sum of all values for all economic activities (including market use and non-use value of water supply, fishing, hunting, recreation, boating, ecotourism, agriculture, and navigation/port benefits in the basin), natural capital or ecosystem services value of natural goods and services provided by habitat (wetlands, forests, farms and open water) and jobs and wages directly and indirectly associated with the Delaware River Basin. Although Kauffman (2011) does not provide a formal computation of environmental and resource costs associated with water uses, it offers one of the most comprehensive economic analyses of water use at the river basin level.

Bithas et al. (2014) have proposed a method for calculating the environmental and resource cost. They rely on a monetisation for internalising the external costs of water users. This method is applied to Water Districts of Central and Western Macedonia, Greece. Results have been published in the Integrated River Basin Management Plans of Western and Central Macedonia Water Districts (WFD Directive) which is a formal legal document, under the Special Secretariat for Water of the Ministry of Environment and Climate Change in Greece, funded by Strategic National Reference Framework 2007-2013 (co-funded by the EU).

Sources: Brouwer R. and R. van der Veeren (2004), "Assessment of environmental and resource costs for the economic analysis in the WFD" , *RIZA working paper 2004.115x*, Lelystad, The Netherlands; Scottish Environment Protection Agency (n.d) , "An economic analysis of water use in the Scotland river basin district: Executive Summary" https://www.sepa.org.uk/media/37271/economic-analysis_water-use_scotland.pdf; Kauffman G. (2011), "Socioeconomic Value of the Delaware River Basin in Delaware, New Jersey, New York, and Pennsylvania", University of Delaware – Water Resources Agency; Bithas, K. et al. (2014), "The Water Framework Directive in Greece. Estimating the Environmental and Resource Cost in the Water Districts of Western and Central Macedonia: Methods, Results and Proposals for Water Pricing", *Procedia Economics and Finance*, Vol. 8, 2014, pp. 73-82

Information on water abstraction, return flows, and pollution loads should be consistent with the ambition and design of abstraction and pollution charges. Examples of information systems are provided in Box 5.3. Many countries, including Brazil, struggle to gather compelling and accurate information about who abstracts how much water, where, for what purpose and how much water is discharged and of what quality. As mentioned in Chapter 3, when abstraction charges are grounded on volumes of water used, sites must be routinely monitored for compliance, and the accuracy of the volumetric information submitted as the basis for billing. Yet, compliance remains a major challenge and very much influenced by cultural factors. The large number of small water users and the lack of a culture of compliance contribute to the problem, as do the limited use, high cost and maintenance issues associated with water meters (OECD, 2015b).

In relation to the effluent discharges, most charging schemes have a factor relating to the net loss, or proportion returned to the river. This can be assessed from the process involved, but in many cases the measurement of the effluent volume is a useful cross-check. More importantly, pollution charges should reflect the pollution load since this is a critical factor in discharge permits. The concentration of pollutants, and the volume discharged, both need to be monitored and enforced in order to manage load.

Box 5.3. Examples of information systems from Spain and Danube River

In **Spain**, SIA (National Integrated Water Information System) is aimed at collecting information on water management at a Central Government level (Ministry of Agriculture, Fisheries and the Environment) and a homogenised fashion (on the basis of common language and protocols).

It is also considered a support tool for the implementation of the EU Water Framework Directive (WFD), in other words, a reporting tool to report WFD data to the European Commission and EEA, through WISE (Water Information System for Europe) and to exchange data between river basin authorities (and regional water authorities) and the Central Government (nation-wide water authorities). SIA also promotes public participation and information use. It contains a database with information on the institutional and administrative framework, water management practices, the physical environment, meteorological data, water status, water uses, impacts, and infrastructures.

SIA interacts with other national information systems on water: SAIH (Automatic Hydrological Information System) and SIAR (Agro-climatic Information System for Irrigation). SAIH is an information system aimed at providing data (and graphic and geo-localised information) in real time for managing floods, droughts, associated risks, ecological flows (e-flows), water quality, and additional knowledge.

The International Commission for the Protection of the **Danube River** (ICPDR) also provides valuable insights on the possible uses of the information system of the EU Water Framework Directive for assessment of economic instruments. The ICPDR is the intergovernmental Commission responsible for co-operation in water management in the Danube Basin, which covers 600 000 km2 and has a population of about 80 million inhabitants. Although the ICPDR has not yet carried out any overarching assessment of the use of economic instruments in the Danube Basin, the information systems needed to facilitate collection of the necessary information in support of decision making, assessment and evaluation in river basin management exist. The information systems contain the information reported by Contracting Parties about the state of the water resources in the basin and the pressures on them. The information has so far been used by the Contracting Parties and the ICPDR to support the assessment of recovery of environmental costs and financing needs at the level of Contracting Parties or of the Basin.

The main elements of the information systems are:

- Water quality through the Transnational Monitoring Network (TNMN), which has been in operation in the Danube River Basin District (DRBD) since 1996. The major objective of the TNMN is to provide an overview of the overall status and long-term changes of surface water and, where necessary, groundwater status in a basin-wide context (with particular attention to the transboundary pollution load).
- Pollution discharges: Data are collected on treatment types or industrial technologies, on annual waste water, organic matter, nutrients and hazardous substances discharges at agglomeration or facility level over certain population or capacity thresholds, respectively. Data are integrated into the ICPDR database and are available for the stakeholders.

Box 5.3. Examples of information systems from Spain and Danube River *(cont.)*

- Groundwater abstraction (national information only): the concept of registers of groundwater abstractions is well developed throughout the Danube River Basin District. The Ministry of Environment and Water in Bulgaria maintains a national register of abstraction permits. A central register of groundwater abstractions based on the National Water Law is updated annually in Slovakia. In Hungary, a Groundwater Abstractions register is published yearly and it contains data on the withdrawals of the operating, monitoring and reserve wells. In Bavaria, water suppliers are obliged to report annual data to local authorities on overall water abstraction and specific abstractions from spring sources. Bavaria and Austria cooperate on the annual preparation of a register of abstractions from the thermal water of the Lower Bavarian – Upper Austrian molasses basin. In Romania, the National Administration "Romanian Waters" maintains the national register of abstraction permits according to the National Water Law.
- Danube GIS: This platform supports the ICPDR in its tasks related to spatial data, including data collection, management, and reporting. It is open to public users as well – providing access to data and maps for the whole Danube Basin. It is a common basis for data usage in the ICPDR supporting its reporting tasks – such as the implementation of the EU Water and Floods Directive (FD).

Source: Gonzalo Delacámara, Peer-Reviewer, IMDEA Water Institute (Spain) and Igor Liska, Alex Höbarth and Adam Kovacz of the ICPDR Secretariat.

The situation in Brazil

Register-entitle-enforce are three pillars of the Brazilian legislation and they have been implemented for a long time, although more or less effectively. While users' registries are reliable in the case of federal rivers for which water charges are implemented, this is not always the case in state basins. At federal level, a National Register of Users of Water Resources (Cadastro Nacional de Usuários de Recursos Hídricos, CNARH) was set up in 2003, data collection is in progress and integration with state systems is ongoing, although challenging. The CNARH is considered robust, especially where water charges have been implemented (São Francisco, Paraíba do Sul, PCJ and Doce River basins) but does not cover the entire country (OECD, 2015b). Water permits are important prerequisites for water charges, but there is still some uncertainty both for abstraction and discharges on how permits are assessed and enforced, conditions are applied, and how volumes are measured and reported. Finally, greater enforcement on permits could generate additional revenues from water charges. Illegal water abstraction, especially from groundwater, is also a problem that has proven difficult to quantify. Some statistics would be informative to guide decision-making as the size of the problem (illegal abstraction) may ultimately lead to over-abstraction of water resources.

Brazil counts with a National Water Resources Information System (Sistema Nacional de Informações sobre Recursos Hídricos, SNIRH); however, the availability of data for economic analysis is still lacking. Overall, there is little knowledge on the economic value generated by water uses (agriculture, industry, households, environment), useful to provide estimates of the impact of water charges on water users. The current lack of economic assessment of the actual impact of economic instruments, where they are used, weakens the case for reform. Some economic assessments of water use and water value at river basin level should be conducted. These assessments should serve as planning tools at river basin level.

In some cases, the lack of data or projections on users' ability to pay and wider needs of the basin has led to opt for rates that are generally similar across different basins and fail to reflect local conditions. The current state of play may actually reflect the low willingness to charge rather than affordability issues. In Brazil, at the level of the National and State Councils, estimates of the impacts on the cost structure of water users are carried out based on secondary data, in order to verify that the levels agreed within the river basin committees cause very low impacts.

Ways forward to strengthen the information base in Brazil

Having access to reliable water use data is a prerequisite for the economic instruments (including water charges) to potentially drive water use efficiency. Reliable data would make it possible to revise water entitlements so that, over time, they reflect actual use, thereby generating some room to reallocate available water, possibly to new comers, in basins where water was over-allocated but not over-used. Monitoring and modelling can help know how much water is available, who uses it, what the quality of effluents is and how it affects environmental sustainability and people's health; monitoring and modelling have a role also in assessing the interaction of charging policies with the multifactorial developments that impact on water resources and the related issues of economic development and welfare.

Economic assessments of water use and water value at river basin level should be conducted more systematically. These assessments should serve as planning tools at river basin level. Economic valuation provides the initial frame within which a discussion about the potential benefits – or lost opportunities – for the community of alternative allocation rules, who wins and who loses, the potential needs for compensation and orders of magnitude can take place. This information can support discussions about the opportunity cost of using water, or the cost of pollution and how these costs should be allocated among different categories of water users. Economic analyses can help investigate in detail the impact of water charges on affordability and competitiveness. As highlighted in Chapter 3, the use of simple proxies can help send consistent messages to water users, when sophisticated methodologies for economic assessment are difficult to be used.

For water charges to achieve expected outcomes, it is essential to have a clear understanding on who pays for what and with what consequences. Water charges are very often seen in Brazil as "the last instrument to be implemented": a robust *ex post* evaluation would help to understand what is the value added of water charges in this system and increase their acceptability. In addition, education and awareness raising would be essential to enhance the willingness to pay and the effectiveness of water charges.

The issue of scale

The situation in Brazil

The issue of double dominion raises the question of the "appropriate" scale for water resources management, stakeholder engagement and investment (Box 5.4). It also challenges the implementation of water charges. As highlighted in OECD (2015b), although hydrographic and administrative boundaries do not coincide in most countries, this "administrative gap" is exacerbated in the case of Brazil because of the double dominion and jurisdiction over state and federal rivers add complexity to the water resources management system. For example, it is difficult to enforce water quality regulations and water abstraction rules where two or more water management bodies are in charge of different sections of one river.

There are several consequences of the double dominion on water charges. One issue concerns the management of water charges through delegated water agencies, which in some cases are not foreseen by the state legislation or they are differently regulated across state and interstate river basin. In the case of Paraíba do Sul River Basin, for example, the AGEVAP is the delegated water agency for the Federal Government, and the States of Rio de Janeiro and Minas Gerais, while in the case of São Paulo is the DAEE, within the State Secretariat for Sanitation and Water Resources that carries out these duties. The 1998 law established that water agencies in the State of São Paulo are foundations and therefore are not compatible with the AGEVAP. The Agência das Bacias PCJ is the water agency for the rivers basin's portions that belong to the State of São Paulo and acts as delegated water agency for the Federal Government, but not for the Minas Gerais's portion of the basins, since the State of Minas Gerais would not be able to delegate foundation to act as delegated water agency. Nevertheless, the Agência das Bacias PCJ must act in compliance with all the different regulations of São Paulo and the Federal Government, as well present its accountings to each of them. In the Paranapanema River Basin waters are shared among the States of São Paulo, Paraná and the Federal Government. In this case the legislation of the State of Paraná do not foresees water agencies and the state authority for water management (*Instituto das Águas do Paraná*) plays this role. If the State of São Paulo will establish a water agency with the status of foundation for its portion in the Paranapanema River basin, there will be two different water agencies in the basin. The National Water Resources Council (CNRH) will then be able to delegate functions of water agency (for the Paranapanema River basin committee) to any of these institutions, or to both, or to a third one (ANA, 2016).

Another issue relates to the fact that there can be different governance models and charging systems within a same interstate river basin. Some have a single, integrated river basin committee where all stakeholders are gathered and take decisions on planning, charges and other management instruments; while others count many of such committees covering different parts of the basin. For instance, in the case of Rio Verde Grande, a common charging system needs approval by two different State Water Resources Councils as well as the National Water Resources Council. In interstate river basins charges have to be approved by their corresponding Water Resources Councils, regardless the existence of only one or more river basin committees.

Box 5.4. The double dominion and water charges in Brazil: Options to cope with challenges

The system of double dominion deriving from the Constitution raises problems of consistency in the criteria for granting permits for water abstraction or licenses for effluent discharge. Those inconsistencies result from the fact that the ANA is responsible for those criteria in the main channel of a river of the federal domain, but the states are responsible for the criteria in the tributaries of that same river if those tributaries are in the state dominion. Changing these prerogatives would require constitutional change, political negotiations and trade-offs. Therefore, the best option is to accept this double role, perform it as effectively and consistently as possible, and to consider low-cost options and alternatives based on specific problems to solve. A possible way of circumventing this problem is for the ANA to delegate to states some of its prerogatives on water allocation following commonly agreed guidelines and

Box 5.4. The double dominion and water charges in Brazil: Options to cope with challenges (*cont.*)

when capacity is in place, while retaining reserve powers to intervene if something is not in conformity with those guidelines. This approach can be implemented by the ANA to the extent considered convenient, overcoming the constitutional limitations imposed by the double dominion without requiring any change to the Constitution.

Devolution of responsibility may be a solution to some allocation issues. This is consistent with the Constitution and with the 9433 Water Law (Article 14, 1st paragraph) and there has been a precedent: the ANA has signed an agreement on the management of federal rivers with the Federal District, Minas Gerais, São Paulo and Ceará; these precedents confirm that devolution works well and is in line with the decentralised approach to water management in Brazil. Devolution will be contingent on sufficient capacity at the local level, which appears to be an issue in many states and can also be subject to "tenders": such an "à la carte" decentralisation process ensures consistency with the Constitution, gives the ANA the opportunity to warrant that federal waters will be allocated in ways that are consistent with policy objectives, and provides an incentive for states to strengthen their capacity. An instrument such as the Pact could be used to accompany such a gradual devolution of responsibility.

Source: OECD (2015b), *Water Resources Governance in Brazil*, OECD Publishing, Paris, http://dx.doi.org/10.1787/9789264238121-en.

Finally, there is the issue concerning the implementation of water charges. There are basins where charges have been applied at federal level, but not yet at all state levels, as in the case of the São Francisco, Doce and Paranaíba River basins.[5] This may also create limitations in terms of the financial autonomy of the water agencies, given the fewer resources available (ANA, 2016). Some delegated water agencies have to deal with both federal and state authorities and face difficulties in applying different set of rules, inspections and more or less stringent regulation.

Charges are agreed in river basin committees at levels that guarantee a consensus between their members. OECD (2015b) highlighted that river basin committees are endowed with strong deliberative powers, but have limited implementation capacity. In many instances, they play an advocacy role, while in most OECD countries their role is to build consensus on priorities and planning to guide decision making. One of the recommendations (from OECD, 2015b) called for strengthening the effectiveness of basin-level institutions for results-oriented engagement of stakeholders and full-fledged implementation of river basin plans (Box 5.5). In the case of water charges, one could wonder whether or not river basin committees are the right platforms to set the level of charges given the vested interest that can proceed from the most vocal users who will eventually pay the charge. This consultation capture can be conducive to defining charges at levels that will not deliver because they are too low to drive behavioural change from users (economic function) and to catalyse the needed funding for water management (financial function).

The lack of effectiveness of river basin committees has led to a downgrading in the representation of the various members. Municipalities are much less represented and quasi absent from these deliberative bodies. In practice, the Interest-Pay-Say principle is applied in a way that limits the impacts of decisions due to short term interests. Water charges can certainly bring new dynamics to river basin committees, by triggering greater engagement of water users. However, it seems that keeping the *status quo* represents the easiest and less risky option, making nobody either happy or unhappy.

Box 5.5. The role of river basin committees in Brazil: Options for reform

River basin committees should act as co-ordination mechanisms to bridge the "administrative gap" and fit water policies to places; in practice, however, they face challenges. River basin committees have deliberative functions that give them significant powers with limited means of implementation, contrary to public authorities. The divide between public authorities and civil society in the committees is increasing with respect to priorities for water decision making. Water plans lay out what needs to be done, but they are not always implemented, which discourages water users, especially when river basin committees mainly complain and denounce problems rather than provide a forum to help executive powers find solutions.

Some actions could be foreseen:

- **Create committees only when executive powers in a river basin are clarified and effective:** this may require specific legislation and an investment in improving the capacities of relevant institutions first, before formalising such institutions as, according to the specific circumstances, a basin agency linked to the state water agency; or the state water agency itself.
- **Define "forms" of institutions according to their intended "functions":** indeed, there is some paradox in giving deliberative powers to the river basin committees and keeping all executive powers in the state agencies. The committees approve river basin plans, but frequently do not have means for implementing them and the state agencies cannot either, because plans are not diligent enough, realistic nor feasible. This situation is at the origin of frustration and abandonment.
- **Reinforce the consultative role of the councils and committees (from basin to national level), and concentrate deliberative powers and executive powers in the state (and federal) agencies:** This would match decision making to capacity and accountability lines, and result in less unimplemented decisions. This way forward does not imply deflating the role of the national and state water resources councils or overlooking the role of basin committees. The flip side of a change in this direction should be the strict obligation of the state (and federal) agencies to consult with the "advisory" councils and the committees, and give thorough explanations when they do not follow their advice, in order to guarantee transparency and accountability.

Source: OECD (2015b), *Water Resources Governance in Brazil*, OECD Publishing, Paris, http://dx.doi.org/10.1787/9789264238121-en.

The geographical scales of governance structures for existing river basins in Brazil have an impact on efficiency and inclusiveness of water charges. While France faces the challenge of bringing the six major committees closer to local actors, Brazil faces the opposite challenge of building governance structures at the regional scale from existing and consolidated committees at the local level. In France, since the seventies, the Seine-Normandie Committee has managed to convince its members that the water charging system was an efficient one, thus contributing to its acceptance by water users and opening up the possibility to increase the values for the agency's second intervention programme (1972-75). Such a collective dynamic was only possible because the City of Paris, the main beneficiary of financial aid from the water agency and the main source of recovery, was located in the basin and its representatives were influential members of the committee. In Brazil, the level of charges in the PCJ in 2013 was ten times lower than the charges applied in 1975 in Seine-Normandie. A committee on the scale of the River Tietê unit, in addition to the interstate Committee PCJ would allow water management issues to be discussed at a relevant hydrological scale, bringing together representatives from the

Metropolitan Region of São Paulo and representatives of the PCJ basin where the Cantareira System is implemented. A basin agency at the Tietê River scale would be comparable to the Seine-Normandie agency, including in the possibility of raising larger amounts by charging water uses (OECD, 2015b).

Ways forward to manage water charges at the right scale

River basin committees would gain influence, credibility and effectiveness in having a consultative rather than deliberative role in setting the charges. As underscored above, the main issue is that river basin committees are run mainly by water users that ultimately will pay the charges, and that water charges are agreed between the users that may have interest in keeping the *status quo* (no or low water charges).

Decisions on charges should be backed up by economic analyses made by technical/managing bodies. Water agencies could have this role, but should be independent from any user interest within the river basin committees. At the moment, the administrative councils (the 'assembly of members' and fiscal councils) of each of delegated water agency is composed, amongst others, by users. Delegated water agencies should ensure independent advice on water charging.

A realistic distinction between the role assigned to stakeholders in the "consultation" and "decision-making" process needs to be made. Public authorities and democratic platforms can secure the public interest and manage trade-offs as they arise. Although against prevailing winds in Brazil and the historical background for creating councils throughout the country in different policy domains, an open and documented debate on the effectiveness of current "deliberative" bodies in water resources management and their capacity to be outcome and result-driven is much needed.

Experience from OECD countries shows that river basin committees are best-placed to identify and try to reconcile diverging interests after thorough consultation of all those who have a stake in the outcome at a given scale. Stakeholder engagement for water charge setting could follow some basic principles, including the need to clarify the different levels of engagement (from information-sharing to consultation all the way through co-production) as well as the ultimate decision-making line (stakeholder engagement does not necessarily imply co-decision) and how the inputs from stakeholders are used in the latter (OECD, 2015c).

Given the co-existence and complementarity of federal and state water resources management systems in Brazil, guidance on how to design and govern water charges should also be provided at both scales. First, as highlighted in Chapter 3, there is scope and need for national rules or principles setting the rationale for water charges and providing advice on their level, process and structure. Such a role could be discharged by the CNRH, which technical chamber on water charges has been discussing room for improvement in this area, building on its multi-stakeholder representation. The process for developing such a guidance could be supported by the ANA. Second, there is also scope for more detailed, place-based and tailored guidance at basin/state level, which takes into account local conditions, risks and hydrography to set minimum and maximum thresholds needed for water charges, to contribute to sustainable growth.

Delegated water agencies play a key role in managing revenues of water charges. Although their future requires some clarifications in the legal framework, there may be room for considering further opportunities to create a single water agency in big interstate basins to foster co-ordination across states. The creation of actual water agencies for each basin (not delegated ones) as well as a single water agency in big interstate river basins holds potential to ensure a common *modus operandi* at a larger scale. However, this much relies on states' sovereignty to choose their preferred management model. To fulfil their role of technical bodies in supporting decision making for water charges, they should be independent by any users influence.

The issue of scale is compounded by the fact that different agencies acting within and across states have different levels of expertise, capacity, and knowledge. This severely affects their ability to set appropriate charges. The ambition should be, for each river basin, a common level of understanding of the state of the water resources, the pressures, the actions needed to protect and improve the resource, the controls on permits, and how all these translate into a coherent and consistent charging regime across the various agencies that operate within the basin.

Planning and spending issues

The situation in Brazil

Water charges and water resources management plans are strongly interrelated. Water resources management plans, or river basin management plans set policy priorities to which water charges are expected to contribute. However, this hardly occurs in practice in Brazil. OECD (2015b) concluded that plans are poorly co-ordinated and weakly implemented partly because of the disconnection between those (stakeholders) who design them and those (public authorities) in charge of prioritising actions and finance. Although technically valid, basin plans often are a collection of "to do-s", lacking assessment of implementation costs and financial feasibility, thus creating a risk of setting unrealistic objectives. As reported in OECD (2015b) plans could shift from a "programme" approach, which always requires someone else to implement, to a "target" approach. An example would be to define water quality targets, limits in water consumption and pollution loads, and standards for water use efficiency to be reflected into water permit systems. Targets not met could then be subject to sanctions.

The non-mandatory nature of the basin plans makes them mostly unable to ensure the necessary constructive engagement in the various sectors; in OECD (2015b), they were qualified as "paper tigers" or "promises for others to fulfil". Prerequisites for effective planning should rely on both proactive actions (e.g. public organisations like the ANA taking steps to develop permits) and reactive levels (developing a set of rules for those requesting permits). Planning as a multi-level, multipurpose and multi-stakeholder governance instrument raises three main questions: planning for what (e.g. collection of charges, co-ordination, and implementation); planning with whom (which institutions need to be engaged); and lastly planning at which scale (local, basin, state, federal).

The reason why water charges in Brazil do not bite or are considered irrelevant also derives from the fact that they are collected with no visible purpose and therefore are seen as mere fiscal instruments. Sometimes revenues are allocated to investment programmes (such as water supply and sanitation) which are several orders of magnitude larger: hence, they do not make a difference, and users cannot appreciate their added-value. Or collected funds, when used, are scattered in minor expenses that are not recognised by the payers as being important. This can affect water users' willingness to pay water charges.

Poor performance in the allocation of revenues raises criticism towards the federal water resources management system and is used as an argument to reinforce the view that there is actually no need to increase the amounts collected because they do not play their intended role in any case. There is a strong concern, especially from the representatives of water users, that amounts collected might be quickly disbursed in order to achieve water resources improvements. There is no acceptance that some resources should be available for eventualities. In turn, the delegated water agencies claim that with the amounts currently collected, they cannot properly structure themselves to fulfil their duties and, consequently, their capacity to disburse resources effectively is affected. The approach adopted by Ceará (see Chapter 2) may be a way of circumventing deadlocks, although it is not clear if it can be replicated under different circumstances. International examples on how revenues are spent are reported in Box 5.6. Table 5.3 reports the unbalance between money transferred and disbursed in four river basins from the federal domain.

Table 5.3. The use of resources from water charges in four interstate river basins

Year 2016

Interstate River Basins	Delegated Water Agencies	Transfer of Funds + Income	Disbursement of Resources	Disbursement Resources Index
Paraíba do Sul	AGEVAP	137 860 770	91 036 060	66%
Piracicaba, Capivari e Jundiaí	Fundação Agência das Bacias PCJ	173 535 992	147 676 543	85%
São Francisco	Agência Peixe Vivo	137 812 342	90 658 028	66%
Doce	IBIO – AGB Doce	38 669 895	20 947 124	54%
TOTAL		**519 776 716**	**284 633 350**	**72%**

Source: ANA (2017), "Valores Cobrados e Arrecadados", http://www2.ana.gov.br/Paginas/servicos/cobrancaearrecadacao/cobrancaearrecadacao.aspx (accessed August 2017).

Since water charges are considered public resources, control on the expenditure is the same as that applied to public entities managing public funds. It requires going through a bidding process, which limits how money can be spent. At federal level, legal and administrative procedures hamper access to the resources of private sector borrowers. The 1997 Federal Water Law does not contain restrictions on financing private organisations. Instead, art. 22 provides that the amounts collected will be used to finance actions included in water resource plans, which contain measures to be undertaken by public or private organisations. The amounts may be applied as non-refundable investments in projects and construction works that change, in a way considered beneficial, for the community, the quality, the quantity and the flow regime of a body of water (ANA, 2016). However, legal interpretations of public administrations refer to other regulations hindering aid for investments to be incorporated to the assets of private companies for profit.

It is also not possible to use the amounts collected to compensate users financially, for example, when during a water restriction period their water usage is restricted in favour of other uses. Another example of restrictive administrative constraint is the 70% obligation to assign the revenue to sanitation in the State of Rio de Janeiro (see Annex B).

Box 5.6. Spending revenues from water charges: International experiences

Revenues from water abstraction or pollution charges are commonly earmarked.

- In **Germany** revenues from abstraction charges are spent on, among other things, restoration and maintenance of surface water, protection of groundwater, and to finance water-related projects in agriculture and forestry.
- In **Belgium**, revenues are re-used to fund water-related investments.
- In **South Africa**, as from 1 April 2002, the water resource management charge was introduced to fund a portion of the water resources management activities to protect, allocate, conserve, manage and control the nation's water resources.
- In the **Czech Republic** fees collected from polluters (including wastewater discharge fees) accrue to the State Environmental Fund. This fund, which also receives support from the EU, is then used to offer financial support in the form of subsidies or loans to projects aiming at environmental improvement.
- In **France**, the largest part of this expenditure is aimed at ensuring compliance with the European Water Framework Directive (DCE 2000/60/CE) and French environmental regulation on wastewater treatment and the (good) ecological status of surface water (including addressing the problem of nitrate and pesticide pollution originating from agriculture).

Source: Acteon (2010), "Economic instruments for mobilising financial resources for supporting IWRM", additional information and illustrations for the OECD initiative, https://search.oecd.org/environment/resources/46228724.pdf; DWA (n.d.), Water Resources management charges; www.dwa.gov.za/projects/warms/docs/pdf/leafletforest.pdf; DWA (2013), "Revised Water Pricing Strategy for Raw Water III Draft for comment", https://www.dwa.gov.za/projects/perr/documents%5crevised%20pricing%20strategy%2027-09-2013.pdf.

Even when funds are available, their allocation is jeopardised by the lack of capacity of small municipalities in submitting projects. Small municipalities show low levels of capacities when it comes to set projects, access the funds and finally implement the actions. This follows a lack of technical and human resources. In some OECD countries the creation of co-ordination mechanisms such as inter-municipal co-operation helped to share information, build capacities and create the critical mass for investment.

Ways forward for basin plans to drive decisions on charging and spending

Plans should be robust and practical enough to guide decisions on the allocation of revenues (when available). They should identify the priority areas for action on water resources management, on the basis of objective criteria that would take into account primarily health risks, social issues, the environment and the economy. This is only possible if quantitative information about the state of the environment is available. Otherwise it is difficult for plans – and actions – to deliver any meaningful benefits. Plans should quantify realistically the financial resources needed to take action, and list specific actions for specific organisations that can help drive behaviour change and foster water use efficiency.

Discussions on water charges and their expenditures tend to overshadow the importance of the plan itself. The plan could specify what kind of measures should be financed by the public administration, and what would fall under the private domain. Basin plans should be accompanied by strategic financial plans, tailored to an agreed action plan and affordable timescales for implementation. River basin plans should be integrated with other plans (e.g. for agriculture development or sanitation) as they can contribute to enhance water security. Charges should effectively address the issues of scarcity and pollution and that they are co-ordinated with other policy priorities.

Municipalities should be incentivised to participate in river basin plan development and implementation because they deal with critical areas related to water management including environment licensing, land use and solid waste management. Further discussions would be needed to determine incentives that can be set at state and federal levels to upscale municipalities' engagement in water resources management and to raise their level of awareness on the negative impact of poor water management on their core fields of intervention and the other way around. Management pacts, such as the Progestão, could be applied between states and municipalities in setting priorities and deliver agreed objectives.

Revenues from water charges should be allocated to expenditures in line with the initial objective and where they can make a difference. For instance, it is counterproductive to allocate revenues from water charges to large infrastructure projects, to which their contribution is minimal. The issue of the access by private borrowers should be solved in order to favour initiatives that can allow the achievement of the objectives foreseen in the river basin plan, such as water conservation measures, but also to trigger greater willingness to pay through a clearer understanding of the direct benefits/return of charges to users.

Promoting transparency on how revenues from water charges are used could ultimately be an incentive for users to pay and even understand and accept increases. Federal authorities (e.g. ANA) could consider setting guidelines or principles to design spending programmes that will be funded by revenues from charges and that will have a positive impact for users in the basin. The decentralised nature of the system would however need to be preserved, with river basin committees deciding on the specific modalities for adapting these guidelines to their context.

Notes

1. EA (n.d.), Environmental Agency, www.gov.uk/government/organisations/environment-agency (accessed August 2017).

2. Federal Minister for Environment, Nature Conservation, Building and Nuclear Safety (n.d.), Water protection policy in Germany, www.bmub.bund.de/en/topics/water-waste-soil/water-management/policy-goals-and-instruments/water-protection-policy-in-germany/ (accessed August 2017).

3. EA (2013), Water Appraisal Guidance; Assessing Costs and Benefits for River Basin Management, www.ecrr.org/Portals/27/Publications/Water%20Appraisal%20Guidance.pdf (accessed August 2017).

4. CCME (2010), Water Valuation Guidance Document, www.ccme.ca/files/Resources/water/water_valuation/water_valuation_en_1.0.pdf (accessed August 2017).

5. In São Francisco Basin there is the *cobrança* in the Rio das Velhas and Rio Pará (State of Minas Gerais), while in the Doce Basin, the cobrança is implemented for all the 6 Minas Gerais' RBCs, but not for the Espirito Santo State.

References

Acteon (2010), "Economic instruments for mobilising financial resources for supporting IWRM", additional information and illustrations for the OECD initiative, https://search.oecd.org/environment/resources/46228724.pdf.

ANA (2017), "Valores Cobrados e Arrecadados", http://www2.ana.gov.br/Paginas/servicos/cobrancaearrecadacao/cobrancaearrecadacao.aspx (accessed August 2017).

ANA (2016), "Background report on setting and governing economic instruments for water policy in Brazil", Agência Nacional de Águas, Brasilia.

Birol, E., K. Karousakis and P. Koundouri (2006), "Using economic valuation techniques to inform water resources management: a survey and critical appraisal of available techniques and an application", Science of the Total Environment, Vol. 365, pp. 1055-122, http://dx.doi.org/10.1016/j.scitotenv.2006.02.032.

Bithas, K. et al. (2014), "The Water Framework Directive in Greece. Estimating the Environmental and Resource Cost in the Water Districts of Western and Central Macedonia: Methods, Results and Proposals for Water Pricing", Procedia Economics and Finance, Vol. 8, 2014, pp. 73-82

Brouwer R. and R. van der Veeren (2004), "Assessment of environmental and resource costs for the economic analysis in the WFD", RIZA working paper 2004.115x, Lelystad, The Netherlands

CCME (2010), Water Valuation Guidance Document www.ccme.ca/files/Resources/water/water_valuation/water_valuation_en_1.0.pdf (accessed August 2017).

DWA (n.d.), Water Resources management charges; www.dwa.gov.za/projects/warms/docs/pdf/leafletforest.pdf.

DWA (2013), "Revised Water Pricing Strategy for Raw Water III Draft for comment", https://www.dwa.gov.za/projects/perr/documents%5crevised%20pricing%20strategy%2027-09-2013.pdf.

EA (n.d.), Environmental Agency, www.gov.uk/government/organisations/environment-agency (accessed August 2017).

EA (2013), Water Appraisal Guidance; Assessing Costs and Benefits for River Basin Management Planning, www.ecrr.org/Portals/27/Publications/Water%20Appraisal%20Guidance.pdf (accessed August 2017).

EEA (European Environment Agency) (2013), "Assessment of cost recovery through water pricing", Technical report No. 16, http://waterfund.go.ke/toolkit/downloads/cost%20recovery%20through%20water%20pricing%20(eea).pdf.

Federal Minister for Environment, Nature Conservation, Building and Nuclear Safety (n.d.), Water protection policy in Germany, www.bmub.bund.de/en/topics/water-waste-soil/water-management/policy-goals-and-instruments/water-protection-policy-in-germany/ (accessed August 2017).

Kauffman G. (2011), "Socioeconomic Value of the Delaware River Basin in Delaware, New Jersey, New York, and Pennsylvania", University of Delaware – Water Resources Agency

OECD (2015a), "OECD Principles on Water Governance", welcomed by Ministers at the OECD Ministerial Council Meeting on 4 June, www.oecd.org/cfe/regional-policy/OECD-Principles-on-Water-Governance-brochure.pdf.

OECD (2015b), *Water Resources Governance in Brazil*, OECD Publishing, Paris, http://dx.doi.org/10.1787/9789264238121-en.

OECD (2015c), *Stakeholder Engagement for Inclusive Water Governance*, OECD Publishing, Paris, http://dx.doi.org/10.1787/9789264231122-en.

OECD (2011), *Water Governance in OECD Countries: A Multi-level Approach*, OECD Publishing, Paris, http://dx.doi.org/10.1787/9789264119284-en.

OECD (2010), *Pricing Water Resources and Water and Sanitation Services*, OECD Publishing, Paris, http://dx.doi.org/10.1787/9789264083608-en.

Santato, S., J. Mysiak and C. Dionisio Pérez-Blanco (2016), "The Water Abstraction License Regime in Italy: A Case for Reform?", *Water 2016*, pp. 8-103.

Scottish Environment Protection Agency (n.d). , "An economic analysis of water use in the Scotland river basin district: Executive Summary", https://www.sepa.org.uk/media/37271/economic-analysis_water-use_scotland.pdf.

Annex A

The Paraíba do Sul River basin

The Paraíba do Sul River Basin: Water charges pioneer in Brazil

The Paraíba do Sul River basin represents an interesting case-study on the implementation of water charges in Brazil for two primary reasons: i) it was the first interstate basin in the country to implement water charges, helping to improve the legal and institutional framework for the water charges system and serving as example for other basins; ii) it presents socio-economic characteristics that deserve special attention when implementing water charges aiming at changing users' behaviour towards greater water security, e.g. highly urbanised and industrialised area subject to conflicts over multiple-uses.

The Paraíba do Sul River basin covers an area of 55 500 km^2 in the southeast region of Brazil, 37.7% of which is located in the State of Rio de Janeiro, 37.3% in the State of Minas Gerais, and 25% in the State of São Paulo. It covers 184 municipalities, the majority of which is in Minas Gerais (88), and has a total population of 5.2 million. The basin is an urbanised (96% of population lives in the urban areas) and industrialised area, producing about 13% of the country's GDP. It accounts for 1.75% of the country's hydroelectric potential and supplies 85% of water in the metropolitan area of Rio de Janeiro, transferring water from the Paraíba do Sul River basin into the Guandu River basin. Another water transfer is foreseen from Jaguari River (a Paraíba do Sul's tributary) to the dams of the Cantareira System (PCJ River basins).

The area is exposed to critical water risks that include drought, pollution and competing uses. The Paraíba do Sul hydraulic system, which encompasses three reservoirs (called equivalent reservoir- *reservatório equivalente*), has a total reserve capacity of 7 294.70 million cubic meters (Da Costa et al., 2015). Currently, it accounts for above 50% of its capacity, but by the end of 2014 the stock was only 2.7%. A new reservoir management model was recently adopted to address overdrawing issues (see Box A.1). The area also confronts other issues related to water pollution and conflicts over multiple water uses (ANA, 2016a).

Figure A.1. The Paraíba do Sul River basin

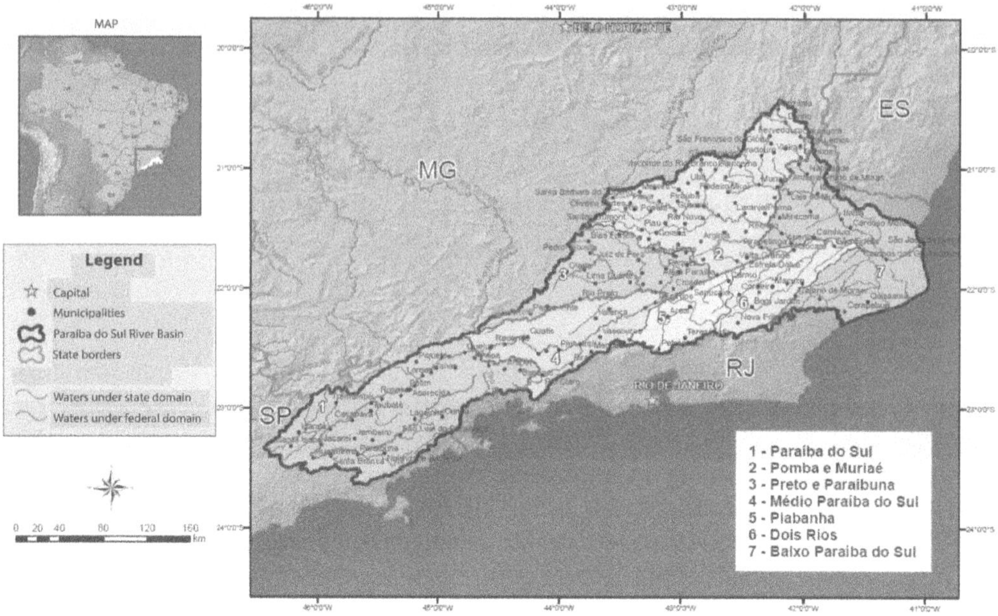

Source: ANA (2017), Mapa da Bacia Hidrográfica do Rio Paraíba do Sul, http://arquivos.ana.gov.br/institucional/sag/CobrancaUso/BaciaPBS/_img/MapaPBS_05062013.pdf.

Box A.1. The New Management of Reservoirs in the Paraíba do Sul River Basin

The Water crisis in 2014 led to a new reservoir management system for the Paraíba do Sul River Basin. The new system seeks to promote more integrated use of water, guaranteeing water security to meet drinking water and sanitation needs, energy production, and future uses, e.g. the expansion of the Guandu treatment station and the interconnection between Jaguari reservoirs in the Paraíba do Sul and Atibainha in the Cantareira System.

A Joint Resolution by ANA, DAEE, IGAM and INEA No. 1.382/2015 provides for new operating conditions of the river basin's reservoirs. It was a joint resolution encompassing waters under federal and state domain: ANA for waters under federal domain, DAEE for waters under domain of the State of São Paulo, IGAM for waters under domain of the State of Minas Gerais, and INEA for waters under domain of the State of Rio de Janeiro. The resolution reduces levels of minimum flow and defines depletion (reduction) stages for each of the reservoirs installed in the river basin. The new management system also seeks to foster co-ordination and joint decision-making across state and federal governments for decisions on the reservoirs.

Source: ANA (2016b), Entram em vigor novas regras de operação para a bacia do Paraíba do Sul www2.ana.gov.br/Paginas/imprensa/noticia.aspx?List=ccb75a86-bd5a-4853-8c76-cc46b7dc89a1&ID=13131 and interviews with stakeholders during the second OECD mission.

Water charges in practice

In 2003, the Paraíba do Sul River basin was the first to implement water charges under federal domain. Water charges rates employed in the basin and the methodology used were a benchmark for other river basins at state and interstate level, which have employed similar methodologies and rates (although after 2006, the methodology developed in the PCJ River basin was used in the Paraíba do Sul River basin).[1] Water charges exist also under the state domain: first in the State of Rio de Janeiro (2004), followed by in the States of São Paulo (2007) and Minas Gerais (2010).

In 2016, abstraction and consumption (quantitative use) represented 81% of the total charged, while BOD (qualitative use) accounted for the remaining 19% (ANA, 2017; Figure A.2). Over a ten-year period starting in 2003, the number of users (and payers) increased from 186 to 307 (ANA, 2014). Between 2003 and 2016, the Paraíba do Sul River basin collected about BRL 141 million (excluding revenues from the Guandu transfer). In 2016 from the sanitation sector contributed the most (70%), followed by the industrial sector (27%) (Figure A.3).

Figure A.2. Water charges by type of use in the Paraíba do Sul basin

2016

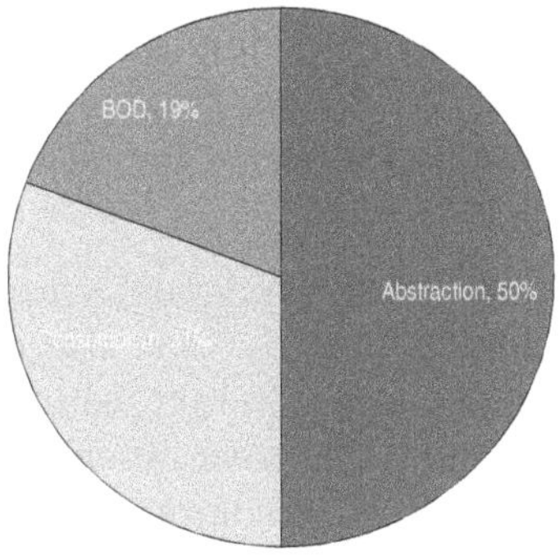

Source: ANA (2017), "Valores Cobrados e Arrecadados", www2.ana.gov.br/Paginas/servicos/cobrancaearrecadacao/cobrancaearrecadacao.aspx (accessed August 2017).

Figure A.3. Proportion of water use charge by sector in the Paraíba do Sul basin

2016

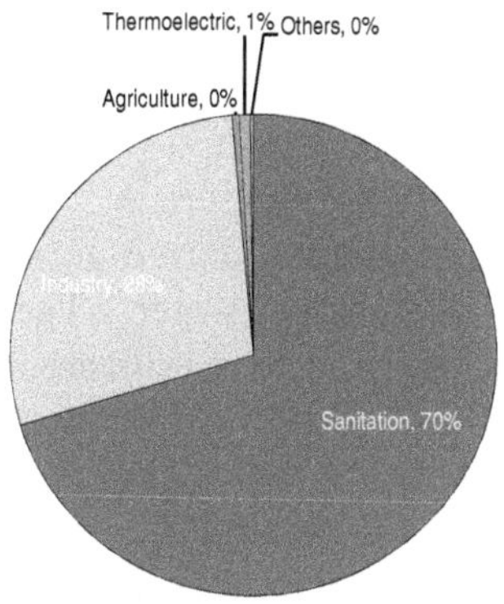

Source: ANA (2017), "Valores Cobrados e Arrecadados", http://www2.ana.gov.br/Paginas/servicos/cobrancaearrecadacao/cobrancaearrecadacao.aspx (accessed August 2017).

According to empirical studies water charges in the Paraíba do Sul River basin may act as an effective instrument to entice firms to undertake water reuse investments. Since plants are more likely to adopt water reuse, policymakers could increase the value of water charges so as to provide firms with incentives to implement water reuse practices. Alternatively, as reuse decisions also seem to be influenced by the price of capital, part of the water charge revenues collected within the Paraíba do Sul River basin could be used to direct subsidies to firms intending to adopt water reuse practices (Féres and Reynaud, 2012). Féres et al. (2012) investigate which factors play a role in explaining firms' decision making concerning water reuse and whether the structure of intake water demand differs between firms that do and do not adopt water reuse practices. Data used come from the industrial water use survey conducted by the Institute for Applied Economic Research (IPEA) in the Paraíba do Sul River Basin. The survey collected comprehensive water-related information on 488 industrial plants located within the basin area for the year 2002.

The legal and institutional framework for water charges

According to the 1997 Federal Water Law, water charges for federal waters are proposed by the interstate river basin committee, set by the Nacional Water Council, and operationalised by a delegated water agency that manages the revenues collected and transferred by ANA as agreed through a management contract. In practice, the Paraíba do Sul River Basin Integration Committee (Comitê de Integração da Bacia Hidrográfica do Rio Paraíba do Sul, CEIVAP) sets the charges and the National Water Resources Council (CNRH), which establishes general criteria for the charges for federal waters, approves the proposal of the CEIVAP.

The CEIVAP was created in 1996 (Federal Decree No. 1.842/1996, modified in 2008). It is composed of 60 members: 40% water users (drinking water and sanitation companies, industries, hydropower, agricultural, fishing, tourism and leisure sectors); 35% public authorities (federal and state governments and prefectures) and 25% civil society organisations. The CEIVAP is in charge of approving the river basin water resources management plan, establishing mechanisms for calculating the charges, and suggesting the values for the charges. There are eight river basin committees for the Paraíba do Sul River: one at interstate level (CEIVAP), one in the State of São Paulo and two in the State of Minas Gerais, and four in the State of Rio de Janeiro. Not all the river basin committees within this area have drafted a state plan. In some cases, a list of actions is available that was drafted following CEIVAP's guidelines.

The ANA is responsible for billing water charges and transfer revenues to AGEVAP, which is in charge of managing them within the whole basin and according to the river basin plan (Figure A.4). The AGEVAP is a non-profit organisation created in 2002, six years after the creation of the CEIVAP (Figure A.5). Through a management contract signed with ANA in 2004, the Association started acting as delegated water agency for managing revenues collected in federal water. The AGEVAP also signed other management contracts for managing revenues collected in state waters (for the State of Rio de Janeiro in 2010 and the State of Minas Gerais in 2014). By Law, the creation of the agency represented a prerequisite for water charges implementation and in particular to make sure that revenues generated through charges would return to the basin. The Paraíba do Sul River Basin pilot experience was used to solve ambiguities in the legislation and to clarify the relationship across levels of government regarding managing revenues from water charges. Before delegating water charges management to the AGEVAP, the ANA served as the water agency. As such, revenues were considered part of the National Treasury raising concerns that revenues from water charges would not return to the basin (Abers and Keck, 2013). The AGEVAP is a key basin institution that carries out capacity building programmes for municipalities, especially those below 5 000 inhabitants, which the lack human and technical capacities to design projects and access necessary funds to put them in practice.

Figure A.4. The water use charge cycle in the Paraíba do Sul River basin at federal level

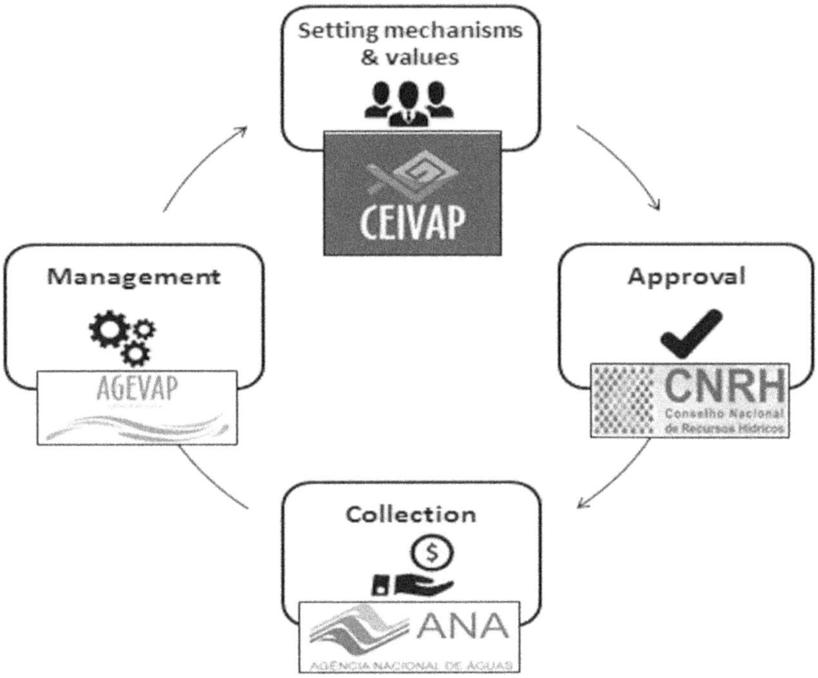

Source: Authors' elaboration.

The water charge in the Paraíba do Sul River basin was established in 2003 to improve the quantity and quality of the waters within the basin. The current mechanisms and rates are regulated by the CNRH Resolution 162/2014; however, formal discussions on mechanisms and values started within CEIVAP in 2001. The charge is linked to the emission of permits for abstracting and consuming water and discharging effluents. Users register with the Integrated Management System of the Paraíba do Sul River Basin (Sistema de Gestão Integrada da Bacia do rio Paraíba do Sul, GESTIN) that is linked to the National Register of Users of Water Resources (Cadastro Nacional de Usuários de Recursos Hídricos, CNARH).

The AGEVAP carried out an assessment on the implementation of the water charge *cobrança* for the period 2001-06. Although some obstacles were identified, the report encourages the use of these instruments in other basins as well as in depth review of the collection mechanisms for the transposition of Paraíba do Sul into the Guandu River (AGEVAP, 2012).

Figure A.5. Timeline of the water charges implementation in the Paraíba do Sul River basin

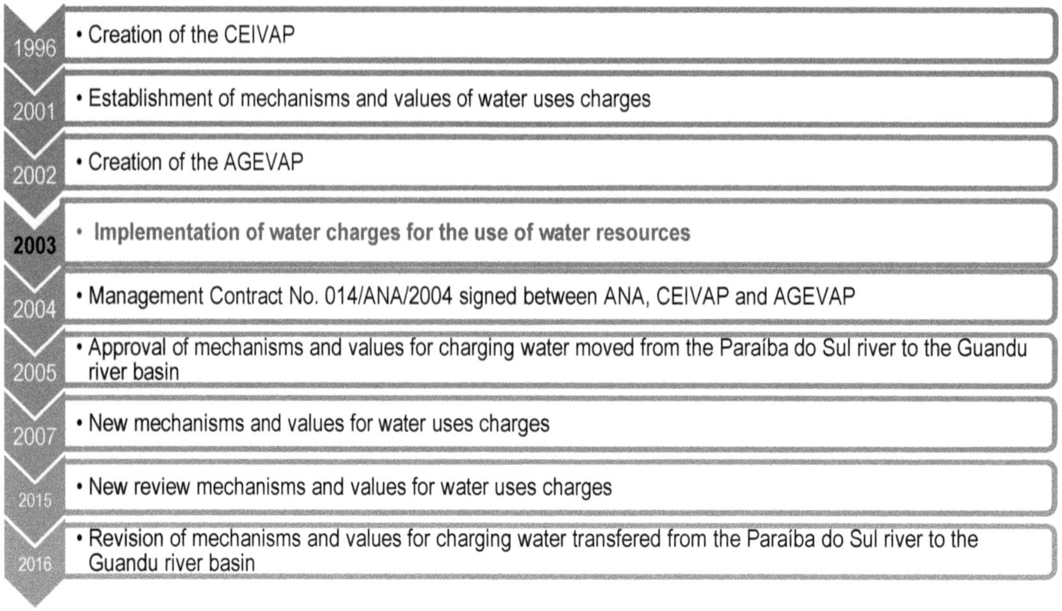

Source: Author's elaboration.

Challenges

The double dominion generates some bottlenecks in the case of Paraíba Do Sul. The interstate river basin includes three states, with advanced institutional systems and some differences in the governance models for water charges, in particular related to the regulation of the delegated water agencies. This may hinder a more strategic vision for investment across states. At federal level, the AGEVAP is the delegated water agency for the whole interstate basin. At state level, the AGEVAP is a delegated water agency only for the States of Rio de Janeiro and Minas Gerais, but not for São Paulo, because by Law water agencies should have the status of foundations. The AGEVAP disburses revenues in accordance with the plans approved by the four management units of the State of Rio de Janeiro and two management units of the State of Minas Gerais. In the State of São Paulo, DAEE collects charges, and 100% of the funds are transferred to the State Water Resources Fund (Fundo Estaduao de Recursos Hidricos, FEHIDRO).

The application of water charges across federal and state domain in the Guandu River basin is another issue the area faces. The water transfer from the Paraíba do Sul River to the Guandu River Basin (1 000 km^2 in the State of Rio de Janeiro) has been ongoing for decades with the main objective of generating hydropower. The operator of the transfer is LIGHT, an electricity company, which pays 0.75% of the value of the energy produced in the four plants located in the Guandu River Basin. A water charge is also applied in the river basin within the State of Rio de Janeiro. Although about 80% of the water flowing through the Guandu River comes from the Paraíba do Sul River, those waters, once flowing in the Guandu River, are considered waters under domain of the State of Rio de Janeiro, as stated by the Federal Constitution. Because of that, industry, sanitation and irrigation sectors, as well as the treatment plant serving the City of Rio de Janeiro and its metropolitan area are charged for using water within the State of Rio de Janeiro. Water charges are implemented by the INEA. In 2006, the State of Rio de Janeiro, the CEIVAP and the Guandu River Basin reached a delicate political agreement to transfer 15% of revenues from water charges to the AGEVAP to be used for projects in the Paraíba do Sul River Basin. Implementation of this policy started in 2010 with an increase in share shift to 20% introduced in 2016. Permits were not granted for concessions for hydropower generation issued before the creation of ANA; therefore, the transfer from the Paraíba do Sul River will receive a permit when the concession is renewed.

The 2007-2020 river basin plan underscores the need for significant investment; however, at present, revenues generated from the basin do not meet current investment needs. Studies show that it would take 470 years to meet investment needs based on the annual collection average and the investment needs assessment set forth in the river basin water resources plan to 2020 (COPETTEC, 2007, Bernardes and Broch, 2015). Despite these findings, no significant revision to the charges has been applied.

Ways forward

Widen the range of pollutants covered by the pollution charge

In 2016, about 30% of charges were paid by the industrial sector; however, payment was not completely based on the Polluter Pays principle, which is not totally applied, especially looking at the composition of the industry and the pollutants they generate. In an industrialised basin such as the Paraíba do Sul, this has great relevance in terms of internalising the costs of pollution. As highlighted in Chapter 3, taking into account only BOD is a limiting factor for the application of the Polluter Pays principle. The base of the pollution charge does not reflect the range of industries and effluents that affect water quality in the basin. In addition, compensation for those improving water quality could be employed, while putting in place monitoring and control.

Expedite the expenditure process

Since the signature of the management contract between AGEVAP and ANA in 2004, about 70% of resources have actually been used in the basin over the last four years. This is an important signal towards breaking the vicious circle of low collection and low delivery. Before starting discussions on increasing charges, it is crucial to clarify priorities for spending and accelerate the expenditure process. Speeding up investment decisions (and actual implementation of projects) requires a move away from institutional lock-in to cut red tape and to streamline administrative processes for greater participation of the private sector. Making these types of changes, however, goes well beyond water policy and water charges, and relates to public governance at large.

Give access to funds to the industry

Water users and payers should be able to see the benefits of their payment in return or apply the revenues themselves towards the improvement of the water management system of the basin in which they operate. In theory, the revenues collected in Paraíba do Sul River basin could be accessed by borrowers from the private sector that are located inside that basin; however, red tape makes this option difficult to occur in practice. The Federal Water Law does not explicitly prevent private borrowers from accessing the fund, but does not provide specific guidance or make it explicit either. Giving access to funds to the industry would be an incentive for the sector to accept water charges and their increase. However, in order to provide the right incentives, revenues made available to the industry should meet some eligibility criteria such as linking those revenues to circular economy projects (i.e. reclaimed wastewater reuse), supported by the dissemination of Best Available Technologies (BATs). The basin has the potential to look at ambitious innovative projects, involving the circular economy and renewable energy, going beyond the domain of water. There could be room for the ANA to negotiate a framework to be applied with the Brazilian competition authorities, to avoid distortion of competition. The framework could contain guidance both on the criteria to access the funds and on the nature of projects allowed for their disbursement.[2]

Consider a single agency at basin level

Different management models co-exist across the three states within the Paraíba do Sul river basin. This could be streamlined and made more efficient. For revenue management, a single water management agency could enhance co-ordination across state and federal rivers and authorities as well as foster convergence in setting priorities and targeting joint investment. Such an agency would need to remain neutral to all users to effective carry out its roles.

Review the collection mechanism in Guandu and return part of the revenues to the Paraíba do Sul

Eighty percent of the water in Guandu comes from Paraíba do Sul; however, historically, in accordance with the Constitution, water charges for the area have been paid to the State of Rio de Janeiro. In 2015-16, there was an agreement between Guandu and AGEVAP to transfer 15% (then increased to 20%) of the revenues to the Paraíba do Sul River Basin. Most of the water in Guandu originates in the Paraiba do Sul, passing through a hydroelectric plant, which pays the standard compensation for hydroelectric use of water. Revenues are not earmarked for water, but enter in the general budgets of the beneficiaries. Redirecting part of the current compensation would depend on the future of the hydroelectric compensation. Under current conditions, the transfer of a greater part can take place either on a negotiated basis between the parties, or by enacting changes in the legislative framework for water charges. Further discussions to review the collection mechanism in Guandu and return additional revenue to the Paraíba do Sul River Basin should be considered, in the first place through a negotiated solution.

Notes

1. The only revision took place in 2007 when the Paraíba do Sul river basin adopted mechanisms and prices similar to those applied by the PCJ Committee. Charges are basically the same: the only difference with the PCJ River basin consisted in charging BRL 0.07/kg for the discharge of organic matter, rather than BRL 0.10/kg. In 2015, there was a 9% increase.

2. An example in the European Union is the Guidelines on State aid for environmental protection and energy 2014-2020 (28.6.2014), http://eur-lex.europa.eu/legal-content/en/txt/pdf/?uri=celex:52014xc0628(01)&from=en.

References

Abers R.N. and M.E. Keck (2013), Practical Authority: Agency and Institutional Change in Brazilian Water Politics, Oxford University Press, Oxford.

ANA (2017), "Valores Cobrados e Arrecadados", http://www2.ana.gov.br/Paginas/servicos/cobrancaearrecadacao/cobrancaearrecadacao.aspx.

ANA (2017), Mapa da Bacia Hidrográfica do Rio Paraíba do Sul, http://arquivos.ana.gov.br/institucional/sag/CobrancaUso/BaciaPBS/_img/MapaPBS_05062013.pdf.

ANA (2016a), "Background report on setting and governing economic instruments for water policy in Brazil", Brazil.

ANA (2016b), Entram em vigor novas regras de operação para a bacia do Paraíba do Sul www2.ana.gov.br/Paginas/imprensa/noticia.aspx?List=ccb75a86-bd5a-4853-8c76-cc46b7dc89a1&ID=13131.

AGEVAP (2012), Avaliação da implementação da cobrança pelo uso de recursos hídricos de domínio da União na bacia hidrográfica do rio Paraíba do Sul, 2003-2011, http://arquivos.ana.gov.br/institucional/sag/CobrancaUso/Cobranca/RelatorioAvalImplCobPBS03_11.pdf.

Bernardes F. S. and Broch S.O. (2015), "Historico de cobrance pelo uso de agua em bacias hidrográficas de domínio da união", XXI Simpósio Brasileiro de Recursos Hídricos, 22-27 November, Brazil, www.evolvedoc.com.br/sbrh/.

COPETTEC (2007), "Plano de Recursos Hídricos Consolidado Resumo", Relatório Contratual R-10.

Da Costa et al., (2015) in INEA (2015), INEANA revista julho dezembro 2015, Vol. 3/1, July, Rio de Janeiro.

EU (2014), Guidelines on State aid for environmental protection and energy 2014-2020 (28.6.2014), http://eur-lex.europa.eu/legal-content/en/txt/pdf/?uri=celex:52014xc0628(01)&from=en.

Féres, J., A. Reynaud and A. Thomas (2012), "Water Reuse in Brazilian Manufacturing Firms", *Applied Economics*, Vol. 44/11, pp. 1 417-1 427.

Annex B

The State of Rio de Janeiro

Rio de Janeiro: A leader in water charges implementation

Key features

The State of Rio de Janeiro is one of Brazil's pioneers in the creation of a water charge system and its experience is important to understanding water charges implementation. From an institutional point of view, all the conditions are in place for water charges to achieve the expected goals (e.g. technical capacity, information and monitoring system); however the state's economic (financial crisis) and environmental (drought) health are currently barriers to implementation. As a result, there are some questions concerning the future of water charges in the state as a management instrument to enhance water resilience in a very industrialised and urbanised state.

The State of Rio has the second largest economy of Brazil, is largely urbanised and industrialised and hosts over 8.4% of the population. The state is situated in the hydrographic region of Southeast Atlantic and includes a river basin under the federal domain (Paraíba do Sul) and nine hydrographic districts organised in river basin committees (Figure B.1).The state hosts the highest population density of the country with 16 million inhabitants (2011) with about 75% of the population living in the urban areas. Its economy mostly relies on services and industry. There are 92 municipalities, including the capital city Rio de Janeiro. The State Water and Sewerage Company of Rio de Janeiro (Companhia Estadual de Águas e Esgotos do Rio de Janeiro, CEDAE) supplies water to 66% of municipalities. The others are served by municipal services or private companies. A total of 92% of municipalities have sewage collection and59% have wastewater treatment (IBGE, 2011; ANA, 2010).

Water availability in the State of Rio de Janeiro is quite heterogeneous due to climate conditions and anthropic activities. The Southeastern Atlantic Hydrographic Region (HR) is endowed with 1.25% of water availability over the total water availability. Industry and human consumption are responsible of 85% of the total water demand. The Paraíba do Sul River and its tributaries directly and indirectly supply (through water transposition in the Guandu River) 75% of the State's population, including 83% of the population of the metropolitan area of Rio de Janeiro. There is a pressing need in the state to enhance water security given the simultaneous increase in population and economic activities as well as decrease in water availability as a consequence of drought (INEA, 2015).

Figure B.1. Hydrographic regions and river basin committees in the State of Rio de Janeiro

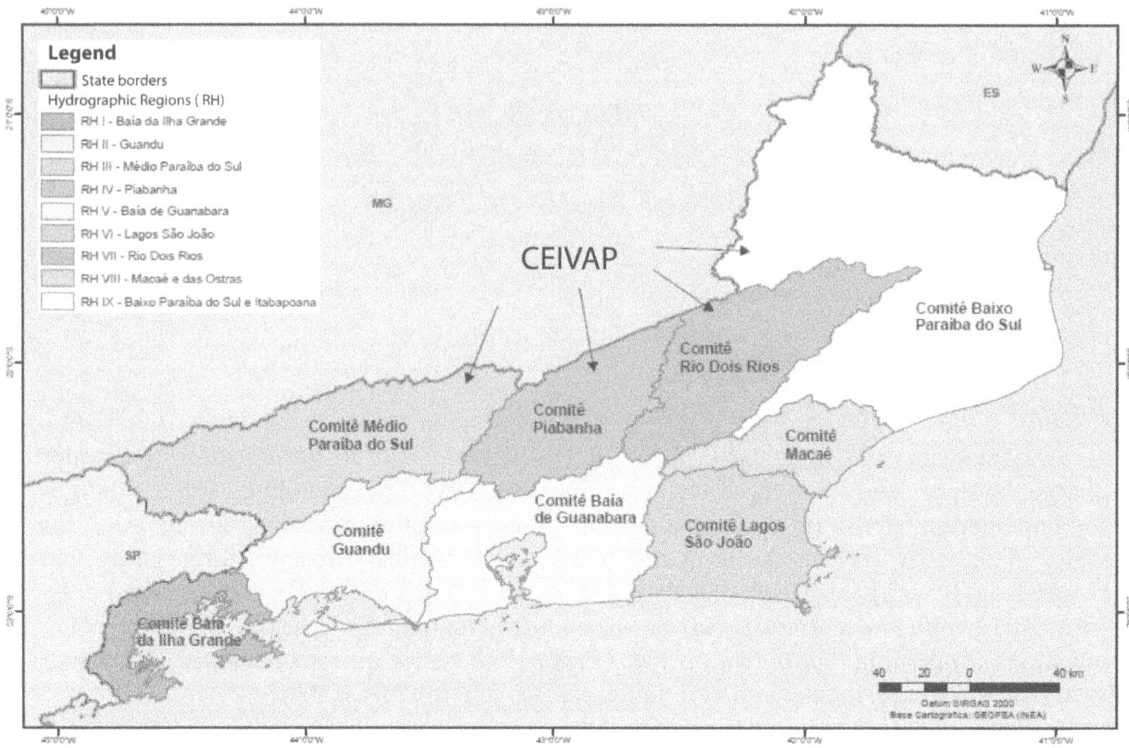

Notes: Legend translation: Inside the map translation: Ceivap – Paraiba do Sul river basin; Comité – committee.
Source: COPPETEC (2014), Elaboracao do Plano Estadual de recursos hídricos do estado do Rio de Janeiro, www.hidro.ufrj.br/perhi/documentos/perhi-r7.pdf.

Water charges in practice

In Rio de Janeiro water charges have been implemented by law since 2004. In 2016, revenues are estimated at BRL 24 million for the nine river basin committees, but there are important disparities in terms of revenue collection across basins (OECD, 2015; ANA Database, 2017). After more than ten years of flat charge collection, the total volume of charges collected doubled in 2016-17 (in all basins but Lagos São João). In 2016, revenues from water charges came mostly from the sanitation sector (83%), followed by industry (10%) and other sectors (6%) (ANA Database, 2017).

In 2010, drinking water and sanitation companies were required by law to pay for water use. In conjunction with the change, State Law 5 234/08 was passed, which allowed these companies to review the tariff for water supply services according to the increased costs due to water charges up to 2% of their revenues (Acselrad et al., 2009 and 2015). Before 2008, in fact, it was forbidden to pass the charges to the users. As a result, the collection rates increased.

Figure B.2. Water charges in the State of Rio de Janeiro (by type of users)

2016

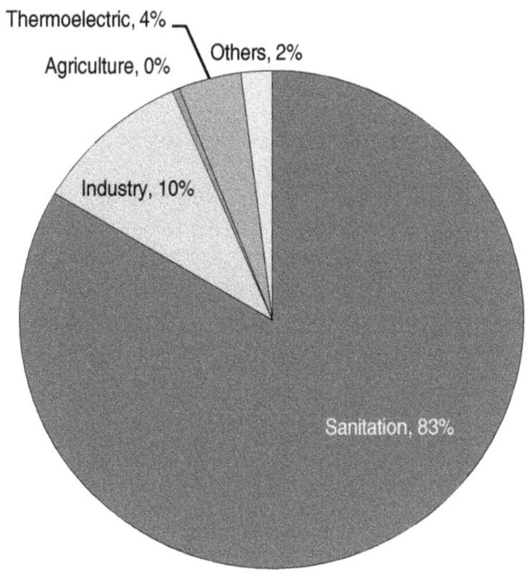

Source: ANA (2017), "Valores Cobrados e Arrecadados", http://www2.ana.gov.br/Paginas/servicos/cobrancaearrecadacao/cobrancaearrecadacao.aspx.

The institutional and legal framework for water charges

The institutionalisation of water charges with State Law (No. 4247/ 2003) gave way to a more advanced governance system that could also incentivise the implementation of the charges. This included the establishment of management contracts with delegated water agencies, the creation of river basin committees in basins where they did not exist, and the design of river basin plans.

The 2003 Law established that 90% of the amount collected must be applied in the basin of origin and 10% in the state managing body. The legislation is flexible, empowering the State Water Resources Council (Conselho Estadual de Recursos Hídricos do Estado do Rio de Janeiro, CERHI) to define this percentage by hydrographic region. Since 2009, 70% of revenue collected from the drinking water (urban water) and sanitation sector must be invested in urban wastewater treatment systems until achieving the target of 80% of wastewater collected and treated in the river basin (art. 6 of Law 5234 / 2008).

Charges for water uses are applied for each category and centralised into the State Water Resources Fund (Fundo Estadual de Recursos Hídricos, FUNDRHI), whose main revenues are collection and compensation from the electric sector (Compensação Financeira pela Utilização pelo Uso dos Recursos Hídricos, CFURH). The FUNDRHI is part of the Single Treasury Account (Conta Única do Tesouro Estadual, CUTE), managed by the State Treasury Department (Secretaria da Fazenda, SEFAZ) (Box B.1). It centralised revenues from water charges (BRL 24 M/y) and the financial compensation from the electric sector (BRL 6 M/y).

Box B.1. The management of FUNDRI in the State of Rio de Janeiro

The management of FUNDRHI is done through sub-accounts for each basin.

Water charge (*cobrança*):

- 10% INEA and 90% to the respective basin committees
- 15% until 2016 and 20% from 2017 (water charge for the transposition to the Guandu basin)
- 70% investment in sewage collection and treatment under the so called "Pact for sanitation", whereby most of the resources from FUNDRHI should be allocated to sewage collection and treatment. According to art. 6 of Law 5234/2008 at least 70% of revenues should be devoted to sewage collection and treatment until the share of sewage collected and treated in the respective Hydrographic Region reached the 80% target.

Financial Compensation for the Use of Water Resources for Hydroelectric Power Generation (CFURH):

- 50% INEA
- 50% Delegate entities of committees with low collection

The Financial Compensation for the Use of Water Resources for Hydroelectric Power Generation (CFURH) is a charge to hydroelectric power plants, collected directly by the National Electric Energy Agency and redistributed according to the share established by law, to federal government, states and municipalities. It is not a charge for water use. The annual amount allocated to FUNDRHI is approximately BRL 6 million, a smaller amount compared to what is received by the States of Minas Gerais and São Paulo, for example. For this reason, Rio de Janeiro's water management system heavily depends on the revenues from water charges at state level.

Source: Acselrad M. et al. (2015), "Dez Anos de cobrança pelo uso das aguas do Estado do Rio de Janeiro: situação atual e proposta de aperfeiçoamento", XXI Simpósio Brasileiro de Recursos Hídricos, 22-27 November, Brasilia, DF; Interview, written inputs from INEA/SEA 2017.

Authorities in charge of implementing the water charge system are the following:

- The Secretary of State for the Environment (Secretaria de Estado do Ambiente, SEA) proposes and guides public policies related to the implementation of the charge.
- As a management body, the State Environmental Institute (Instituto Estadual do Ambiente, INEA) is responsible for the implementation of the water charges, through: i) the management of user-payer registry, calculation of rates, billing users; ii) the management of the State Water Resources Fund (FUNDRHI): control of collection and financial management of resources; iii) technical support to river basin committees, in setting and revising water charges. The INEA holds monitoring and inspection powers (ANA, 2016).
- The basin committees have the legal prerogative to define methodology, criteria and collection values, for a subsequent approval by the CERHI.

- The Delegated water agencies manage revenues from water charges. The State of Rio de Janeiro followed the institutional framework of the Paraíba do Sul River Basin characterised by the Federal Committee (CEIVAP) and its delegated water agency (AGEVAP). This has encouraged the state to create similar legislation (Law 5639 / 2010) and delegate to the same entity (AGEVAP), the agency functions of the river basin committees in the Paraíba do Sul River Basin. Where delegated water agencies are in place, revenues from water charges can be disbursed through a management contract. Where there is not a delegate body, the INEA/ SEA is in charge.

Since 2008, revenues collected have been published on the INEA website bi-monthly by river basin committees and annually in basin committees reports.

Basin committees expenditures are based on their multi-annual implementation plans, which are developed and revised annually. The first state plan for water resources, approved in 2014 by the CERHI, sought to provide guidance at macro level for targeting the budgets of each committee. However, revenues vary widely across committees (Table B.1).

Table B.1. Water charges in the State of Rio de Janeiro

2016, BRL million

River Basin	Charge	Collection
Médio Paraíba do Sul	0.87	0.87
Piabanha	0.68	0.66
Rio Dois Rios	0.41	0.42
Baixo Paraíba do Sul	0.33	0.31
Baía de Guanabara	3.53	3.56
Baía da Ilha Grande	0.30	0.30
Guandu	16.10	16.13
Itabapoana	0.05	0.05
Lagos São João	1.29	1.23
Macaé e Rio das Ostras	1.04	1.04

Source: ANA (2017), "Valores Cobrados e Arrecadados", http://www2.ana.gov.br/Paginas/servicos/cobrancaearrecadacao/cobrancaearrecadacao.aspx.

Water users in the State of Rio de Janeiro have very different perceptions and understandings regarding water charges: while some industrial users are willing to pay higher water charges, others are more reluctant. The main argument is the lack of access from the private sector to the funds raised through water charges. This creates frustration about the capacity of the system to deliver tangible improvements in water management and hinders the willingness-to-pay of industrial water users. Irrigators are minor users in the state: there are 55 000 rural producers, half of which are family farmers; therefore they are exempted from paying water charges. As a result, they have little knowledge about the water charge system in place and of the role of the river basin committees. Not all the drinking water and sanitation companies have a clear picture of how the charge is calculated and the funds used.[1]

Challenges

Revenues from charges are not commensurate with investment needs: the State Water Resources Plan (Plano Estadual de Recursos Hídricos do Estado do Rio de Janeiro, PERHI) estimated investment needs at approximately BRL 15.7 billion by 2030. Improvement in the sewage collection and treatment systems represents 64% of the total investment for the future. The annual collection of water charges is able to meet less than 2.5% of the investment needs: BRL 1 billion/year (2015-2030), with BRL 670 million/year (2015-30) allocated to sewage (Acselrad et al., 2015). Regardless, revenues from water charges from water supply and sanitation should not be directed toward this type of investment: as explained above, water supply and sanitation is not a legitimate destination for water charges.

The state went through a very difficult situation in the aftermath of the State's financial crisis in 2014, when, revenues from water charges were internalised in the State's treasury and trapped in lengthy bureaucracy and red tapes. The activity of the river basin committees was blocked, creating financial insecurity in the water sector. Also, one of the consequences of the State's financial calamity", declared one month before the Olympics (July 2016), concerned privatisation of the State Sanitation Company (CEDAE), which provoked strong reactions and public protests.

There is quite a vocal resistance to water charges from the current largest payers: water supply and sanitation and industry. On one hand, the overall process of implementing water charges was heavily criticised since the very beginning: some argued that water charges have not been defined in a democratic way, as little consultation was carried out within state deliberative bodies to build consensus on the criteria and amounts. This created strong opposition to any increase from representative of stakeholder groups within the river basin committees, which eventually occurred only recently (2016-17).

Charges do not reflect the degree of scarcity or saturation of hydrographic basins either in the State of Rio de Janeiro, and so far they have not been able to change users' behaviour toward greater water use efficiency. Charge rates are almost the same for all the river basin committees under the State's responsibility and as such the criteria and values used to determine the charges are not appropriate for local realities, e.g. pollution charges do not reflect the dilution capacity.

To enhance water security, policy coherence should be carefully considered. Further synergies should be sought across soil management, land use, environmental and solid waste. The State of Rio de Janeiro is currently discussing three items related to policy coherence, which represent a great challenge for the future: i) combine climate change and water resources management and improve hydro security; ii) establish a state policy for floods; iii) consider reforms in drinking water and sanitation sector, including for CEDAE.

The exponential increase in the number of registered users and permits calls for greater enforcement. At the moment, the water user registry reports on users holding permits, as prescribed by the State Law. In the future, an enhanced methodology for water charges may require further information. For example, the state water resources plan for groundwater estimated that about 70% of groundwater users do not hold yet a permit at present. It would be key to focus on the large users; and document potential effects of large numbers of small users at places.

Ways forward

Allocate funds where they make a difference

A different approach that disconnects the use of revenues from water charges to large infrastructure investments in the drinking and sanitation sector should be considered. For users to be convinced of the economic and financial results and impacts of water charges, their revenues need to be directed to where they can bring actual benefits. Greater flexibility should therefore be granted in the application of resources collected. Funds should match the reality of the revenues and of the investments.

Expansion of charging parameters for effluent discharge

Given the variety of the industry and the pollutants that industrial activities generate, charged only BOD does not suffice to internalised negative environmental externalities. Therefore an expansion of charging parameters for effluent discharge should be considered. Action could focus on the monitoring of the harmful consequences of a wide range of pollutants in industrial charges, attempts to monitor them and to monetise them. Similar attention should be paid to the economic consequences of such adjustments. Some industries may win, while others may lose; but the process would help transition towards less polluting processes, at least for a set period of time.

Adapt charges to local circumstances

The state should continue to raise charges so that they reflect tensions in the basin. Charges should be tailored to *places* (hydrography, rural-urban) to induce more rational use of water in regions characterised by chronic scarcity; *people* (users) by targeting largest water users. In addition, it is estimated that including small hydropower plants would increase water charges collection by almost BRL 500 000 a year. A way to improve the acceptability of water charges in agriculture is to refund part of the charged levied through subsidies to the sector (e.g. to water saving technologies such as drip irrigation) where this is not already the case at present. Finally, water sources, both surface and groundwater, should be considered in the calculation of charges.

Enhance water resilience for future and sustainable growth in Rio de Janeiro

Recently the City of Rio de Janeiro experienced the worse drought of the last 80 years. The city is growing at a fast speed and will count by 2030 an additional 2 million people in the metropolitan area (UN-HABITAT, 2016). Urbanisation and industrialisation trends call for water security and resilience. The overarching challenge is to secure water for the greater Rio de Janeiro, through reliance on neighbouring basins, and the systematic promotion of water use efficiency in the basin (essentially for industrial and domestic users). Water charges can help raise awareness on these challenges and catalyse the revenues needed for monitoring and management functions. Technical innovations for conserving and reusing water and for managing water-related risks are crucial, but should be combined with soft, green infrastructure and nature-based solutions to make the most of policy complementarities and minimise investment needs. Another option would be to explore business models for storm water management and finance and future-proof of the City of Rio de Janeiro. In this context, institutions play a determinant role in raising awareness; triggering behavioural and policy change; and managing trade-offs across actual rural and urban areas, water users, current and future generations (OECD, 2016). A city that is resilient from a water management perspective is one that can manage water in a sustainable, integrated and inclusive way, at an acceptable cost, and in a reasonable timeframe (OECD, 2015).

Note

1. Interviews to representative of each stakeholder group in February 2017, Rio de Janeiro, Brazil.

References

Acselrad M. et al. (2015), "Dez Anos de cobrança pelo uso das aguas do Estado do Rio de Janeiro: situação atual e proposta de aperfeiçoamento, XXI Simpósio Brasileiro de Recursos Hídricos", 22-27 November, Brazil.

Acselrad, M.V. et al. (2009), "O processo de implementação da cobrança pelo uso da água no Estado do Rio de Janeiro", XVIII Simpósio Brasileiro de Recursos Hídrico 2009, Brasilia.

ANA (2017), "Valores Cobrados e Arrecadados", http://www2.ana.gov.br/Paginas/servicos/cobrancaearrecadacao/cobrancaearrecadacao.aspx.

ANA (2016), "Background report on setting and governing economic instruments for water policy in Brazil", Brazil.

ANA (2010), "Atlas Brasil Abastecimento Urbano de Água", *Panorama Nacional*, http://atlas.ana.gov.br/Atlas/forms/Home.aspx, Brazil.

IBGE (Instituto Brasileiro de Geografia e Estatistica) (2011), "Atlas de Saneamento 2011", *Revista Ineana*, Vol. 3/1.

INEA (2015), INEANA revista julho dezembro 2015, Vol. 3/1, July, Rio de Janeiro.

OECD (2016), *Water Governance in Cities*, OECD Publishing, Paris, http://dx.doi.org/10.1787/9789264251090-en.

OECD (2015), *Water Resources Governance in Brazil*, OECD Publishing, Paris, http://dx.doi.org/10.1787/9789264238121-en.

UN-HABITAT (2016), "World Cities Report 2016: Urbanization and Development: Emerging Futures", http://wcr.unhabitat.org/ (accessed November 2017).

Annex C

The Piancó-Piranhas Açu River basin

The Piancó-Piranhas Açu River Basin: Water charges in the semi-arid region

Key features

In the Piancó-Piranhas Açu River basin demand for water exceeds supply. Human consumption and irrigation draw heavily on available resources, which are constrained due to drought and intermittent rivers and pollution from domestic sewage. The institutional framework and governance structure for water charges in this area are under development, including strengthening stakeholder participation into the basin committee's activities and the awareness raising around water scarcity. The São Francisco River's water transfer project (Projeto de Integração do Rio São Francisco, PISF) is paving the way for a concrete discussion on the implementation of water charges as they would impact of user behaviour and raise revenue for water management.

The Piancó-Piranhas Açu (PPA) Interstate River Basin covers an area of 43 000 km^2 in a semi-aridterritory in Northeast region of Brazil (Figure C.1). It is located in the States of Paraíba and Rio Grande do Norte. There are 147 municipalities: 100 in the State of Paraíba and 47 in Rio Grande do Norte. The total population is 1 280 000 inhabitants with 67% of the population located in Paraíba (IBGE, 2011). Irrigated agriculture is one of the main economic activities and has been key to regional development since the 1970s. The irrigated area is about 81 000 hectare (IBGE, 2006). Irrigators are the main water users (65.7%), followed by aquaculture (23.6%), human consumption (7.6%), industry (1.6%) and livestock (1.5%) (ANA, 2014; CBH PPA.org.br).

The basin is characterised by intermittent rivers and prolonged droughts, raising specific issues around water scarcity and related conditions. The two reservoirs Curema-Mãe d'Água, in the State of Paraíba, and Armando Ribeiro Gonçalves, in the State Rio Grande do Norte are considered strategic for the socio-economic development of the two states (OECD, 2015). The Piancó-Piranhas Açu river basin committee operates at federal and state level (for both the states).

Water pollution is a significant challenge for the Piancó-Piranhas Açu river basin due to insufficient sewage treatment fertiliser run off (ANA 2014, 2016a, IBGE, 2006; IBGE, 2011). About 96% of the urban population has access to drinking water in the State of Paraíba and 92% in the State of Rio Grande do Norte. However, sewage collection rates are much lower in the State of Paraíba (2.46%) and the State of Rio Grande do Norte (13.95%) (ANA, 2014; CBH PPA org.br).

Figure C.1. The Piancó-Piranhas Açu River basin

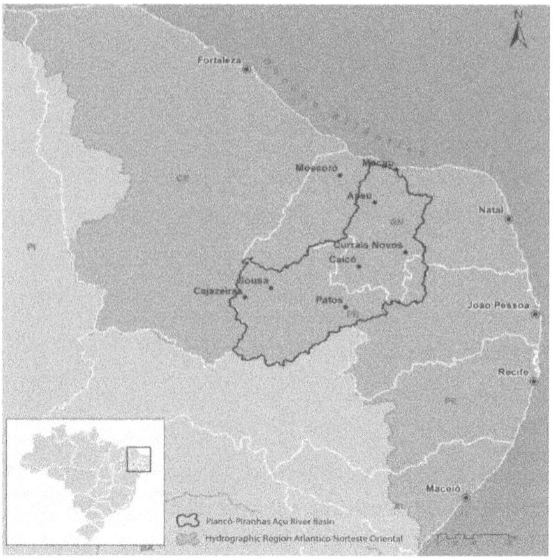

Source: ANA (2017), Sistema Hídrico Curema-Mãe D'Água e rios Piancó e Piranhas http://arquivos.ana.gov.br/institucional/sof/acudessemiarido/LocalizacaodaBaciaHidrograficadoRioPiranhas-Acu.png (accessed August 2017).

Water charges in practice

Water charges are not yet implemented in the Piancó-Piranhas-Açu interstate river basin. In the State of Rio Grande do Norte, the implementation of water charges is under discussion within the Technical Committee of the State Secretariat for Water Resources Management (see Chapter 2). However, the severe drought challenged the operationalisation of water charges. Implementation of water charges in the State of Paraíba have been slow with a low collection rate (less than 10%).

Simulations carried out within the Piancó-Piranhas Açu basin's water resources plan showed that revenues from water charges would be insufficient to ensure the financial sustainability of a water agency. Results from economic analysis showed that using unit prices employed in other river basins, revenues would amount at BRL 257 525/year. This is mainly due to economic base and population of the area, i.e. strong agricultural base exempt from water charges and sparsely populated area (75% of municipalities with less than 10 000 inhabitants). Through a partnership agreement, ANA is currently providing about the double of the above mentioned amount for water charges to support the activities of the operative unit (*Centro de Apoio*) of the Piancó-Piranhas Açu River basin.[1]

The institutional and legal framework or water charges

The institutional framework of the Piancó-Piranhas-Açu River basin includes the Piranhas-Açu River Basin Committee, which was created in 2006 and became operational in 2009. In addition and beyond the CNRH and the ANA, at state level, there are the Water Resources Councils of the States of Paraíba and Rio Grande do Norte; the State Secretariat for the Environment, Water Resources and Science and Technology of Paraíba (Secretária de Estado do Meio Ambiente e dos Recursos Hídricos, SEMARH / PB) and Rio Grande do Norte: Secretária de Estado do Meio Ambiente e dos Recursos Hídricos, SEMARH / RN); the Executive Agency for Water Management of the State of Paraíba (Agência Executiva de Gestão das Águas do Estado da Paraíba, AESA) and the Institute of Water Management of the State of Rio Grande do Norte (Instituto de Gestão das Águas do Estado do Rio Grande Do Norte, IGARN). As in the Verde Grande River basin, there is a single river basin committee that covers whole interstate river basin, which was agreed upon by the federal level and both states. The National Department of Constructions Against Drought (Departamento Nacional de Obras Contra as Secas, DNOCS) has an important role as well given as the Department that manages 321 reservoirs (70% of water resources are accumulated).[2] Support from federal level is also provided to the Piancó-Piranhas Açu River basin through the partnership and contract agreements with ANA.

The Piancó-Piranhas-Açu river basin plan is a reference agenda for the river basin committee and for the water resources management bodies of federal and state rivers. The plan was approved in 2016[3] has a budget of BRL 150 million for the first five years, and undertake three types of actions targeted at enhancing water security and water quality due to the low level of sanitation infrastructure: management, complementary studies, and projects. Actions will be implemented by the river basin committee, ANA, IGARN and AESA. The plan considers water allocation and operation of the reservoirs of the region as central issues. Governance is key to put these actions in place from improving knowledge on strategic issues to establishing negotiated processes for water allocation.

Challenges

Due to its socio-economic and hydrological characteristics, the basin is very fragile in terms of securing water supply now and in the future. There is a lack of investment in water security (e.g. dams, reservoirs, wastewater collection and treatment), due to the limited capacity to invest of the basin. Therefore, targeted measures are needed to enhance the basin's resilience, cope with supply and pollution issues, and competition across water users.

The transfer of the São Francisco River will reduce uncertainty over water availability from 2017. It creates a momentum for taking actions as regard to pressing issues such as water pollution and freshwater contamination, to which water charges can contribute. The project is being implemented by the Ministry of Integration with a USD 3 billion budget. Revenues from water charges could contribute to its operability and maintenance.

The main cause of too polluted water in the area is lack of proper wastewater treatment, which comes under the responsibility of municipalities. The municipalities face constraints (human, technical and financial) and despite their important role in managing sanitation, including environmental licensing and solid waste management, they seldom participate in river basin committees meetings. The poor engagement of municipalities in water resources management, which is a common feature in Brazil, hinders any strategic vision for the Basin. In addition, the basin culture enables the use of rivers for liquid and solid waste dumping. There are programmes at federal level to support municipalities in the sanitation sector, which is their responsibility (Box C.1).

Water scarcity and water pollution increase competition across water users. In periods of water scarcity, human consumption takes priority over re-allocation of water, which causes frequent water interruptions for farmers that come with uncompensated economic consequences. In addition, the monitoring of abstraction and discharge is not done on a routine basis due to lack of staff at relevant state environmental agencies, which hinders real inspections on the ground.

Box C.1. Building capacities of municipalities in Rio Grande do Norte

By Law, municipalities are required to design a sanitation plan. A total of 27 plans are in place in Rio Grande do Norte. Plans aim to identify the infrastructural and operational needs and the, State Sanitation Company in Rio Grande do Norte (Companhia de Águas e Esgotos do Rio Grande do Norte, CAERN) operationalises them through concession contracts, since municipalities lack financial resources. The CAERN supplies 167 municipalities, more than 90% of which have a population below 50 000 inhabitants. These municipalities are eligible to access National Health Foundation (Fundação Nacional de Saúde, FUNASA) funds, a federal programme that makes funds available for municipalities or rural areas below 50 000 inhabitants. Currently, there are 20 projects financed by the FUNASA, for which the CAREN carries out the execution of the construction. However, even with the funds made available by the FUNASA, sometimes municipalities are not able to submit projects. Most of the investment in infrastructure is made possible through the Growth Acceleration Program (Programa de Aceleração do Crescimento, PAC). As for the ownership of the infrastructure, pipelines are property of the state and the distribution network in towns is property of the municipalities. About 70% of municipalities get water from pipelines, with water losses around 80-90%.

The plan is a prerequisite to sign a contract with the CAERN for the concession, which lasts 50 years. The CAERN provides to municipalities assistance and technical support for drafting proper sanitation plans. Political discontinuity is an obstacle for capacity building at local level.

Source: Interviews with local stakeholders during the policy dialogue case-study mission, February 2017.

Ways forward

The following recommendations are built upon a common objective to increase water resilience in the Basin.

Promote water efficiency

In the "land of scarcity", no drop of water can be wasted and every drop should be valuably used. Where social and economic development depends on inter-basin transfers, simply augmenting supply, namely transfers from other basins will not be enough. It is crucial to manage demand and there is a menu of options to do so, such as:

- Promoting wastewater reuse, sludge management and biogas: Reclaimed water is the most reliable source of water in contexts of water scarcity. Sludge can be used as a resource for farming, while biogas collected from wastewater treatment plants is also a source of revenue and can have positive consequences for the economy in the whole region. Redirecting treated wastewater to reuse may reduce the risk of polluting the clean water supply with wastewater that may cause costs and/or health issues elsewhere. Investment in wastewater collection and treatment also generate new jobs and revenues.
- Linking water management with land use, soil conservation, cropping patterns: There should be incentives for using water wisely, such as water-efficient crop production and prices on water use. Water charges can be used to urge farmers to change the kind of crop that they grow towards less water intensive crops in regions where water is scarce. Differentiated tariffs can also be designed to promote the use of treated wastewater. The transition towards this model may not be easy and need to be achieved through accompanying measures that could be financed through revenues form water charges.

- Protecting freshwater from untreated sewerage: Revenues from water charges can be used to protect freshwater from untreated sewage and catalyse more revenues.

Set solidarity mechanisms

Access to funding from FUNASA and existing agreements and partnerships with ANA are solid bases for the Piancó-Piranhas Açu River basin to make further steps in addressing water quality and water scarcity risks (with impacts on competing uses). At the same time, the Ministry of Cities can provide funds for water supply and sanitation for the very few cities with more than 50 000 inhabitants. The Ministry of Integration is responsible for the PISF and the building of new dams (e.g. the Oiticica) and can also provide support. Additional solidarity mechanisms or budgetary transfer from the federal level or other parts of the countries are needed to initiate investment for more sustainable development.

Invest in monitoring and modelling, to support staged reductions of abstraction

Revenues from water charges are too low to make a difference in addressing the need for additional infrastructure (e.g. reservoirs) or be devoted to investments in sanitation. Instead, revenues can support the improvement of the information and knowledge systems that can guide better public action, shed better light on risks, and foster transparency on how they are managed. While monitoring water flows would help to get a better picture of who uses water and when, modelling could also help anticipate crises based on the knowledge of precipitations upstream and water availability in the basin. Investment in monitoring and modelling in this area is very important. Climate change may have an impact not only on natural water availability, but also on the amount of additional water that the São Francisco River transfer can deliver in the area. Assessing water resources status and demand now and in the future, implies embracing a flexible (rather than rigid) water allocation approach.

Differentiate water rights by level of security

Water charges do not work in isolation and cannot be the panacea to solve all water problems in a given basin. They can be used in combination with re-designed water rights. There are different categories of rights, which would benefit from different levels of security. In the case of farmers, different categories of rights could be linked to the type of crop needing different quantity of water, as well as to the capacity of managing risk, investing, innovating and adjusting cropping patterns. This would be particularly relevant in the case of the Piancó-Piranhas Açu River Basin given the prominence of agriculture in the state economy, and the large numbers of small farmers who would require tailored and place-based responses.

Educate, raise awareness

Education programmes for municipalities, farmers, citizens are important to make the case for charges, convince user payers of their direct benefits and increase their willingness to pay. Information sharing and capacity building are also key for shedding light on how to use water more efficiently and should be pursued. Water charges can help incentivise the scarce use of water and raise awareness at the same time. A positive signal during the policy dialogue interviews underlying the preparation of this report is that many water users, including farmers, now have a higher level of awareness of current and future risks. State authorities should build on this momentum to devise collective and consensus-based strategies that can feature water charges as one of the management tools to foster behaviour change and catalyse revenues.

Notes

1. Partnership Agreement No. 001/2015/ANA with the NGO Seridó Sustainable Development Agency (ADESE) supports the river basin committee's actions through the implementation of a Support Centre acting as an Executive Secretariat (to organise meetings, document flow control, handle communication and social mobilisation, build capacity, and organise the electoral processes). Contract No. 063/2016/ANA with the firm Projecte – Engenharia, Arquitetura, Construções e Consultoria Ltda provides technical support services in the field of water management and regulation actions in the basin (identification, registration, updating data and monitoring of water uses, campaign of flow measurement and monitoring of the operation of reservoirs, and monitoring of the conditions of maintenance of hydraulic and hydro-mechanical structures of water flow in rivers). ANA (2016b), Plano de recursos hídricos da bacia hidrográfica do rio Piancó-Piranhas-Açu, http://piranhasacu.ana.gov.br/produtos/PRH_PiancoPiranhasAcu_ResumoExecutivo_30062016.pdf (accessed August 2017).

2. CBH PPA (n.d.), Relatorio, http://cbhpiancopiranhasacu.org.br/docs/relatorio/tdrplanopiranhasacu_final-1.pdf (accessed August 2017).

3. ANA (2015), ANA seleciona organização para apoiar as atividades do Comitê da Bacia Hidrográfica do Rio Piancó-Piranhas-Açu, www2.ana.gov.br/paginas/imprensa/noticia.aspx?id_noticia=12657 (accessed August 2017).

References

ANA (2017), Sistema Hídrico Curema-Mãe D'Água e rios Piancó e Piranhas http://arquivos.ana.gov.br/institucional/sof/acudessemiarido/LocalizacaodaBaciaHidrograficadoRioPiranhas-Acu.png (accessed August 2017).ANA (Agência National de Agua) (2016a), "Background report on setting and governing economic instruments for water policy in Brazil", Brazil.

ANA (2016b), Plano de recursos hídricos da bacia hidrográfica do rio Piancó-Piranhas-Açu, http://piranhasacu.ana.gov.br/produtos/PRH_PiancoPiranhasAcu_ResumoExecutivo_30062016.pdf (accessed August 2017).

ANA (2015), ANA seleciona organização para apoiar as atividades do Comitê da Bacia Hidrográfica do Rio Piancó-Piranhas-Açu, www2.ana.gov.br/paginas/imprensa/noticia.aspx?id_noticia=12657 (accessed August 2017).

ANA (2014), "Cobrança pelo Uso de Recursos Hídricos", *Cadernos de capacitação em recursos hídricos*, Vol. 7.

CBH PPA (n.d.), Relatorio, http://cbhpiancopiranhasacu.org.br/docs/relatorio/tdrplanopiranhasacu_final-1.pdf (accessed August 2017).

IBGE (Instituto Brasileiro de Geografia e Estatistica) (2011), "Atlas de Saneamento 2011", *Revista Ineana*, Vol. 3/1, www.ibge.gov.br/home/estatistica/populacao/atlas_saneamento/default_zip.shtmlnea.

IBGE (2006), Censo Agropecuário, https://biblioteca.ibge.gov.br/visualizacao/periodicos/51/agro_2006.pdf

OECD (2015), *Water Resources Governance in Brazil*, OECD Publishing, Paris, http://dx.doi.org/10.1787/9789264238121-en.

Annex D

Action Plan

Building on a policy dialogue that aimed to stimulate a discussion about water charges and provide governments and stakeholders with means to enhance water charges uses and impacts, this Action Plan was designed to set out concrete actions and suggests champions or institutions that can lead implementation over the short, medium and long run. It identifies key steps for the implementation of the main policy recommendations and the ways forward set out in this report. The ultimate goal is to create the conditions for the effective design and efficient implementation of water charges in a shared responsibility across levels of government as well as the public, private and non-profit sectors.

The Action Plan provides a roadmap to put in place effective instruments that contribute to water policy objectives. It recommends a staged and place-based approach, whereby proposed actions could be first tested in the most institutionally advanced basins/states with high capacities to prepare and implement plans, as well as to spend revenues (avoiding accumulation of unspent revenues). Results from these pilot experiences could then be shared to illustrate the benefits of the water charges systems to other basins/ states engaged in or thinking about implementing similar practices.

Objective	Action	Possible champions/partners	Timeline
Review existing charges and design effective ones	Use the Checklist proposed in the Annex V to work through the steps in designing and implementing a scheme of charges, and as a self-assessment tool of the state of play of water charges at a given scale.	ANA, National Water Council, state water councils, river basin committees, state water authorities, delegated water agencies	Short
	Assess (with a view to improve significantly or phase out) programmes and subsidies that lead to degradation of water quality and increased scarcity. They include policies that support unsustainable agriculture production, and input subsidies (e.g. for fertilisers, biocides) which cause diffuse pollution of waterways.	ANA, state water authorities, Ministry of Agriculture	Short
	Carry out economic analyses to support decision making on water charges. Such analyses should build on existing or new methods to assess, in particular: • Impacts of the water charges on the distribution of economic welfare • Social consequences of charges • Potential wider impacts on competitiveness.	ANA, river basin committees and their executive agencies	Medium
	Identify a range of proxies and promote their use when detailed information is unavailable or sophisticated schemes are not appropriate, strengthening consistency between: • Charging schemes • Other command-and-control instruments (i.e. pollution standards) • Information mechanisms (i.e. metering)	ANA	Short

Objective	Action	Possible champions/partners	Timeline
Build capacities	Provide guidance and incentives at national and river basin levels for designing, setting and implementing water charges and spending related revenues, including rules for expenditure and publishing of accounts.	ANA	Short-Medium
	Develop technical capacities to carry out regular *ex-post* evaluations to monitor the effectiveness of abstraction and pollution charges.	ANA, state water authorities, delegated water agencies	Medium
	Review skills and capacity for carrying out all the activities associated with designing, setting, implementing and monitoring a charges scheme, and deal with any shortfall.	Delegated water agencies	Short
Enhance the knowledge & information base	Provide or improve data and information on the state of environment and water resources and quality, including pressures on water resources (related to availability and quality; demand by sector, location and timing), and others.	ANA, state water authorities, delegated water agencies	Short-Medium
	Update states' registries of water abstractions and discharges to charge accordingly Continue synchronising with the National Registry (CNARH) to cross-check the relevant information for interstate basins.	ANA, state water authorities	Short-Medium
Strengthen the institutional framework and enhance co-ordination	Allocate roles and responsibilities amongst federal and state authorities for setting, implementing, monitoring, evaluating, and regulating water charges. ANA could negotiate agreements with states, avoiding any legal revisions. Adjust where need be based on results.	National and state water council, ANA, state authorities	Short-Medium
	Facilitate co-ordination when a delegated agency deals with different states. At inter-state level, when different managing models co-exist across the states within the interstate river basin, consider the creation of a single delegated agency.	ANA, state authorities and delegated water agencies	Medium
Make the most of stakeholder consultation	• Consult first on different options of water charges schemes, and then on the final scheme after rounds of consultations • Explain clearly the objectives for the charging scheme; how the scheme would be administered, and the sort of billing system needed. • Describe to charge payers how the money will be spent, and what benefits it will bring to themselves and other water users. • Explain consequences on non-payers in terms of chasing bad debts as well as using administrative responses such as revoking the permit	ANA, state water authorities, delegated water agencies	Short-Medium
Develop plans that drive water charges decisions	Make sure that plans identify the priority areas for action on water resources management, on the basis of objective criteria that would take into account primarily health risks, social issues, the environment and the economy.	National and state water councils, river basin committees, ANA, state water authorities, delegated water agencies	Short
	Setting guidelines for the design of plans supported by realistic funding strategies.	CNRH/ ANA	Short
	Consider explicit support for plans that meet the guidelines.	State water authorities	Short
	Incentivise municipalities to participate in river basin planning efforts and implementation for example through performance agreements, along the lines of the *Progestao.*	State water authorities	Medium
Develop accompanying measures	Identify and promote a suite of options to accompany the reform of water charges in agriculture.	River basin committees and water agencies.	Medium
	Consider nudging to accompany the reform of water charges.	ANA, state water authorities, water agencies	Short

Objective	Action	Possible champions/partners	Timeline
	Promote instruments – independent from charges – to address affordability and other equity issues.	ANA, state water authorities, river basin committees	Short
	Promote programmes such as agro-environmental schemes aiming to reduce the negative impact of agriculture on water resources.	ANA, state water authorities, river basin committees	Medium
	Facilitate the reform of water allocation regimes so that they encompass and benefit from well-designed abstraction charges and contribute to improved water management, enhancing water security in normal times and in episodes of scarcity.	ANA and National water council , in consultation with states water authorities and river basin committees	Long
	Strengthen sound inspection and control mechanisms, as well as sanctions and penalties in case of non-enforcement and compliance.	ANA, state water authorities	Short-Medium
Facilitate spending that contributes to enhanced water security and enhance transparency	Change rules so that agencies can improve effectiveness of spending revenues collected through water charges, through: • Procedural rules for public expenditure and the transfer mechanisms between different public authorities to make the handling of the revenues faster and more efficient • Harmonising bidding rules across ANA and the states for the delegated agencies to adopt a single set of rules in a river basin • Harmonising the audit and accountability processes that delegated entities must adopt for the control to be carried out by public authorities, both federal and state • Allowing the disbursement of resources through repayable financing to private sector borrowers, to carry out actions envisaged in the river basin plans • Allowing delegated agencies to use part of the revenues collected to compensate users who in periods of severe drought have their water use restricted in favour of the supply of the cities (which is a priority) • Allowing delegated agencies to maintain funds for emergencies	ANA, state water authorities, delegated water agencies, legislatives bodies	Medium
	Share experience with mechanisms to recycle revenues from water charges in order to demonstrate collective benefits from water charges.	River basin committees and water agencies	Short
	Promote transparency on how revenues from water charges are used (water agencies) and demonstrate that revenues are being spent in an accountable way, effectively, equitably and efficiently for the benefit of the river basin and its several users.	Water agencies	Short
Monitoring and evaluation	Promote regular monitoring and evaluation of the adequacy, implementation and results of water charges to assess to what extent they fulfil the intended outcomes and adapt where necessary.	ANA, state water authorities and water agencies	Medium-Long

Annex E

Charging for water abstraction and discharges – A checklist

By Professor Ian Barker, Water Policy International Ltd

Why do you want to charge?

- What is the problem you are trying to solve, and over what timescale? What policy outcomes do you want to achieve and how will charges (alone or in combination with other measures) help you deliver them? Charging is just one mechanism among many that can be used to deliver sustainable water management. It is not an end in itself, and for the purposes of managing a public good it cannot operate effectively without other delivery systems. In particular, permitting systems – "command and control" regulation – are essential for effective water allocation and pollution control. But charging can also help to ensure that water users internalise at some of the costs of their activities, and, over time, change their behaviours.
- What do you want the charges to fund, and why? Are you looking to ensure full cost recovery for water monitoring, assessment, modelling, management, regulation, compliance monitoring (inspection), enforcement and operational and strategic planning activities – in other words, the full range of costs of water management? If your costs include the operation of major sources such as reservoirs, for the benefit of different sectors, do you want to recover not only operational costs, but also a rate of return on the capital outlay and depreciation of the asset?
- Do you want to target particular sectors (and if so, why, and how will you justify not charging some other sectors or classes of water users), or do you want an equitable system of charges for all abstractors and dischargers – perhaps above some *de minimis* threshold for volume or impact?

How will the charges scheme link with permitting systems?

- How will your charging scheme fit in with other mechanisms to manage water resources? In particular, the use of permits to set limits and conditions on abstraction and discharges. And will your permitting and compliance monitoring systems ensure that charges are calculated fairly and accurately?
- Ideally, you would know the locations of all abstractions and discharges, and they would all be controlled (or nearly all if a risk-based approach is taken) through permits backed up by routine compliance monitoring, and enforcement where necessary. The permits would then form the basis for the approach taken in the charging scheme, and the specific charge related to each user.

- All abstractions would have a means of measurement designed to ensure compliance with volumetric limits. Other permit conditions, such as restrictions on abstraction at low flows, would also have a means of ensuring compliance. Discharges should also have a volumetric limit and means of measurement, as well as emission limits to protect the environment and human health for the parameters in the discharge. There should be an agreed basis for monitoring the quality of the discharge at a frequency that meant that the results were statistically significant, auditable and appropriate to the type of process involved.

Designing the charging scheme

- How will you structure the charges so that they align with the policy objectives? For both abstractions and discharges, will you use the volume authorised on the permit, or the actual volumes abstracted or discharged? The latter requires more effort to oversee: the water user or your inspector will need to record and report the volumes, there must be a means of measurement of certified accuracy in place (e.g. a calibrated meter) because otherwise you could be over-or under-charging. Your billing system must also be capable of calculating different charges according to volume at the billing frequency that you choose.
- Do you want to impose a separate administrative charge to cover the costs of managing and carrying out the technical determination of applications for new permits, or revisions to existing ones?
- Do you want your abstraction charges to send signals about the degree of water stress, and incentivise reduced consumption? And what do you mean by 'water stress' or 'water scarcity': if it is stress as a result of excessive abstraction will you rely on charges alone to achieve a sustainable balance with the available resource, or will you also take other measures to reduce abstraction (e.g. by buying out entitlements or by forcible reductions in authorised volumes)? If scarcity is more dynamic, such as from low rainfall and the risk of drought, what will trigger the charging response? And how will you ensure that charge payers are aware of what is happening on a dynamic basis, and where possible, have access to advice about how to reduce their consumption?
- For discharges, what signals do you want to send to polluters, and how costly do you want to make the act of pollution? If you want to incentivise a reduction in pollution load from toxic substances, do the permits specify limits on, for example, pesticides, hydrocarbons, metals, cyanides etc? And how will you reflect this in the charges scheme through a sliding scale from cooling water through to discharges from chemical works and mining operations? If you want to see improved water quality to protect human health and support target ecosystems can you use charges to help achieve this faster than through the use of progressively tighter limits in Environmental Quality Standards-based permits?
- Do you want to send signals about the value of effluent as a resource? In other words, where, when and in what volumes effluent discharges are made is important to other water users (providing that the quality is within permitted limits) and although these matters can be specified in permits, do you want to reward discharges that benefit resources? Similarly, do you want to penalise abstractions through higher charges where the net return is low because the water

has been evaporated, incorporated in a product, lost through leakage or taken up by growing crops?

- How will you ensure that your charging schemes are flexible and adaptable to changes in water demand, environmental stress, climate change and droughts? And what feedback mechanism will you build in to allow for periodic reviews of its effectiveness?

Engaging with charge payers

- In developing the options for the charges scheme, have you modelled the potential costs on different sectors, as well as individual permit holders? And if you are making changes to an existing scheme, what is the incidence effect by sector, and who are the winners and losers? Is affordability likely to be an issue, and how will you deal with it? A good practice approach is to carry out a Regulatory Impact Assessment, and to publish this simultaneously with the charges consultation.
- How you consult is critical. Who you consult with, and with what questions, in what timescale and for what purpose are important issues to consider. The consultation document should be as simple and concise as possible, and freely accessible. The consultation should make it as easy as possible for consultees to respond, either by a simple online questionnaire on the key issues, or by using lengthier arguments and evidence as necessary.
- It is good practice to consult first on different options, listen carefully to what consultees say in response, and then to consult on the final proposed scheme, identifying how you have taken account of consultees' comments. After the final consultation, consultees will also want to know what has been said in response, and the basis for your decision on the charges scheme.
- Developing a consultation document can help you think about how easy it is to describe the objectives for the charging scheme and how easy (or otherwise) the scheme itself is to explain. It will also help you to think about how the scheme would be administered, and the sort of billing system you will need.
- Importantly, charge payers will want to understand how the money will be spent, and what benefits it will bring to themselves and other water users. Will they be able to influence priorities?
- How will the scheme be approved, and by whom? And how will you demonstrate that the money is being spent transparently, effectively and efficiently, and to whom are you accountable for delivering these tests?
- What terms will you offer for payment (annual, quarterly, monthly?) and if you are relying on information from the permit holder or a third party (e.g. on volumes used, or discharge quality monitoring) how will the billing arrangements work in practice?
- How will you deal with non-payers in terms of chasing bad debts as well as using administrative responses such as revoking the permit?

Conclusion

If you are charging for the first time you will be concerned (or should be) about whether you have the information you need to do so. Ideally, you would have brought into regulatory control all the abstractions and discharges that you are concerned about, and will have a programme of compliance monitoring backed up by enforcement where necessary. You will also have a comprehensive network of groundwater monitoring boreholes, and river flow measurement stations to provide a sound understanding of water availability, or lack of it. In addition, you will also have a comprehensive water quality and ecological monitoring network to provide information on the state of the environment and the issues to deal with, and a clear, costed plan for achieving sustainability targets.

In practice, you are unlikely to have all these measures in place, particularly if the reason for charging is to introduce charges to provide the revenue to fund water monitoring and management activities to the level necessary for adequate control. The critical issue is whether you believe that you have enough information to introduce charging with reasonable confidence. And then to design the scheme in such a way that it can be reviewed and improved over time as more information about water resources and their use becomes available. Although over time it might be possible and desirable to move towards greater sophistication in terms of economic signals, initially it might be prudent to start simple, but ensure that you have built in feedback loops to progressively refine how you charge.

Annex F

List of stakeholders consulted during the policy dialogue

Institution	Name
ABAS – Associação Brasileira de Águas Subterrâneas (Brazilian Groundwater Association)	Humberto José Tavares Rabelo de Albuquerque
ABES/SP- Associação Brasileira de Engenharia Sanitária e Ambiental São Paulo (Brazilian Association of Sanitary and Environmental Engineering)	Luiz Roberto Barretti
ABHA-Associação Multisetorial de Usuários de Recursos Hídricos da Bacia Hidrográfica do Rio Araguari (Multisectoral Association of Water Resources Users of Araguari River Basin)	Sergio Gustavo Rezende Leal
ABRAGE – Associação Brasileira das Empresas Geradoras de Energia Elétrica: (Brazilian Association of Electric Energy Generation)	Marcelo de Deus Melo
ABRAGEL/ENERGISA	Maria Aparecida Borges Pimentel Vargas
ADASA – Agência Reguladora de Águas e Saneamento do Distrito Federal (Regulatory Agency for Water and Sanitation of the Federal District	Eduardo Carvalho
	José Queiroz Filho
	Viviana Almeida
	Igor M. Silva
ADESE- Agência de Desenvolvimento do Seridó (Development Agency of Serido)	Jose Vanderli
	Marcone de M. Nunes
	Emídio Gonçalves de Medeiros
Escritório de Advocacia MGM (MGM Law firm)	Rodrogo Pereira de Mello
AEDIN- Associação das Empresas do Distrito Industrial de Santa Cruz e Adjacências (Association of the Industrial District of Santa Cruz and surroundings)	Abilio Souza Faia
AESA/PB -Agência Executiva de Gestão das Águas do Estado da Paraíba (Executive Agency for Water Management of the State of Paraíba)	João Fernandes da Silva
	Noemia Leitão
AESBE – Associação das Empresas Estaduais de Saneamento (Association of State Companies for Basic Sanitation)	Ubiratan Pereira da Silva
AGB PEIXE VIVO – Associação Executiva de Apoio à Gestão de Bacias Hidrográficas Peixe Vivo (Executive Association to Suport River Basin Management)	Alberto S. Schvartzman
Agência PCJ – Agência das Bacias dos Rios Piracicaba, Capivari e Jundiaí (Agency of Piracicaba, Capivari and Jundiaí River Basin)	Sergio Razera
	Eduardo Leo
	Ivens Oliveira
AGERH – Agência Estadual de Recursos Hídricos dos Estadio do Espírito Santo (Agency for Water Resources of the Espírito Santo State)	Paulo Paim
AGEVAP – Agência Pró-gestão das Águas da Bacia Hidrográfica do rio Paraíba do Sul (Agency of Paraíba do Sul River Basin)	Edson Brasil de Matos Nunes
	André Luis de Paula Marques
Águas do Brasil (Waters of Brazil)	Nelson Carvalho
	Adelfran Lacerda de Matos
AIBA – Associação de Agricultores e Irrigantes da Bahia (Assocation of Bahian Farmers and Irrigators)	José Cisino Menezes
ANA- Agência Nacional de Águas (National Water Agency)	Paulo Varella
	João Lotufo
	Flavia Gomes de Barros
	Carlos Motta Nunes

Institution	Name
ANEEL- Agência Nacional de Energia Elétrica (National Agency for Electric Energy)	Tiago B. Correia
	Larissa Mamed
	Ludimila Lima
Apedema/RJ (Environmental association/Rio de Janeiro)	Marcus S. W. Büdzynhz
	Viviane Logullo
ASFLUCAN- Associação dos Plantados de Cana (Sugar Cane Association)	Tito Livio Inojosa de Andrade
Autônomo	Gilberto Valente Canali
Independent expert	Antonio Eduardo Leão Lanna
Bamin- Bahia Mineração (Bahia Mining Company)	Claudio Menezes
	Delfim Rocha
	Aildo Fonseca
Banco Mundial (World Bank)	Paula Freitas
	Marcos Thadeu Abicalil
	Maria Ines Muanis Persechini
BRK Ambiental – Macaé S.A. (Sanitation Company)	Vinicius Soares da Silva
CAERN – Companhia de Águas e Esgotos do Rio Grande do Norte (Water and Severage Company of the State of Rio Grande do Norte)	Rosy Gurgel
	Claudio Alves Maciel
	Francisco Nehilton
	Wellington Assis Queiroga
	Sayonara Medeiros
	Maria Geny Formiga de Farias
CAESB – Companhia de Saneamento Ambiental do Distrito Federal (Environmental Sanitation Company of the Federal District)	Raquel Brostel
	Fabio Bakker Isaias
CBH BG –Baia de Guanabara (Basin Committee of Guanabara Bay River)	Izidro Paes Leme Arthou
CBH BIG - Baía de Ilha Grande (River Basin Committee of Ilha Grande Bay)	Tiago Oliveira Menezes
CBH BPSI- Baixo Paraíba do Sul e Itabapoana (River Basin Committee of South Paraíba do Sul and Itabapoana)	Hilário de Magalhães Santos
	João Gomes de Siqueira
CBH dos Rios Macaé e das Ostras (River Basin Committee of Macaé e das Ostras Rivers)	Affonso Henrique de Albuquerque Júnior
CBH dos Rios Preto e Paraibuna (River Basin Committee of Preto e Paraibuna Rivers)	Matheu Cremanesa
CBH Rio Dois Rios (River Basin Committee of Dois Rios River)	Lícius de Sá Freire
CBH Paranaíba (River Basin Committee of Paranaiba)	Bento de Godoy Neto
CBH PCJ (River Basin Committee of Piracicaba, Capivari and Jundiaí)	Gabriel Ferrato
CBH Piabanha (River Basin Committee of Piabanha)	Lara Valverde
CBH Preto e Paraibuna – PS1 (River Basin Committee of Preto and Paraibuna)	Matheus Machado Cremonese
CBH São Francisco (River Basin Committee of São Francisco)	Jose Maciel Nunes de Oliveira
CCRON Conselho Comunitário da Região Oceânica de Niterói (Community Council of the Ocean Region of Niterói)	Leila Heizer
CEIVAP- Comitê para Integração da Bacia Hidrográfica do Rio Paraíba do Sul (Commitee for the Integration of the Paraiba do Sul River Basin)	Maria Aparecida Borges Pimentel Vargas
CENIBRA S.A. – Celulose Nipo-Brasileira S/A (Celulose Company)	Jacinto Lana
	Edson Valgas De Paiva
CERHI – RJ- Conselho Estadual de Recursos Hídricos Rio de Janeiro (State Council of Water Resources Management of the State of Rio de Janeiro)	Maria Aparecida Borges Pimentel Vargas

Institution	Name
CESAMA – Companhia de Saneamento Municipal de Juiz de Fora (Municipal Sanitation Company of Juiz de Fora)	Ricardo Stahlschimdt Pinto Silva Ana Maria Laque Marinho
CHESF – Companhia Hidro Elétrica do São Francisco (Hidroelectric Company of São Francisco)	José Carlos de Miranda Farias Ricardo Jucá Sonáli Cavalcanti Oliveira
CIA – Saneamento de Minas Gerais (Sanitation Company Minas Gerais)	Elizabeth Lamego Noce
CNA- Confederação da Agricultura do Brasil (Brazilian Confederation of Agriculture and Livestock)	Nelson Ananias Evilásio da Silva Fraga Gustavo dos Santos Goretti
CNI – Confederação Nacional das Indústrias (National Confederation of Industry)	Percy Baptista Soares Neto José Quadrelli Neto Rafaela Aloise
CNRH – Conselho Nacional de Recursos Hídricos (National Water Resources Council)	Thereza Christina Pereira Castro Patricia Boson Tarcísio Nunes Jefferson Nascimento
CODEVASF – Companhia de Desenvolvimento dos Vales do São Francisco e do Parnaíba (Development Company of São Francisco and Parnaiba Valleys)	Athirson Ferreira Flávio D. Aragão Márcio A. Andrade
COGERH – Companhia de Gestão dos Recursos Hídricos do Ceará (Water Resources Management Company of Ceara)	Denilson Marcelino fidelis Marcílio Caetano de Oliveira
COMPÉ – CBH estadual	Maria Aparecida Borges Pimentel Vargas
Consórcio Intermunicipal Lagos São João (Lakes São Joao Intermunicipal Consortium)	Adriana Saad Arnaldo Vilanova
Consórcio PCJ- Consórcio Intermunicipal das Bacias dos Rios Piracicaba, Capivari e Jundiaí (Inter-municipal consortium in the Piracicaba,Capivari and Jundiaí basins)	Francisco C.C.Lahoz Murilo Ferreira de Sant'Anna
COPASA- Companhia de Saneamento de Minas Gerais (Sanitation Company of Minas Gerais)	Elizabeth Lamego
Copel Geração e Transmissão S.A.- Companhia Paranaense de Energia (Energy Company of the State of Parana)	Mônica Irion Almeida
CRH/SP (Water Resources Council of the State of São Paulo); SSRH/SP (Secretaria de Saneamento e Recursos Hídricos do Estado de São Paulo)	Rui Brasil Assis
CSN – Companhia Siderúrgica Nacional (National Steel Company)	Cláudio César Boscov Graffunder Antônio Carlos Simões de Santana Filho
CTCOB-Câmara Técnica de Cobrança pelo Uso de Recursos Hídricos (Technical Chamber for Water Use Charge)	Livia Soalheiro
DAEE – Departamento de Águas e Energia Elétrica (São Paulo Water and Energy Department)	Fabricio Cesar Gomes Wandeley de Abreu Soares Júnior Hélio C. Suleiman
DIG – Distrito de Irrigação do Perímetro Gorutuba (District of Irrigation of Gorutuba)	Gustavo W. Drumond Lage
Diretoria de Vigilância Ambiental-SVS-SES-DF (Directorate of Sanitary Surveillance)	Guliver Brito de Azevedo
DNOCS- Departamento Nacional de Obras Contra as Secas (National Department of Constructions Against Drought)	Robeisia Herbenea Miranda de Holanda Ângelo José de Negreiros Guerra Maria de Lourdes Barbosa de Sousa Clésio Jean Saraiva Aluísio Ferro
DPIVAS- Distrito de Irrigacao do Perimetro Irrigado Varzea de Sousa (Irrigation Perimeter District of Varzea de Sousa)	Demilson Lemos de Araújo Francisco Dias
DRM- Departamento de Recursos Minerais (Departmernt of Mineral Resources)	Wilson Ferreira Giozza Elisa Bento Fernandes

Institution	Name
EBP – Estrutura Brasileira de Projetos SA (Brazilian Structure of Projects)	Maria Eduarda Berto
Embrapa Cerrados– Empresa Brasileira de Pesquisa Agropecuária Cerrados (Brazilian Agricultural Research Agency)	Eduardo Cyrino de Oliveira Filho
Embrapa Solos- Empresa Brasileira de Pesquisa Agropecuária Solos (Brazilian Agricultural Research Agency)	Rachel Bardy Prado
FABHAT – Fundacao Agencia da Bacia Hidrografica do Alto Tiete (Agency of the Alto Tiete River Basin)	Francisco José Toledo Piza
FAERJ – Federação da Agricultura do Estado do Rio de Janeiro (Agriculture Federation of the State of Rio de Janeiro)	Rodolfo Tavares Leopoldo Carrielo Erthal
Fazenda Oriente/DIG/PGO	Gustavo Wagner Drumond Lage
FECOMÉRCIO – DF– Federação de Comercio de Bens, Serviços e Turismo do Distrito Federal (Federation for theTrade of Goods, Services and Tourism)	Gutemberg Uchoa
FIEMG – Federação das Indústrias do Estado de Minas Gerais (Federation of Industries of Minas Gerais State)	Patricia Helena Gambogi Boson
FETARN – Federação dos Trabalhadores na Agricultura do Estado do Rio Grande do Norte (Federation of Agricultural Workers of Rio Grande do Norte)	Francisco de Assis Araújo
FGV – Fundação Getulio Vargas (Getulio Vargas Foundation)	Joisa Dutra Irene Altafin Teresa Nunes Daniel Augusto Diniz Vila-Nova
Fibria Celulose (Cellulose Company)	Camila Reggiane da Silva
FIEMG – Federação das Indústrias do Estado de Minas Gerais (Federation of Industries of the State of Minas Gerais)	Wagner Costa Deivid Lucas de Oliveira
FIEP – Federação das Indústrias do Estado do Paraná (Federation of Industries of the State of Parana)	Francisco José Bernardino
FIESP – Federação das Indústrias do Estado de São Paulo Paulo (Federation of Industries of the State of São Paulo)	Alexandre Vilella Zeila Piotto
FIRJAN – Federação das Indústrias do Estado do Rio de Janeiro (Federation of Industries of the State of Rio de Janeiro)	Jorge Perón Luiz Mario Concebida
Fonasc APEDEMA-RJ – Forum Nacional da Sociedade Civil – APEDEMA Rio de Janeiro (National Forum of Civil Society)	Markus Stephan Büdzynkz
Fonasc Cbh – Forum Nacional da Soc Civil nos CBH (National Forum of Civil Society for River Basin Committees)	João Clímaco
FUNASA/MS- Fundação Nacional de Saúde (National Foundation of Health)	Ricardo Frederico de Melo Arantes Geraldo Melo Correa Alberto Venturier
FURNAS CENTRAIS ELÉTRICAS S.A. (FURNAS power plants)	Milena Ferreira Leticia Leite Luiz Felipe Mattos dos Reis Marcelo Roberto Rocha de Carvalho Alexandre Moreira Lopes
Ministério da Fazenda/SPE (Ministry of Finance- Secretariat for Economic Policy)	Aloisio P.de Melo
IAVARP/MG- INSTITUTO AMBIENTAL VALE DO RIO PRETO (Institute of Environment Vale do Rio Preto)	João Emídio Lima da Silva Marilda Cruz Lima da Silva
IDEMA/Rio Grande do Norte- Instituto de desenvolvimento Sustentável e Meio Ambiente (Institute for Sustainable Development and Environment of the State of Rio Grande do Norte)	Sérgio Luiz Macedo
IFPB, Sousa/PB- Instituto Federal da Paraiba (Federal Institute of Paraiba)	Hermano de Oliveira Rolim
IGAM – Instituto Mineiro de Gestão das Água	Felipe Silva Marcondes

Institution	Name
(Minas Gerais Water Management Institute)	Sônia de Souza Ferreira
	Maria de Fátima Chagas
IGARN – Instituto de Gestão das Águas do Estado do Rio Grande do Norte (Institute of Water Management of the State of Rio Grande do Norte)	Antonio Righetto
	Nelson Césio Fernandes Santos
	Josivan Cardoso Moreno
INEA – Instituto Estadual do Ambiente do Rio de Janeiro (State Environmental Institute of Rio de Janeiro)	Moema Versiani Acselrad
	Monica P. Lima
	Marcos de Almeida Lima
	Edson Falcao
	Maicon Guerra De Miranda
	Lorena Procopio
	Paolo Vitor RM da Silva
	Luiz Firmino Martins Pereira
	Samuel Muylaert
	Antoin Lousco
	Marcia Chaves de Souza
	Giselle de Sá Muniz
	Wallon Pas
IBIO – Instituto BioAtlântica (Bio Atlântica Institute)	Eduardo Figueiredo
	Ricardo Alcântara Valory
IPEA, Instituto de Pesquisa Econômica Aplicada – Ministério do Planejamento, Orçamento e Gestão (Institute of Applied Economic Research, Ministry of Planning, Budget and Management)	Jose Gustavo Féres
	Demetrios Christofidis
IRGA – Instituto Rio Grandense do Arroz (Rio Grande do Sul Institute of Rice)	Ivo Mello
Irrigação (Irrigation sector)	Antônio Pereira da Costa
	Armando Almeida Martins
JLG Consultoria / Comitê Guandu	José Luiz Governo de Souza
Light Energia	Humberto Duarte de Andrade
	João Vieira de Araujo
Man Latin America	Alex Carvalho Nogueira
MCTIC- Ministério da Ciência, Tecnologia, Inovações e Comunicações (Ministry of Science, Technology, Innovation and Communication)	Rodrigo Roubach
MDS – Ministro do Desenvolvimento Social e Agrário (Ministry of Social and Agrarian Development)	André Mattana
	Vitor Santana
MDIC-Ministério da Indústria Comércio Exterior e Serviços (Ministry of Industry, Foreign trade and Services)	Antônio José Juliani
MDS-Ministério do Desenvolvimento Social (Ministry of Social Development)	Yara Farias
	Lilian Rahal
MDIC- Ministério do Desenvolvimento, Indústria e Comércio (Ministry of Development, Industry and Commerce)	Gustavo Fontenele e Silva Demetrio de Toledo
MF-Ministério da Fazenda (Ministry of Finance)	Andrey Goldner Baptista Silva
MI Ministério da Integração Nacional (Ministry of Integration)	Jonathas Assunção
MMA- Ministerio do Meio Ambiente (Ministry of the Environment)	Jair Oliveira Tannus
	Sérgio Antonio Gonçalves
	Adriana Lustosa
	Geraldo Sandoval Góes
MME-Ministério de Minas e Energia (Ministry of Mining and Energy)	Renato Dalla Lana
	Thomaz Toledo
	Luciano Teixeira

Institution	Name
MP-Ministério do Planejamento, Orçamento e Gestão (Ministry of Planning, Budget and Management)	Gilma dos Passos Rocha
	Paulo Henrique Siqueira Isobe
	Manoel Renato Machado Filho
	Marcel Barbosa
MPS- Ministério da Previdência Social (Ministry of Social Security)	Vera Lúcia Teixeira
MRE-Ministério das Relações Exteriores (Ministry of Foreign Affairs)	Luciano Pereira de Souza
	Thiago Cavalcanti
MTPAC- Ministério dos Transportes, Portos e Aviação Civil (Ministry of Transport,Ports and Civil Aviation)	Eimair Bottega Ebeling
O nosso vale! A nossa vida	Fátima de Lourdes Casarin
Observatório da Governança das Águas (Water Governance Observatory)	Angelo José Rodrigues Lima
Odebrecht Ambiental Macaé	Thais da Costa
OMA Brasil	Ricardo Lima
ONS – Operador Nacional do Sistema Elétrico (Electric System national Operator)	Saulo Guerreiro
	Paulo Diniz
Especialista (Expert)	Paulo Roberto Ferreira Carneiro
	Irene Guimaraes Altafin
	Joisa Dutra
	José Gustavo Féres
	Rodrigo Pereira de Mello
	Marcos Thadeu Abicalil
	Rosa Maria Formiga Johnsson
PETROBAS	Fernando Carvalho Ribeiro
PGE/RJ- Procuradora Geral do Estado do Rio de Janeiro (Attorney General of the State of Rio de Janeiro)	Carlos da Costa e Silva
PM de Assú/RN- Prefeitura Municipal de Assú/Rio Grande do Norte (City Hall of Assú/Rio Grande do Norte)	Sônia Maria de França
	Alexander Douglas de Souza
PM de Pombal/PB (City Hall of Pombal)	Halana O. Trigueiro Severo
	Aline Cristina A. F. Silva
PM Santana do Seridó/RN- Prefeitura Municipal Santana do Seridó /Rio Grande do Norte (City hall of Santana do Seridó /Rio Grande do Norte)	Tatiana Fatima Ferrira
PM de São Fernando, RN- Prefeitura Municipal de São Fernando /Rio Grande do Norte (City Hall of São Fernando /Rio Grande do Norte)	Paolo Maia
Prefeito (Mayor)	Roberto Salim
Prefeitura B.Jesus (Town Hall B.Jesus)	Evaldo G. Junior
REBOB – Rede Brasil de Organismos de Bacias Hidrográficas (Brazilian Network of River Basin Organisms)	Lupércio Z. Antônio
Representante Turismo (Tourism representative)	Wilson de Azevedo Filho
SAAE-Barra Mansa- Serviço Autônomo de Água e Esgoto (Barra- Mansa Autonomous Service of Water and Sewage)	Jardel Souza de Azevedo
SABESP – Companhia de Saneamento Básico do Estado de São Paulo (Basic Sanitation Company of the State of São Paulo)	Silvio Renato Siqueira
	Marco Antonio Lopes Barros
	Jerson Kelman
SEAE/MF- Secretaría de Acompanhamento Economico do Ministerio de Fazenda (State Secretariat for Economic Mnitoring of the Ministry of Finance)	Jefferson M.Marinho
SAEG – Companhia de Serviço de Água, Esgoto e Resíduos de Guaratinguetá (Service Company for Water, Sewage and Waste of Guaratinguetá)	Miguel Sampaio Júnior
	Gonçalo Ferraz Cardoso
	Marcos Guimarães Silva Filho
SAG- Salzburger Aluminuim Group	Marcelo Guaranys

Institution	Name
SANASA Campinas Sociedade de Abastecimento de Água e Saneamento S/A (Campinas Enterprise for Water Supply and Sanitation)	Marco Antonio Santos Pedro Cláudio da Silva
Schmidt Valois Miranda Ferreira Agel Advogados (Law firm Schmidt Valois Miranda Ferreira Agel)	Márcio Silva Pereira
SDS/SC- Secretaria de Estado do Desenvolvimento Sustentável (State Secretariat of Sustainable Economic Development)	Bruno Beilfuss
SEA – Secretaria Estadual de Meio Ambiente do Rio de Janeiro (State Secretariat of Environment of Rio de Janeiro)	André Corrêa Antônio da Hora Eliane Pinto Barbosa Gabriela Campagna Lívia Soalheiro Romano
SEAPAC, Secretaria de Agricultura e Pecuária Caicó/RN (Secretariat for Agricutlure and Livestock Caicó/ Rio Grande do Norte)	José Procópio de Lucena Damião Santos de Medeiros Ulyanc Lima
SEAPEC/ Secretaria de Agricultura e Pecuária do RJ (Secretariat for Agricutlure and Livestock Rio de Janeiro)	Nelson Teixeira Alves Filho Helga Hissa
SEGETH – Secretaria de Estado de Gestão do Território e Habitação do Distrito Federal (Secretariat of State for Territory and Housing Management of the Federal District)	Sílvia Borges De Lázari
SEMA DF – Secretaria de Estado de Meio Ambiente e Recursos Hidricos Distrito Federal (State Secretariat for the Environment and Water Resources of the Federal District)	Maria Silvia Rossi
SEMARH-RN-Secretaria de Estado do Meio Ambiente e dos Recursos Hídricos do Rio Grande do Norte (State Secretariat for the Environment and Water Resources of Rio Grande do Norte)	José Mairton Figueiredo de França Mairton França
Sentinela Ambiental (Non governmental organisation)	D. Ribeiro
SEPLAN/MP- Secretaria de Planejamento e Assuntos Econômicos/ Ministério do Planejamento, Desenvolvimento e Gestão (Secretariat for Planning and Economic Affairs / Ministry of Planning, Development and Management)	Fabiano Chaves
Sindicato Rural de Campos (Rural Union of Campos)	José do Amaral Ribeiro Gomes Ronaldo Bartholomeu dos Santos Júnior
SMMA- Secretaria Municipal do Meio Ambiente (Municipal Secretariat of the Environment)	Rodolfo de Oliveira Alfredo Peixoso Oineto
SNSA/MCidades – Secretaria Nacional de Saneamento Ambiental/Ministerio das Cidades (National Secretariat of Environmental Sanitation/ Ministry of Cities)	Gustavo Frayha
SOAPEDRA- Sociedade Amigos da Pedra da Mina (Enterpise Friends of Pedra da Mina)	Rutnei Morato Erica
SPI-Secretaria de Política e Integração – Ministério dos Transportes, Portos e Aviação Civil (Secretariat of Policy and Integration - Ministry of Transport, Ports and Civil Aviation)	Katia Matsumoto Tancon Alexandre Vaz Sampaio
SRH/CE – Secretaria de Recursos Hídricos do Estado do Ceará (Secretariat of Water Resources of the State of Ceará)	Francisco José C. Teixeira
SSRH/SP- Secretaria de Saneamento e Recursos Hídricos do Estado de São Paulo (Secretariat of Sanitation and Water Resources of the State of São Paulo)	Ariane Coelho Donatti
STRAF (Sindicato dos Trabalhadores Rurais e Agricultores Familiares do Município de São João do Sabugi) (Union of Rural Workers of the municipality of São João do Sabugi)	Aldenir Araujo De Morais
STTR – (Sindicato dos Trabalhadores e Trabalhadoras Rurais Sousa (Sousa/PB) – (Union of Male and Female Rural Workers of Sousa)	Ailton de Sousa Pereira
Superintendencia do Ibama no Distrito Federal (Superintendence of Ibama- Federal District)	Aline Rezende Peixoto
Suzano Papel e Celulose (Suzano Pulp and Paper)	Ricardo Quadros Yugo matsuda
TCU-Tribunal de Contas da União (Federal Court of Accounts)	André Delgado Marcos Rezende Marcelo Soares
TNC – The Nature Conservancy:	Samuel Barreto

Institution	Name
	Hendrick Mansur
Trutas NR (Fishery Company)	João Mauro Mendes Chio
UERJ – Universidade do Estado do Rio de Janeiro (Rio de Janeiro State University)	Friedrich Wilhelm Herms
UFRJ – Universidade Federal do Rio de Janeiro (Federal University of Rio de Janeiro)	José Paulo Soares de Azevedo
ÚNICA – União da Agroindústria Canavieira do Estado de São Paulo (Union of sugarcane industry of the state of São Paulo)	André Elia Neto
UnB - Universidade de Brasilia (University of Brasilia)	Conceição de Maria Albuquerque Alves
UFRB - Universidade Federal do Recôncavo da Bahia (Federal University of Recôncavo da Bahia)	Jaildo Santos Pereira
FRGS- Universidade Federal do Rio Grande do Sul (Federal University of Rio Grande do Sul)	Guilherme Fernandes Marques
Vale S.A. (Mining enterprise)	David Veiga Soares
	Denes Martins da Costa Lott
	Gleuza Jesué
	Denes Costa Lott
	Vitor Cabral
WWF – World Wildlife Fund – Brazil	Ricardo Novaes

ORGANISATION FOR ECONOMIC CO-OPERATION AND DEVELOPMENT

The OECD is a unique forum where governments work together to address the economic, social and environmental challenges of globalisation. The OECD is also at the forefront of efforts to understand and to help governments respond to new developments and concerns, such as corporate governance, the information economy and the challenges of an ageing population. The Organisation provides a setting where governments can compare policy experiences, seek answers to common problems, identify good practice and work to co-ordinate domestic and international policies.

The OECD member countries are: Australia, Austria, Belgium, Canada, Chile, the Czech Republic, Denmark, Estonia, Finland, France, Germany, Greece, Hungary, Iceland, Ireland, Israel, Italy, Japan, Korea, Latvia, Luxembourg, Mexico, the Netherlands, New Zealand, Norway, Poland, Portugal, the Slovak Republic, Slovenia, Spain, Sweden, Switzerland, Turkey, the United Kingdom and the United States. The European Union takes part in the work of the OECD.

OECD Publishing disseminates widely the results of the Organisation's statistics gathering and research on economic, social and environmental issues, as well as the conventions, guidelines and standards agreed by its members.

OECD PUBLISHING, 2, rue André-Pascal, 75775 PARIS CEDEX 16
(42 2017 52 1 P) ISBN 978-92-64-28570-5 – 2017

www.ingramcontent.com/pod-product-compliance
Ingram Content Group UK Ltd.
Pitfield, Milton Keynes, MK11 3LW, UK
UKHW051501290926
15471UKWH00008B/1335

9 789264 285705